Boost!

Boost!

*How the Psychology of Sports
Can Enhance Your Performance in
Management and Work*

MICHAEL BAR-ELI

OXFORD
UNIVERSITY PRESS

Oxford University Press is a department of the University of Oxford. It furthers the University's objective of excellence in research, scholarship, and education by publishing worldwide. Oxford is a registered trademark of Oxford University Press in the UK and certain other countries.

Published in the United States of America by Oxford University Press
198 Madison Avenue, New York, NY 10016, United States of America.

Library of Congress Cataloging-in-Publication Data
Names: Bar-Eli, Michael, author.
Title: Boost! : how the psychology of sports can enhance your performance in management and work / Michael Bar-Eli.
Description: New York, NY : Oxford University Press, [2018]
Identifiers: LCCN 2017007200 | ISBN 9780190661731 (hardcover : alk. paper)
Subjects: LCSH: Performance. | Sports—Psychological aspects. |
Management—Psychological aspects.
Classification: LCC BF481 .B275 2018 | DDC 650.101/9—dc23
LC record available at https://lccn.loc.gov/2017007200

9 8 7 6 5 4 3 2 1

Printed by Sheridan Books, Inc., United States of America

To Asaph, my reason for everything

CONTENTS

INTRODUCTION

It's now or never . . .

—ELVIS PRESLEY

July 7, 1974 was a bright summer Sunday. As a young Israeli soldier on vacation, I watched West Germany and Holland compete at the Olympic Stadium in Munich in the final game of the World Cup. Dutch star player Johan Cruyff had just received the ball, dribbled up field, and then suddenly accelerated and dashed into the penalty area. Before the Germans even touched the ball, Cruyff was fouled and the Dutch team was awarded a penalty kick.

Johan Neeskens, who took the penalty, struck a forceful shot right to the center of the goal, yet goalkeeper Sepp Maier dove, as goalkeepers usually do. The ball flew directly into the net. Holland was now leading 1 to 0, and the game was only in its second minute. Though Holland ultimately lost 1 to 2, that single penalty kick could have cost West Germany the cup. But why did Maier jump? If he had simply stood still and not moved, the ball would have practically fallen into his arms!

In retrospect, my interest in sports psychology dates back to that wonderful evening. Over the next twenty years, the goalkeepers' question continued to nag at me, as I saw similar situations play out time and again—it seemed that goalkeepers almost had some type of predisposition to leap for the ball, even when staying in the center of the goal would have probably proven much more effective. After leaving the military, receiving my doctorate, and becoming a university professor, I would still often ponder why. It wasn't until 1995 that a group of colleagues and I managed to approach the question from a scientific standpoint and empirically research goalies' actions, resulting in a study that was published in 2007.

We conducted a study of penalty kicks collected from actual games in top male soccer leagues and championships worldwide. We found that even though the chances of stopping a kick were shown to be higher when the goalkeeper stayed in the center than when he jumped to one of the sides, goalkeepers almost always jump to the right or left instead of staying put. Further study and analysis over this obviously nonoptimal behavior led to the finding that an "action bias"—in which a personal or group expectation to perform an action causes someone to act even when it goes against his or her best interest—is at play. Simply put, goalkeepers believed they should "do something" during a penalty kick, implying that a goal scored would cause the goalkeeper to feel worse following inaction (i.e., staying in the center) than following action (i.e., jumping), leading to a bias for action.

"Interesting," you may say, "but so what?" And you're right, I could have stopped there, and simply used these findings to help goalies perform better in the future. But it occurred to me that the applications of this study were much broader. I came to a simple maxim: sometimes, the best course of action is inaction. And not just in the world of soccer. Whether it's selling a stock when the market is low (instead of waiting for the inevitable upturn), or practicing a speech so many times it comes across as over-rehearsed and stiff (instead of just winging it), or rehashing the pros and cons of a decision (instead of just going with your gut), or micromanaging a team or office (instead of giving them their independence to work), we all waste valuable time and energy "doing things" when we'd be better off sitting back and letting nature take its course.

This unique, nonintuitive maxim received a great amount of resonance in both the scientific community and among popular media as well. The study was chosen in 2008 by the *New York Times Magazine* as one of the most innovative research breakthroughs of the year. I realized then that much of my research, which has dealt for many years mainly with sports, is truly about human performance overall.

The concept of performance—a goal-directed behavior—plays a central role in contemporary Western culture. Every one wants to perform better—not only in their careers, but also in their hobbies, relationships, and in pretty much everything else they do. And to perform better in any situation, it is necessary to focus on and develop the psychological skills that help lead to success.

Just like physical skills, psychological ones can be taught, learned, and practiced. In understanding human behavior, both in individuals and in groups, you can develop these psychological skills and use them to heighten your awareness, foster your talents and abilities, and reach your peak performance. What I'm really talking about here is mental preparedness and psychological awareness—the ability to *thrive* in any environment.

As one of the first researchers to concentrate on the various psychological determinants of human athletic performance—from stress and arousal to motivation, aspiration to self-confidence, decision processes and creativity to social dynamics, and mental preparation to morality—I found that these determinants were integral to more than just sports. I began drawing connections between the behaviors and mental preparedness of high-performing athletes and entrepreneurs; the creativity seen in famous high-jump champions and exhibited at today's most innovative companies; the ability to motivate and lead a team whether you're a baseball coach or the CEO of a Fortune 500 company; how specific goals must be set in the office and on the court; how optimal levels of stress lead to better presentations and sinking more foul shots; and many more.

The thought processes and behavioral patterns associated with athletic excellence produce high performance in so many other human undertakings. Lessons from sports psychology can be applied to the understanding of human behavior across the board, but nowhere more so than in the world of business, economics, and finance.

With contemporary advances in the understanding of individual and group behavior, lessons for leaders in an increasingly diverse, international business and economic environment are more necessary now than ever before. Today, it is imperative for team leaders—from middle managers to CEOs—to utilize these lessons in supporting, advising, and inspiring their coworkers and employees, helping them to perform at their highest levels, and create a sustainable, successful working environment and business. By considering the curious psychology that drives human behavior, leaders across industries can learn to find their "sweet spot" and improve and enhance their companies'—as well as their individual—performance.

As a sports psychologist for nearly four decades, not only have I researched, studied, and written on this topic widely, but I have also worked directly with elite athletes, coaches, and teams to help them improve their performance. This book takes the lessons I've learned from sports psychology and applies them to overall human behavior and performance, showing how you can harness this knowledge to perform at your highest levels, succeeding in your careers and personal lives.

So if I had already been thinking about the psychological factors of performance back when I was a soldier in the early 1970s, you may ask why it took me so long to write this book. A major part of the answer would surely be that scientists in general have a problem—they are trained to formulate ideas and write them down in an extremely rigorous scientific manner. Maybe I just felt more comfortable in this familiar scientific playground . . . but then came something that changed my view on life dramatically, and, out of a deep sense of urgency, brought me to write this book. It began with a tiny, virtually unnoticeable tremor in my right hand—nothing to pay attention to. Only later did I find out that it was a greeting from my new partner for life: Parkinson's disease.

It slowly developed into serious movement-related symptoms, such as rigidity, difficulty in walking, general slowness, and occasional shaky hands. Writing became a burden and my handwriting shrank into miniature. My medications have been quite effective at managing my symptoms, specifically the motor ones, though these will probably lose their efficacy as the disease progresses. As a result, I underwent a soul-searching process, thinking about my past and future, and considering what I would like to do *now* with the time remaining for a reasonable quality of life.

It became clear that I have a limited time in which it will be possible to work more or less normally with the medications I have been taking. And I understood that even if the grey cells in my brain remained reasonably intact, my hands would sooner or later refuse to entirely obey my brain's instructions to type. That's when I knew that I simply *must* write this book. As Elvis sang, "It's now or never."

In the following chapters, I focus on the sometimes hidden, often overlooked psychological forces that drive human performance. I draw on my own original research and practical experience in sports—and other areas such as education, the military, art, literature, and history—to offer conclusions and insights about broader performance, while showing how individuals, organizations, and teams can apply these insights to any task or endeavor. These findings are universally applicable, particularly in competitive, stressful, or high-stake business situations.

These lessons are invaluable for executives, middle managers, directors, and team leaders—plus business professionals aspiring to these roles—who want to not only improve their individual performance, but who also want to inspire their employees and contribute to the overall success of their organizations or teams.

Now, let's begin!

PART I

Getting Activated

Arousal

Is a Lot of Stress Really That Bad?

Run, Forrest! Run!

—*Jenny to Forrest in* Forrest Gump

As a kid, I was enthusiastic about aviation and wanted to build aircraft models from plastic and balsa wood. The first one I ever built was the Mikoyan-Gurevich (MiG) 17, a Soviet jet fighter that began service in 1952. As a fifteen-year-old adolescent, however, this pursuit clashed with my impatient character, and it turned out this was also the last airplane model I would ever build. Still, I proudly hung my one and only model in my childhood room where I saw it every day, every night, for years.

Years later, on Monday, October 8, 1973, I was stationed in an anti-aircraft Hawk guided missile battery in the Sinai desert as a soldier in the Israeli Army. The Yom Kippur War was bitterly storming around us; Israel had been taken by surprise by the Egyptian and Syrian Armies, and we regular soldiers in the field didn't know exactly what had happened. What we did know was that a warning siren that enabled us to seek shelter preceded each Egyptian aircraft attack.

But not that day.

We were outside, working on the missiles and launchers, preparing them for the next action. Suddenly—without any warning—I saw my model in front of my eyes, as if it was just a few short yards away. I realized that this aircraft had already passed us, but if another one was coming, it would be from the direction of the sun (to blind the anti-aircraft units shooting at it). When I looked toward the sun, there it was, another MiG-17, heading toward us. I could feel my heart beating quickly—I had no time to think, just to react.

"MiGs!" I shouted, and everybody scrambled for shelter. I ran like crazy and jumped into the next bunker just before the entrance was hit by two rockets and completely destroyed. I can still recall the smell of that explosion more than forty years later.

When it all ended, I came out of the half-destroyed bunker and found two huge craters in the sand. It looked like a moonscape, but actually it was the result of two 550-pound bombs landing exactly where I had been running a few seconds earlier. Imagine what would have happened had I not recognized the MiG immediately, cried out, and raced to cover. As I thought about this, I was overwhelmed with shock. I call October 8 "my second birthday," because I know I'm lucky to be alive. For over forty years I have been asking myself: was it coincidence or providence that saved me?

The fact of the matter is that though both of those surely played a role, there was also another major factor: the human sensation of arousal. Arousal—loosely defined as a psychophysiological state of being awake or reactive to stimuli (i.e., general alertness and readiness to respond)—is the underpinning of stress, anxiety, pressure, and even motivation. The concept dates back thousands upon thousands of years to our distant pre-historic ancestors.

When coming face-to-face with a potential bear or other animal attack, prehistoric peoples were already presented with three options: fight, flight, or face the music. They could stand their ground, turn and run, or suffer the consequences. Even then, the human brain and human behavior was developing, and arousal was contributing to performance and survival.

In business, as in sports, you may not be handling life and death situations such as soldiers in battle or a prehistoric person facing off against a bear, but arousal, or high levels of stress, can be used to your benefit in both everyday and extraordinary circumstances. Understanding how to healthily and positively handle and harness stress will not only make you more productive, but will lead to a happier and more inspired life.

THE CONCEPT OF STRESS

It is not the strongest of the species that survives, nor the most intelligent, but the one most responsive to change.

—*attributed to* CHARLES DARWIN[1]

In the 1930s Hans Selye (1907–1982), an Austrian-born Canadian physician, suggested that the general adaptation syndrome (GAS) accounted for the body's short- and long-term reactions to what he labeled "stress." Stress is the body's way of reacting to a threat or a challenge, and it includes three phases: alarm, resistance, and exhaustion or recovery. The logic is simple: when the body is attacked (strained), it must first identify the threat or challenge (alarm), and then recruit and mobilize extra coping resources, namely energy.

During the 1920s Walter Bradford Cannon (1871–1945), a professor of physiology at Harvard Medical School, developed a concept he called "homeostasis," which referred to the daily steady-state balance between the human body and its environment. When this balance is disrupted— let's say, by an acute, sudden threat—our body must recruit its energy stores and focus attention on overcoming the challenge at hand.

After this energy is mobilized, resistance continues at a high, intense level of activation until one of two things occurs: recovery, in which the threat is successfully overcome, removed, or eliminated and homeostasis is regained; or exhaustion, in which all our coping mechanisms are depleted and then we are unable to continue resisting the strain caused by the threat.

Nature created stress to help us survive—it's as simple as that. High levels of stress provide us with the extra strength required to defend ourselves in dangerous situations; then, we recruit all the resources needed to protect ourselves and cope with threats. But what about normal daily performance requiring achievement, not necessarily under threat or danger?

STRESS AND PERFORMANCE

> Stress is not necessarily something bad, it all depends on how you take it.
> —HANS SELYE, *the "father of stress research"*

A classic experiment conducted in 1908 by Robert M. Yerkes (1876–1956), a pioneer of American psychology, and his colleague John D. Dodson, is highly relevant to the question of how stress influences performance. These researchers attempted to investigate "the relation of strength of stimulus to rapidity of habit-formation," according to the title to their renowned study in the *Journal of Comparative Neurology and Psychology*. In short, they discovered that mild electrical shocks could effectively be used to cause mice to acquire the habit of completing a maze. If the electrical shocks were too mild or too strong, however, the mice's performance in the maze decreased. From this they developed what is now called the Yerkes-Dodson law which shows a curvilinear relationship between stress and performance. Performance will increase with arousal, but only up to a certain point, at which time levels of arousal become so high that the result is a negative effect on performance (think of an inverted U, as shown in Figure 1.1). Similarly, when levels of arousal are too low, performance will decrease as well.

In everyday situations, ideal levels of stress and arousal can help you complete tasks, meet or exceed expectations, and overcome difficulties. Think about the added pressure you experience at work when you're

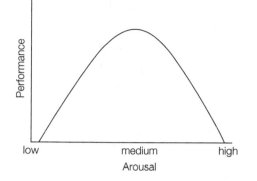

Figure 1.1 Yerkes-Dodson Law Representation.

under a tight deadline—sometimes it can feel overwhelming, but it also contributes to your ability to work quickly and diligently. It's similar to a tied score during the last moments of the fourth quarter of a basketball game. One basket could clinch the win, and the pressure is bearing down; those players who suffer from extreme arousal are likely to make mistakes, but those who are at their most alert, their peak level of performance, will lead their team to the win.

But if stress is so important, how did it get such a bad rap?

Chronic Stress

Part of the answer lays in what is called "chronic stress," that is, exposure to extreme conditions or situations for an extended period of time. This type of stress boomerangs and causes more harm than good (think of the right-hand side of the curved line in Figure 1.1).

Growing research shows that overworking is damaging to personal lives, including your family and health, and also to your productivity at work. A 2015 study even suggested that working long hours might be a contributing factor in 120,000 deaths a year.[2] Obviously, this type of stress isn't good for you, or for any of your employees or coworkers. This is a major lesson for any manager, director, or CEO—if the people below you are in a constant state of stress, they'll perform at a lower capacity.

Much effort has been devoted over the years to identify and locate so-called stressors—the factors in our environment that continuously affect us as if we were under threat. In sports, one main stressor I typically find with the teams I consult is the referee. A top basketball player I worked with had a problem with one particular referee whom he perceived as a threat. According to the player, the ref had a history of calling fouls on him, even when none had been committed.

"Every time I see him on court, I get mad," he said. "With him, I begin each game with two fouls!"

The result?

The player's anger resulted in a high state of arousal, causing him to act aggressively. He would end up starting each game refereed by that particular ref with unnecessary fouls—evidently a self-fulfilling prophecy.

Let's say you really hate your boss. You actually would like to do to him what the prehistoric man could do with the bear—kill him . . . or leave. Of course the first action is somewhat too extreme (and against the law!) and the latter action is impossible since you have bills to pay and a family to feed.

So when you see him each day, anger and aggression rise in you like bile, but instead of taking action, you just smile, try to be nice, and even prepare him a cup of coffee. Repressing your feelings over time may create stress and additional pressure, not only on your psyche, but also on your body. You potentially put yourself at risk of developing an ulcer, heart problems, or even a nervous breakdown. These are called "psychosomatic diseases," which basically come from activating GAS in vain; in essence it is a kind of "imprisoned aggression," which is eventually directed toward oneself—another source of the bad reputation that stress has earned.

If you continuously get angry in such a situation, you unknowingly punish yourself time and time again for something you have no control over. I call it the "full gas in neutral" system, or FGN—racing the engine while the car is in neutral so that you get nowhere. You are angry and agitated, but only under the surface; that's why you may develop the ulcer. Perhaps you put your foot on both the gas and the brake simultaneously, which is even worse and can cause you to eat yourself up from the inside.

As a leader of any team, you need to find the sweet spot when it comes to stress, both your personal state and that of the group you're leading. This optimal functioning zone will be determined by your personality (and those of your team's), the task to be performed, and the nature of the environment in which it is to be conducted. Before finding this optimal zone, you must first consider how your perceptions, or the perceptions of others, contribute to your level of stress.

SUBJECTIVE PERCEPTION

> I really hit the shit out of that discus.
>
> —DALEY THOMPSON

One of the most stunning moments in the history of the modern Olympic Games was the 1984 decathlon duel between track and field stars Daley Thompson of Great Britain and West Germany's Juergen Hingsen. For years, Hingsen and Thompson had been breaking each other's world records, but in their six meetings preceding the Los Angeles 1984 Olympics, Thompson had always prevailed, regardless of Hingsen's world records.

In Los Angeles, the competition developed such that the seventh event—the discus—could be decisive for the final result. Hingsen was excelling, giving his absolute best. In contrast, Thompson's performance was weak (discus was historically his worst event)—until the last throw. When the discus landed, he had set another personal best in competition. Hingsen was so astonished, he broke down: for the rest of the program, he just went through the motions, ending up with the silver medal. Thompson won the gold. Here is how Thompson described the games in his autobiography:

> For that one moment I wasn't interested in winning. Some people shy from the high-pressure moments. It was what I had been looking for, a culmination of all I had trained for. Just to be faced with the situation in an Olympics—the feeling was incredible. And I'd faced

it and overcome the thing I'm least competent in, the discus. I really hit the shit out of that discus.[3]

When he needed it most, Thompson proved that he could peak when it counted. His interpretation of the event was purely functional: he did not perceive this high-pressure moment as a threat, but instead enjoyed the opportunity as he saw it as a chance to prove himself.

Anat Draigor (born 1960)—probably the best female Israeli basketball player of all time, and a good friend of mine for the past quarter of a century—once told me: "You know, in such moments, the game becomes really interesting and challenging; otherwise it would have been quite boring." She has what I call a genuine winner's attitude. For her—as for Thompson—such intense, stressful moments offer great positive opportunities, rather than being perceived as negative "horror" experiences.

Our subjective view plays a major role in how we experience the world around us. Subjective beliefs have a crucial influence on our conduct, as our behavior in many situations is determined primarily by our perception and interpretation of the stressfulness of any given situation.

In 1966 Professor Richard S. Lazarus (1922–2002), a pioneer in the psychological investigation of stress at the University of California, Berkeley, published a seminal book, *Psychological Stress and the Coping Process*, in which he argued that cognitive processes of what he labeled "appraisal" are central in determining whether a situation is perceived as potentially threatening or as benign. Furthermore, Lazarus said that our behavior vis-à-vis the situation is also dependent on our subjective estimation of whether we have the resources required to deal with the problem at hand.

Think about a promotion. Is it positive or negative? Positive, will be your immediate answer—but is it always? Not necessarily, at least according to the famous "Peter principle,"[4] which claims that organizational personnel are promoted based on performance in their current jobs, and will continue to be promoted so long as they work competently. Sooner or later, however, they reach a position in which they are no longer competent—their "level of incompetence." Isn't it highly stressful to function in a job for which you are actually incompetent? Couldn't this lead to chronic stress and other issues?

Such promotions are more common than you may think, and they can happen quite quickly. Those people being promoted will typically start the new position with a positive outlook, seeing any promotion as a good one, but they may find that they are uncomfortable in their new role and simply unprepared for the new challenges and tasks.

The promotion in name only raises similar problems when you or an employee are given a new title but there are no new benefits, monetary or otherwise. Many times these promotions are accompanied by more work, but employees feel as if they can't turn them down. From a subjective point of view, it's possible to consider these promotions more deeply, from different angles, weighing the pros and cons, and deciding what you want out of the next step in your career. You may be happy with your current position or see another place in the organization where you think your talents will fit better. It all depends on your subjective experience and viewpoint.

Understanding your own personal perception of stress will help you better frame the problem or obstacle at hand. If you approach every situation like Daley Thompson and his Olympic discus throw, you're more likely to succeed at your task, finding opportunity where conflict or pressure may exist. In doing so, it will help you to reach your peak level of performance: your optimal functioning zone.

MORE IS MORE, LESS IS MORE: MAXIMIZATION THROUGH OPTIMIZATION

> Because . . . she is not too tall, not too short, she is in the middle; not too
> smart, not too dumb—she is all I wanted, made to measure.
>
> —KAVERET, *Israeli rock band, "Kacha hi ba'emza"*

John M. Hoberman's 1992 book *Mortal Engines* discusses the dehumanization of sports. It argues that in the service of performance enhancement, modern Western sports establishments abuse athletes (such as Olympic sprinter Ben Johnson) by creating "man-machines" through scientific experimentation. This process, says Hoberman, also has immense implications for the science of human performance in general.

His metaphor of athletes—and humans in achievement situations in general—is striking: in fact, we are talking about machines. In older non-Western tribal cultures, sport was often associated with notions like "play" and "games"; these, according to British professor Sir Isaiah Berlin (1909–1997), reflect old traditions in which sport was conceived as an expressive human activity, along with dancing, singing, fighting, or worshipping.[5]

Similarly, many people consider modern elite sport as a contrast to ancient Greek sport, which supposedly advocated a harmony between the body and soul.[6] Currently, however, sport is a product of scientific thinking and rational fabrication; in short, elite athletes are "mortal engines," or human machines, easily comparable to many modern workplaces and employees.

Hoberman was the first to make me think about this deep, pervasive metaphor. Over time, I realized that as a sports scientist, much of what I do is connected to the ideas of "optimization" and "maximization"—sport science is in fact trying to optimize athletes' functioning in the sense of continuously making them more efficient (just like any other machine), in order to maximize their performance. This concept reflects rationality in its so-called instrumental sense, which has to do with the effectiveness of one's application of means toward the accomplishment of a certain goal, an idea associated with the great German thinker Max Weber (1864–1920). Through optimization, sport science strives to aid athletes in the maximization of their performance—this is the ultimate goal of athletes in elite sport.

In order to be the greatest, highest, supreme, paramount, utmost, or topmost (or simply maximal), one must be the best—that is, optimal. In the pursuit of excellence, something must be optimized in order for something else to be maximized. I label this principle "maximization through optimization."

For example, think about Michael Schumacher and his Ferrari. The seven-time Formula One world champion, and undoubtedly one of the greatest Formula One drivers of all times, needs to have a vehicle that performs flawlessly. In order to be the fastest, each and every component of his Ferrari must be at its best, in optimal shape. Moreover, it is of utmost importance that the relations or interconnections between the parts—namely, the ways in which the car's elements influence one another—function optimally to enable the whole Ferrari to produce maximal velocity.

In this case, Schumacher is also a part of the system—where the car fits him and he fits the car. That's why "man-machine-systems" are created. The car is user-friendly, and Schumacher trains with it to understand how it works and how they can work together. The same is true for pilots in a jet fighter, or even in a flight simulator, or for any performer, including athletes. For example, before it was revealed that Lance Armstrong had been using performance-enhancement drugs, author Daniel Coyle, in his bestselling book *The Talent Code*,[7] talked about how he was highly impressed by Armstrong's "desire to optimize every dimension of the race"—evidently, to maximize performance (unfortunately, using illegal means, as it turned out later).

Peak Performance and Flow State

Athletes' maximum performance, also known as peak performance, is often characterized or accompanied by what is called a "flow state" or "peak experience." Athletes describe this state as being "on automatic pilot," "totally involved," "hot," "on a roll," "in a groove," or "in the zone." An excellent example is provided by the great German goalkeeper Oliver Kahn in the 2001 champions league final game, between his team FC Bayern Munich and FC Valencia.

In the shootout that won the game, he saved three of seven penalty kicks, or 42.86 percent. Even if you count the penalty he did not stop during the game, this makes it three out of eight, which is 37.5 percent—still far beyond the base rate (that is, the initial chances of a goalkeeper saving a penalty kick to begin with) of 25 percent. He attributed his success to "a state of absolute concentration, with optimal control over my emotions and thoughts."[8]

A flow state, however, is a rare event—it is an ideal state to which the performer strives, but only infrequently achieves. This is probably one of the reasons why Russian sport psychologist Yuri L. Hanin criticized the Yerkes-Dodson law's inverted-U hypothesis by arguing that it is unlikely that only one optimal arousal state exists that corresponds with the maximal performances of different athletes across contexts. He used a well-known anxiety test, the state-trait anxiety inventory (STAI), developed by the late US psychologist Charles D. Spielberger (1927–2013) and his team,[9] to operationalize arousal. He then conducted systematic retrospective multiple field observations of athletes' state anxiety and performance levels.

Hanin found that all top athletes had an individual zone of state anxiety in which their maximal performance occurred, whereas poor performances occurred outside this zone. He defined this zone as an athlete's mean precompetitive state anxiety score on the STAI, plus or minus 4 points (which is a standard deviation of approximately 0.5), and labeled it the zone of optimal functioning (ZOF).

Thus, Hanin criticized the Yerkes-Dodson law, arguing that an optimal *zone* exists in the relationship between arousal and performance in which the individual's performance is maximal. This (individual) ZOF is an individual's zone of state anxiety in which maximal performance occurs, whereas poor performances occur outside this zone (Figure 1.2).

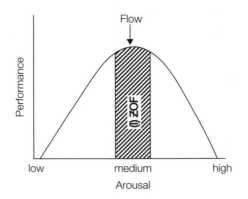

Figure 1.2 Flow and (I)ZOF Representation.

Later on, Hanin extended this idea to include more emotional states and emphasized the individuality of the ZOF (IZOF).[10] What matters for us now, however, is the fact that most of the time, we sport psychologists are satisfied with our athletes being in their (I)ZOF; if they manage to achieve a flow state it would be a great bonus, because of its low probability of occurrence.

Now, if you combine the main ideas reflected by Yerkes-Dodson and Hanin, you actually get two possible nonoptimal arousal states for athletes to be in, and two corresponding strategies for enhancing performance to strive for the maximum:

- Too-low arousal, in which "more is more" would be the right strategy—the athlete is advised to increase arousal to try and create optimal conditions.
- Too-high arousal, in which "less is more" would be the right strategy—the athlete is advised to decrease arousal to try and create optimal conditions.

The same applies of course in other settings as well, such as when you take an exam or interview for a job. If you are tired, apathetic, or simply indifferent, your arousal is probably too low and somebody has to wake you up. However, if you are too tense, anxious, or pressured, then your arousal is probably too high and you need to relax.

Your natural personality also plays a substantial role: for example, if you are a nervous versus relaxed person, or Type A versus Type B. Type A people are those who are achievement-oriented and highly competitive, have a strong sense of time urgency, find it hard to relax, and become impatient and angry with delays or when confronted with people whom they perceive as incompetent. Type B people are able to work without becoming agitated, and to relax without feeling guilty. They have less of a sense of time urgency—including its accompanying impatience—and are not easily roused to anger.[11]

Your level of expertise plays a role, too—it makes a big difference whether you're a seasoned professional or a novice. Starting out in the corporate world, as an assistant, you are likely to defer to more experienced coworkers who have a better understanding of company processes, inter-office politics, or a particular industry in general. There is nothing wrong with that, but understanding your strengths and weaknesses will help you figure out how to reach your own level of peak performance. And don't forget our earlier discussion on subjective perception: how you perceive the task to be conducted (is it easy or difficult for you, have you done it before or is this your first time?) is crucial.

In finding your or your team's optimal level of stress and arousal, the environment should also be taken into consideration. The environment that managers and bosses create and cultivate is crucial to employee per-formance. For example, would you experience more of a threat in a sta-dium full of 80,000 spectators, as compared to training, or do you revel in it, as did Daley Thompson and Anat Draigor? Understanding and know-ing your team, and the individuals that comprise it, will help you create the appropriate environment.

Consider open-plan offices: at the beginning of the twenty-first cen-tury, we find more traditional cubicle structures being eschewed in favor of these new arrangements. As of the end of 2014, about 70 percent of US offices had no or low partitions.[12] Such settings, in which the empha-sis is on large, open spaces with little to no barriers between desks and offices, were at first seen as an exciting new way to break from the typical cubicle mode in an effort to raise transparency, camaraderie, and team-work. Companies like Google, Facebook, Yahoo, eBay, Goldman Sachs, and American Express have all implemented the idea.[13]

What many people didn't foresee were the accompanying issues of high levels of noise and the lack of privacy, all of which have led to greater stress on employees—and not the good kind. Research over the last decade has shown that open office design is negative to employees' satisfaction with both their physical environment and perceived productivity.[14] In addi-tion to stress and reduced satisfaction with the physical environment, poorer coworker relations have developed.[15] What was thought to be a beneficial way to increase employee engagement and conversation has backfired: though conversation between employees has increased in the environment, they are typically short and superficial.[16]

Of course it's hard to please everyone. Some employees may want standing desks, some sitting, or their own offices, or more common spaces, or even different snacks in the vending machines. At the end of the day, it's important to decide what environment will be best for the team to increase performance—finding that sweet spot may be difficult, but it will lead to a stronger, more successful workforce. If your employees are uncomfortable and stressed out, they are likely to reach that too-high arousal stage and their performance will suffer. As a leader, you will then need to figure out how to decrease that stress and get your team back to it's zone of optimal function.

The arousal–performance relationship, such as the Yerkes-Dodson law, is only one classic example of the pervasive principle behind maximization through optimization. The biomechanist, for example, tries to optimize the athletes' movement; the strength and conditioning coach tries to find the balance between strain and recovery (e.g., to avoid overtraining); and the medical doctor prescribes the optimal dose of only the necessary medications—not too much, not too little (as with my Parkinson's medicaments, if I take too much I get so-called dyskinesia, and if it is too little, I simply cannot move). All these parts should be integrated into a functioning whole, known as "optimizing preconditions," just like Michael Schumacher racing in his Ferrari.

MAKING THE COMPLEX SIMPLE

> If you want to spoil a tennis player's game, just ask him to explain what he does.
>
> —Daniel Kahneman, *Nobel Laureate*

As far back as the early 1950s, American psychologists Clark Hull and Kenneth Spence proposed the "drive theory," which claimed that increased arousal facilitates only the performance of well-learned or simple tasks (think of sit-ups, for example: the more aroused you are, the better you perform).[17] Of course many of the tasks that you as a leader or business professional perform are not necessarily simple, nor are those performed by elite athletes. So what happens with complex tasks?

With increased complexity, more and more "unlearned elements" are included in the task to be performed; when these are aroused, performance may become poorer. Think, for example, of a novice trying to learn to drive a golf ball two hundred yards under high stress. This of course leads us back to Yerkes-Dodson and the inverted-U function. So if simple tasks exhibit a linear relationship between arousal and performance, but complex tasks are associated with the inverted U, what should you do? The answer is to try turning complex tasks into simple ones.

You may be thinking, well, that's easier said than done, but there is a systematic way to go about it known as "chunking." Chunking is a deliberate process of knowledge acquisition through concerted practice. For example, Nobel Laureate Herbert Simon investigated chunking with chess players.[18] Novice chess players become experts by acquiring a deeper grasp of the underlying structure of the game. They learn how to organize and reconstruct the various arrangements possible from memory by chunking the separate pieces of information into larger, meaningful units (such as "a king-side attack by black"). New material is then recoded into increasingly larger, more meaningful units and stored in their working memory.

Applying this idea to other areas of human performance, seemingly effortless skill is created by the accumulation of small, discrete units. The skill to be learned is broken down into its component pieces, and those pieces are first memorized separately. Then, the acquisition process continues by linking those pieces together into progressively larger, interconnected groupings. Therefore, the complex task can be made simpler (i.e., because there are now more trained units in the brain and body). This concept should be applied to your own tasks and endeavors.

Simply put, you need to build up your ability to perform complex tasks in the same way you've mastered well-learned tasks—take it one step at a time. This changes the curvilinear arousal–performance relationship into one that is close to linear. As Daniel Coyle points out in *The Talent Code*, a superior gymnast, for example, "doesn't have to think," he or she simply acts. Of course, our individual or group reaction to stress and arousal and our subjective perception still play a role.

For many years, leading German sport psychologist Juergen Nitsch, my one-time advisor when I was a doctoral student from 1980 to 1984, promoted what he called "action theory." In 1994 he wrote an article in which he discussed "the organization of motor behavior," where he suggested that we think about "behavior in situation."[19] And what, pray tell, does that mean? It's actually quite simple. Think about a shot taken by a basketball player. At face value, "a shot is a shot"—but is it? Consider all the potential differences:

- Shots may be taken from different distances.
- Shots may be taken with or without defending players.
- Shots may be taken in "garbage time" or in a decisive stage of the game.
- A shot may be taken by me (novice) or by LeBron James (expert).

Moreover, even a foul shot, which is considered the mother of all routines, is completely different when it is taken in a quiet training atmosphere during garbage time (when nothing matters), or at the highest international level, where that one shot may decide the championship. These are not the same shots!

Taking Nitsch's behavior in situation, simplicity or complexity may be determined by one's own subjective construction of the task. For example, it may be easy for two people to interview well in front of a mirror at home, but much more difficult for one of them to do so in an actual interview. In essence, this approach reflects the philosophy of Friedrich Wilhelm Nietzsche (1844–1900), who once said that "there are no facts, only interpretations."[20]

If we go back to the Thompson and Hingsen decathlon discussed earlier in the chapter and compare the two athletes, Thompson won because the task of "performing X under high arousal" was subjectively constructed as something positive. For Hingsen, the seemingly same task was perceived as negative (perhaps a threat). Therefore, they actually were not performing the same tasks.

Gerd Mueller—a German striker, considered one of the greatest scorers of all times in the history of soccer, alias "the Bomber of the Nation"—is cited as having said that "when you think, it is too late" (in referring to his own phenomenal scoring skills).[21] But notice that Mueller's "chunks" were comprised of not only scoring a goal, but primarily scoring a goal under highly stressful conditions, which he did time and again (including the winning goal he scored in the 1974 Germany–Holland World Cup final, discussed in the introduction).

The deeper meaning of what Mueller said here is actually based on several theories of human reasoning and problem-solving, which argue for what is called "dual-process" of thought. On the one hand, thought processes may be intuitive, instinctive, subconscious, and automatic. On the other hand, they may be deliberative, logical, conscious, and effortful. Nobel Laureate Daniel Kahneman labeled these dual processes as System 1 and System 2, respectively. In an interview given to the Israeli popular economic newspaper *Kalkalist*, Kahneman explains:

> Good tennis players, for example, play almost thoughtlessly, and respond almost automatically to complex shots and feints as well. Actually, if you want to spoil a tennis player's game, just ask him to explain what he does with his hand to produce such a wonderful serve. When System 2 tries to explain something that happens subconsciously, System 1 gets stuck.[22]

It is likely that Gerd Mueller would explain his own goal-scoring performance in terms of Kahneman's System 1, had he only known or heard about it.

SUMMARY

High stress or arousal is not always that bad—it can sometimes save your life. But when you have to perform, carrying out a goal-directed behavior, you have to be in an optimal arousal state. It is a necessary precondition for maximal performance, but your personality and skill level also play a role (e.g., you may be optimally aroused for an exam, but if you don't know the material—forget it. Similarly, Anat Draigor had to have great basketball skills; otherwise even optimal arousal could not help her).

Arousal and performance stand in a curvilinear relationship and the point—or more accurately, the zone—of optimal functioning is determined by three major elements: Who you are (Daley or Juergen? an expert or a novice?); the task to be performed (simple or complex?); and the subjective nature of the environment in which it is to be conducted (training or competition? at home or in class? what is the threat a particular situation represents for you?).

We'll loop back to this idea in chapter 11, when I introduce my research on crisis theory, which argues that the more substantial you deviate from optimal arousal, the higher the chance that you'll experience impaired performance. You have to create optimal conditions in order to maximize performance and increase the probability of a flow state not only before you perform, but also during performance.

This is the entire secret, I'm telling you. How do you do it? That's a somewhat more difficult question, which we'll continue to discuss and answer throughout the book.

DAILY PRACTICES

As an Individual

- Aim for an optimal state of stress and arousal to keep you on your toes, staying involved and productive, without overworking yourself or entering a state of chronic stress.
- Remember that obstacles and tasks are subjective—your personal perception can be a major determinant in how you handle stress and how it affects your performance.
- Make complex tasks simpler by employing chunking techniques, breaking down your actions into smaller, discrete units.

As a Leader

- Find the sweet spot when it comes to your personal levels of stress and that of the group you're leading.
- The environment that managers and bosses create and cultivate is crucial to employee performance—talk to your employees and colleagues about what works best for them and see how you can incorporate their preferences into the surrounding environment.
- Recognize that there will be Type A and Type B people on your staff, and you will have to motivate them accordingly—the Type A group will likely need help decreasing stress and anxiety while Type B will need some added pressure.

NOTES

1. Some scholars argue that this quote is a misattribution, potentially originally stated by Leon C. Megginson, though it is widely considered a distillation of Darwin's main thesis in *The Origin of Species*. More information on the quote is available: Garson O'Toole, "It Is Not the Strongest of the Species that Survives but the Most Adaptable," *Quote Investigator*, May 2014, http://quoteinvestigator.com/2014/05/04/adapt/.
2. Joel Goh, Jeffrey Pfeffer, and Stefanos A. Zenios, "The Relationship Between Workplace Stressors and Mortality and Health Costs in the United States," *Management Science* 62, no. 2 (March 2015): 608–628.
3. As reported by Rob Bagchi in *The Guardian*, "50 Stunning Olympic Moments No21: Daley Thompson Wins 1984 Decathlon," 2012, www.theguardian.com/sport/blog/2012/apr/04/50-stunning-olympic-moments-daley-thompson.
4. L. J. Peter and R. Hull, *The Peter Principle: Why Things Always Go Wrong* (New York: Morrow, 1969).
5. I. Berlin, *Against the Current* (London: Penguin, 1982).
6. This is probably only a myth developed during the nineteenth century in Europe; Ancient Greeks were highly competitive, says University of Florida Classics Professor David C. Young. See his *The Olympic Myth of Greek Amateur Athletics* (Chicago: Ares, 1984).
7. D. Coyle, *The Talent Code* (New York: Bantam, 2009).
8. O. Kahn, *Ich: Erfolg kommt von Innen* [I: Success Comes from Within]. (Munich: Riva, 2008). Kahn will be mentioned several times throughout this book.
9. C. D. Spielberger, R. L. Gorsuch, and R. E. Lushene, *Manual for the State-Trait Anxiety Inventory (STAI)* (Palo Alto, CA: Consulting Psychologists Press, 1970).

10. Y. L. Hanin, "Emotions and Athletic Performance: Individual Zones of Optimal Functioning Model, *European Yearbook of Sport Psychology* (1997): 1, 29–72.
11. M. Friedman and R. H. Rosenman, *Type A Behavior* (New York: Knopf, 1974).
12. Lindsey Kaufman, "Google Got It Wrong. The Open-Office Trend is Destroying the Workplace," *Washington Post*, December 30, 2014, www.washingtonpost.com/posteverything/wp/2014/12/30/google-got-it-wrong-the-open-office-trend-is-destroying-the-workplace/.
13. Ibid.
14. Aoife Brennan, Jasdeep S. Chugh, and Theresa S. Kline, "Traditional versus Open Office Design: A Longitudinal Field Study," *Environment and Behavior* 34, no. 3 (May 2002): 279–299.
15. Annie Murphy Paul, "Workplace Woes: The 'Open' Office Is a Hotbed of Stress," *Time*, August 15, 2012, http://ideas.time.com/2012/08/15/why-the-open-office-is-a-hotbed-of-stress/.
16. Ibid.
17. C. Hull, Essentials of Behavior (New Haven, CT: Yale University Press, 1951); K. Spence, *Behavior Theory and Conditioning* (New Haven, CT: Yale University Press, 1956).
18. W. G. Chase and H. A. Simon, "Perception in Chess," *Cognitive Psychology* 4 (1973): 55–81; H. A. Simon and K. Gilmartin, "A Simulation of Memory for Chess Positions," *Cognitive Psychology* 5 (July 1973): 29–46.
19. J. R. Nitsch, "The Organization of Motor Behavior: An Action-Theoretical Perspective," in *Movement and Sport: Psychological Foundations and Effects, Vol. 2: Motor Control and Motor Learning*, eds. J. R. Nitsch and R. Seiler (Sankt Augustin, Germany: Academia, 1994), 3–21.
20. W. Kaufmann (ed.), *The Portable Nietzsche* (New York: Viking Penguin, 1954), 458.
21. U. Muras and P. Strasser, *Gerd Mueller: Der Bomber der Nation* [Gerd Mueller: The Bomber of the Nation] (Munich: Riva, 2015), 197–201.
22. Oren Huberman, "How Intuition Works," *Kalkalist*, September 27, 2011.

2

Motivation

Defining Our Driving Force

He who has a "Why?" in life, can tolerate almost any "How."
—FRIEDRICH WILHELM NIETZSCHE

I n the late 1980s I began working with the Wingate Institute, Israel's National Center for Physical Education and Sport, where I was appointed—among others—as a psychological consultant to the Israeli national table-tennis team. The first time I watched the players train, I was surprised by their frequent shouting and cursing: "You are an idiot!," "What did you do?," "Are you stupid?," and "Can't you play?" were regularly heard, along with some more colorful language and phrases that I probably shouldn't repeat here. I was amazed by the way the players yelled at each other, and I was thinking that my work was certainly cut out for me. After observing them more carefully, however, I realized that they only shouted or cursed after they themselves had made a mistake; they weren't cursing the other players, they were cursing themselves!

When I asked the players why they did this, they told me it was to "psych themselves up"—they cursed themselves in order to encourage and motivate themselves. A very strange habit indeed, especially given that we as a society are so often taught that success is a matter of thinking positively. But as it turns out, these players believed that self-criticism and negative self-talk were more motivating than any pep talk or cheerleader-like speech.

Strange as it was, at that time, Israel's best tennis table players seriously considered this counterproductive tactic to be highly effective in psyching themselves up. As I later found out, this bizarre habit had traditionally been passed down from generations of coaches and veteran players, creating a culture of motivation. This experience evoked my interest to better understand human motivation in athletic performance environments. To do so, however, I had to first consider the most basic aspects of motivation.

For example, let's assume that you are going to perform a very simple daily action, like driving your car from home to work. What does it take? Essentially, four basic things:

1. Produce energy to power movement by igniting the engine.
2. With the help of the energy produced, move the wheel in order to steer the car in the right direction.
3. Keep going, maintaining your speed and following traffic signals, and continue driving as long as required.
4. Reach your goal by arriving at work.

This four-step description is precisely the process we call "motivation." It deals with what energizes behavior (i.e., motives or drives) as well as what focuses energized behavior in a particular direction toward a goal. Thus, the first element to motivation is our buddy from chapter 1: arousal. The second element is direction, followed by maintenance, and finally the goal—everything we need to accomplish any endeavor in life.

As one of my professors in Jerusalem reasoned many years ago, if loosely defined, *all* psychology is really about motivation, making it an incredibly complex and expansive subject. We must therefore set limits on how we define the concept of motivation, even if they are arbitrary, in a sense. But before doing this, think about the word. "Motivation" comes from the Latin substantive *motivum*, which means "reason to move" or "drive." Why should we motivate people at all? Why should we motivate ourselves? Why should human beings be moved or driven?

The great ancient Greek philosophers, such as Socrates, Plato, and Aristotle, believed in the power of something that can be interpreted in today's jargon as motivation. The same goes for René Descartes—one of the greatest thinkers of the modern era after the Renaissance—whose writings on human will can be seen as one of the first attempts to suggest a philosophical theory of motivation. Some cynics, however, may play devil's advocate and argue, waxing ideologically, that exploitation in the service of big industry lies behind motivation. In the second half of the nineteenth century, together with the process of psychology becoming a legitimate academic discipline, motivation began to play a major role in this context.

Toward the end of the nineteenth century, the word "motivation" became commonplace. The world of psychology began to use it even more frequently in the early twentieth century, precisely the period of accelerated industrialization in many parts of the world, including the United States, Western Europe, and Japan. Within this zeitgeist it is not surprising that people were motivated—that is, "provided with a reason to act in a certain way." Otherwise, they would have probably stayed in homeostasis (a state that you already got to know from chapter 1).

Several theories of motivation portrayed humans as machine-like organisms, controlled and compelled to act by internal or external forces. In a time of accelerated industrialization, such an idea soon evolved, primarily with the spirit of "scientific management," developed by Frederick Taylor (1856–1915). Taylor started as a steel mill laborer, worked his way up to the position of chief engineer, and was later credited with being the first person to recognize the substantial role that motivation plays in job performance.

Taylor believed not only in carefully selecting and training employees to become first-class performers, but also in raising their motivation and production through increased wages, thereby emphasizing the importance of economic efficiency. This concept, Taylorism, was closely tied to the automation and mechanization of work, and was related to the ideas of Fordism. Both Taylorism and Fordism became engrained in the culture at the time, but not without some heavy criticism. For example, Charlie Chaplin's *Modern Times* (1936) took aim at this new culture of work, satirizing a world in which people *had* to be motivated by outside forces, otherwise they'd have no reason to do anything at all.

Later, supposedly more humanistic approaches to work motivation—such as the human relations movement, the human resource/organizational behavior approach, and the systems and contingency approaches—were developed and propagated. In the end, however, all of these approaches were intended in one way or another to achieve one major purpose, namely to motivate employees, thereby increasing their performance and above all—needless to say—the entire organization's productivity.

Of course, whether you believe the devil's advocate position or not, motivation is critical to high performance and success. Today all kinds of motivational techniques are espoused. Take the recent popularity of "bullet journaling"—a new method of journaling and note-taking to help people increase their productivity through a journal-writing framework. A to-do list, diary, and planner hybrid, the bullet journal tracks daily activities but also contributes to long-term goal planning, and acts as a self-motivator.

But what psychological factors are behind motivation? And what are the best ways to motivate others and ourselves?

INTRINSIC MOTIVATION

The only way to do great work is to love what you do.

—STEVE JOBS

As the Beatles sang, in order to become a star, "your car" has to be driven. But driven by what? In Oliver Kahn's book *Ich*, the champion German soccer goalkeeper tells his readers about the motivation that drove another sports hero I introduced in chapter 1, Michael Schumacher. Kahn points out that Schumacher does not drive simply to win. Of course he aims to win, but that's not his actual motive. Instead, winning a race is a byproduct that comes from the love of his sport and profession. Kahn explains that it's not about being first, but that Schumacher strives for perfection in each round every time. With consecutive perfect rounds, Schumacher succeeds in his goal and, as a result, wins the race. He's not doing it to win, he's doing it for himself.

This type of motivation, in which a person loves their chosen profession, is what we call "intrinsic motivation." Needless to say, Schumacher earned a lot of money in his career (his estimated net worth is upward of $800 million), but he had to love what he was doing in order to succeed. Intrinsic motivation is marked by doing something "for the sake of doing it"; *extrinsic* rewards—such as money, fame, or prestige—come later. Schumacher did not wait for somebody to drive him: he drove himself from within.

In fact, the best athletes I consulted really loved what they do. They were even willing and ready to undergo physical pain for their athletic careers, which often include suffering through strength and conditioning training and injuries while playing. To hone this point, I used to advise club presidents negotiating with their "tough" players—those who were hard bargainers—not to give in too soon, because at the end of the day their players would *beg* them to play and typically be willing to "pay" the presidents for this privilege, including all of the tireless work and effort athletes expend on training and in games. This reminds me of the wonderful O. Henry story "The Ransom of Red Chief," in which two kidnappers try ransoming an unruly child, but give up soon since he's so difficult; at the end, they are even ready to pay the child's father to take him off their hands.

When I was an associate professor, the Dean asked me if I would stop writing after I was promoted to a full professor. My immediate answer was, "Can I stop breathing?" After I became a full professor more than a decade ago, one of the strangest questions I ever heard was sometimes posed to me this way: "Miki, you are a full professor now, why do you still publish?"

The question implied that full professorship was some kind of House of Lords or, maybe worse yet, even a nursing home. This indicates that some of my colleagues do not truly love what they are doing—they just publish for extrinsic reasons (i.e., because of the old academic saying, "publish or perish"). Maybe they are in the wrong place: for me, a full professorship is wonderful precisely because I am free to publish whatever I want—the very essence, the raison d'etre, of the university as an institution.

Extrinsic rewards are typified by the infamous industrialist Henry Ford (1863–1947), who actually paid his workers a lot, surprisingly so for those days. Still, employee turnover in his plant was high—today, we would say that many of these workers "burned out." In the twenty-first-century business world, an emphasis on extrinsic motivation still exists at many companies, but there has also been a major shift toward intrinsic motivation as well. No place is this seen more than in the mission-driven companies that are not only breaking the status quo and creating positive change throughout the world, but who are also turning a major profit.

A prime example is the New York City–based eyeglasses and sunglasses company Warby Parker. Their mission is simple and described easily by their "buy a pair, give a pair" model: for every pair of glasses customers purchase online, the company makes a monthly donation to their nonprofit partners, covering the cost of sourcing that number of glasses. In doing so, these nonprofits train people in developing nations to provide eye exams and sell affordable glasses to their communities. This sustainable practice has led to the distribution of over a million pairs of glasses to people worldwide in need.

Warby Parker's motivation is to help others, while also providing fairly cheap glasses, which are considered ultra-hip, to domestic customers at around $95 per pair. It's a win-win, and was only possible because the founders had a mission to help others even before there was any money to be made. Their intrinsic motivation led to a company that they founded in 2010 with only $2,500 in seed investment money. As of April 2015, Warby Parker was valued at $1.2 billion.

Companies who have established a shared purpose or common goal will find greater success than those businesses solely driven by profit. For example, LinkedIn's CEO Jeff Weiner rallies the employees of the professional social network site around a powerful vision to "create economic opportunity for every member of the global workforce" and a mission to "connect the world's professionals to make them more productive and successful."[1] Even if everyday tasks can sometimes be mundane, at the end of the week these employees know they've contributed to something much greater than themselves—a much more powerful motivator than a paycheck.

Intrinsic motivation, however, does not have to manifest itself in a major philanthropic cause; many people find satisfaction in their work when simply creating a product or service *other* people can enjoy and love. As reported by *Forbes*, the O. C. Tanner Institute's *Great Work Study*, which began in 2010, showed that 88 percent of award-winning projects began by an employee asking a question that boiled down to, "What difference could I make that other people would love?"[2]

Such work fulfills you and makes you happy and satisfied. On this issue I completely agree with Steve Jobs, who is quoted as having said that "the only way to do great work is to love what you do." Still, even more than that, our brain and immune system work in a mysterious way so that the love we feel for what we do also helps us in coping with other personal issues, whether mental (e.g., depression) or physical (e.g., diseases like my Parkinson's). For example, while writing this very book, I happily occupied my time, consuming positive energy and imprisoning my "friend" Parkinson's in as small a place as possible, at least for a while.

In a broader sense, such intrinsic motivation provides us with meaning. As the great (and greatly misunderstood) German existentialist philosopher Friedrich Wilhelm Nietzsche (1844–1900) once said: "He who has a 'why' to live, can tolerate almost any 'how.'"

It has also been shown that people who thrive on intrinsic motivation at work will be more productive, feel more fulfilled, become better leaders, and, in turn, motivate others.[3] I have seen similar phenomena throughout the athletic teams I have worked with. Of course, earning money is important, but without intrinsic satisfaction, your success will be limited.

When all is said and done, the basis of intrinsic motivation relies on the subjective meaning you give to a task, event, or occurrence. As concentration camp survivor and existential psychiatrist and professor Viktor Emil Frankl (1905–1997) said, it is precisely the subjective meaning you give to things that may provide you with immeasurable powers to cope with extreme difficulties—such as a concentration camp—or more mundane troubles such as stress at work, divorce, or illness. That's why Nietzsche was right in saying "That which does not kill us, makes us stronger!"

Concentrate on your intrinsic motivation and the rewards will follow.

OVERMOTIVATION

> If you're a plumber and you don't do your job, you don't get any work.
> I don't think a plumber needs a pep talk.
>
> —GREGG POPOVICH

Many coaches, bosses, teachers, and parents are firm believers in the motivational speech, and there certainly are examples throughout history where such a motivational means has been proven effective.

A famous example from my research with Israeli sociologist and Wingate colleague Yair Galily can be found during the so-called golden age of Israeli basketball in the late 1970s.[4] In 1977 Maccabi Tel-Aviv, Israel's perennial champions, had to play against CSKA Moscow in the European Championship league. CSKA Moscow was the Soviet Army team which, during the Cold War, was perceived as a representative of the entire Soviet Bloc. On that occasion, Maccabi's legendary coach, the late Ralph Klein (1931–2008), said to his players prior to the game: "We are fighting for our country as well as for thousands of Jews who cannot immigrate to Israel because of Soviet policy. Let's beat the Soviet Bear!" One of the key players, Lou Silver, an American-born Jew, said that Klein did not have to say anything more, because "we were all [the Americans on the Maccabi squad] raised in the US, where fighting the 'Reds' was something you didn't have to explain at all."

Maccabi won 91 to 79 in an unforgettable game, advancing to the finals against Italy's champion team Mobilgirgi Varese. Before the final game, Coach Klein gave a brilliant speech once again. This time, all he said to the players was, "This evening, an entire state will sit and watch you. Everybody wants you to win. What is Varese? A small town in Italy with a good sweater store. But if you win this evening, you will be heroes of an entire state. You will remember it for all your life." Nothing more. Maccabi beat Mobilgirgi Varese 78 to 77 and won the European Championship for the first time.

In these cases, Klein's speeches were appropriate because he managed to help players focus and give their best on particularly special occasions. In addition, the coach knew his players well so he could talk directly to their sensitive points (e.g., "the Reds"). But such cases are really infrequent, nearly once-in-a-generation examples. More often, I have witnessed instances where coaches or club presidents have come into the locker room prior to a decisive game to psych up their players with a pep talk or motivational speech and failed.

They may have felt the need to explain how important the game was, what was "at stake" or "on the line." What they actually ended up doing, besides insulting the players' intelligence—of course a professional basketball player waiting to go on court for a championship game understands the inherent importance—was adding pressure that could tip the balance of stress from positive to negative, causing the players to choke.

There are successful coaches who seem to take this point to heart and tend to avoid pep talks. For example, on December 8, 2016, Chicago Bulls handed San Antonio Spurs its first road loss (95–91) after a marvelous 13–0 away game start of the season. Spurs coach Gregg Popovich furiously criticized his players' effort as follows:

I don't remember playing tonight. No Knute Rockne speeches. It's your job. If you're a plumber and you don't do your job, you don't get any work. I don't think a plumber needs a pep talk. A doctor botches operations, and he's not a doctor anymore. If you're a basketball player, you come ready. It's called maturity. It's your job.[5]

Coach Popovich seems to believe that mature, professional NBA players do not need motivational pep talks. But he is in a minority, I assume; more frequently, this type of overmotivation is still a common mistake in sports, business, education, and at home.

Just as there is a tendency for people to believe that all stress hurts performance, an issue discussed in chapter 1, many people think that you can never be too motivated. However, the truth is that supposedly motivational techniques can often have the opposite effect. Just as too much arousal can result in a negative effect on performance, too much motivation can produce the same problems.

Here we have, again, a connection to the inverted-U function. For example, in the first chapter of Dan Ariely's second bestseller, *The Upside of Irrationality*, the author discusses the issue of "paying more for less," exploring the relationship between motivation and performance and asking why big bonuses don't always work. It may be surprising, but Ariely and his colleagues found that those people who receive the largest bonuses actually demonstrate the lowest levels of performance. (Participants who could earn a small bonus or a medium-level bonus, however, did not differ much from each other.) After measuring people's performance on a wide range of tasks, they concluded that "paying people high bonuses can result in high performance when it comes to simple mechanical tasks, but the opposite can happen when you ask them to use their brains."

Ariely describes monetary motivation as a "double-edged sword," stating that in the case of work that requires cognitive ability, if the incentive levels are too high, a person may become distracted by the reward. The motivating factor—the additional money—can command too much attention, creating stress and reducing performance. If the incentive is smaller, however, it may help *increase* the person's performance.

In my opinion, it is arousal that underlies these phenomena. When you are highly motivated, your arousal increases—and there you are: just as we see with arousal, if the task is complex, high motivation will be detrimental to performance; if the task is simple, high motivation will help to improve performance. Again, one major solution to the problem is chunking; the more appropriate chunks you have, the more resistant you become to high levels of motivation. Thus, even when people "use their brain," success in task-performance is very often just a matter of intensive training and deep practice.

In today's work environments not just overmotivation, but the wrong *type* of motivation, may also have negative effects. For example, as Ariely pointed out, monetary incentives can only go so far. Many employees are beginning to prefer nonmonetary rewards, such as flexible hours, telecommuting, changes in the typical business dress code, or summer Fridays, which have become increasingly popular in the creative industries, such as fashion and publishing. Seemingly small improvements that make employees happier will not only motivate them, but also help them succeed.

Nonmonetary *recognition* has also become a popular motivator. It has been reported that public recognition of a job well done may prove more effective than a monetary reward.[6] Not only does recognition increase someone's status, but it also creates a more social environment, where people can recognize each other's accomplishments—while those recognized feel that they are performing meaningful work.

Choking Under Pressure

Much of the information on why overmotivation may be detrimental for human performance comes from the "choking under pressure" literature, which includes several studies conducted in the world of sports. For example, in Jose Apesteguia's and Ignacio Palacios-Huerta's famous 2010 article "Psychological Pressure in Competitive Environments," the two economists looked at soccer penalty shootouts where two teams, in alternating order, kicked directly from the 11-meter (36-foot) penalty mark to score a goal.

They collected data from 129 shootouts and found that the first team kicking won 60.5 percent of the cases (78 cases) and the second team only 39.5 percent (51)—despite an assumed a priori winning probability of 50 percent for each team. Apesteguia and Palacios-Huerta argue that this "first mover advantage" results from psychological pressure put on the "second mover." Simply stated, the second team tended to choke much more under the pressure.

Choking effects have also been found in many other sports. For example, Zheng Cao from Oregon State University analyzed the effects of psychological pressure on performance using NBA free throw data between 2002 and 2010. He found evidence that players do choke under pressure, because they shoot on average five to ten points worse than normal in the final seconds of close games.

In her 2010 book *Choke*, University of Chicago psychologist Sian Beilock examines the science behind why we choke under pressure—that is, why we mess up when it matters the most. According to Beilock, choking results from "overthinking," "paralysis by analysis," and worries, which inhibit the performance of well-practiced procedures by experts under pressure. In such a case performance is not only poor but rather worse than expected, given what the performer is capable of doing. This happens not only in sport (e.g., when a golfer botches a swing when she or he should have had it in the bag), but also in organizations, when employees compete for promotions (such as when a candidate tanks an interview), or at school, when students compete for grades (e.g., when the smartest students do poorly on a standardized exam). In all these situations, performers "choke under pressure," says Beilock.

It seems that pressure-induced failure results from the simultaneous influence of neurological, biomechanical, and attention related (e.g., distraction) mechanisms. To cope with the problem, people should try and "just do it" (as the Nike slogan says, or as Gerd Mueller repeatedly did). To develop this skill one is advised to practice under stress: creating stress in practice (just as Nitsch's "behavior in situation" discussed in chapter 1 would argue—remember?) increases the chances of performers to get used to the pressures of competition (so that competition will not be something threatening for them anymore, as you'll recall from Lazarus).

Paradoxically, says Beilock, it is the very desire to perform as well as possible (i.e., extremely high aspirations to function at one's best) in situations with a high degree of personal importance that creates the pressure and subsequently, the choking. So even with the type of positive intrinsic motivation discussed earlier in the chapter, such choking effects are possible—when you're passionate about what you do, this high degree of personal importance may cause higher levels of pressure under certain circumstances, potentially leading to the dreaded choke. In that case, you are overmotivated! It is, again, the subjective element (i.e., perceived importance) that matters.

For example, consider a very important presentation you may have given in the past that you were sure you had down perfectly in practice, but you bombed on the opening line. Of course, don't feel so bad—this is more common than you may think. Even if you know the material backward and forward, have your cue cards in hand, and a flawless PowerPoint prepared, it's possible to flop. Many times such a failure comes from extreme stress, despite any apparent reason to harbor such an intense feeling (don't forget. you know the material).

Issues arise, however, when you subjectively create a highly stressful situation by pressuring yourself. A major presentation may be important, but if you put too much emphasis on it you will reach a level of stress that is just too high (recall the lessons from chapter 1). The question of "How will I look?" is a major motivator in this situation since you want to make a good impression on your colleagues and bosses. You may also hope to gain more social status at work through an extraordinary performance. However, such desires and thoughts are completely irrelevant for successful task performance per se. Moreover, they may distract your attention and concentration from task fulfillment, thereby placing unnecessary pressure on yourself. You need to reconsider the situation—you need to reframe.

REFRAMING AND THE THREE STATES OF MOTIVATION

> The happiness of your life depends upon the quality of your thoughts.
> —MARCUS AURELIUS

In addition to chunking, another method to cope with problems revolving around motivation is to reframe the perceived importance of an event or action. However, let me first elaborate on this idea through a previous study of mine.[7]

Based on my doctoral dissertation, Gershon Tenenbaum (now a professor at Florida State University) and I developed a line of research on what we called "psychological performance crisis in competition." In this context, we wanted to study the athlete's motivation for competition and argued that such motivation will increase (a) when the perceived significance of the competition increases, and (b) the more uncertain the perceived chances of success are. Then we went on to define three possible states, with which you are already acquainted as applied to arousal in the last chapter:

- Too-high motivation, in which the competition is extremely significant for the athlete. The perceived chances of success are about 50/50, which results in extreme uncertainty (and you already know that uncertainty is an important stressor).
- Too-low motivation, in which the competition is of minor personal significance. The perceived chances of success hover around 0 percent or 100 percent.
- Optimal motivation, in which the significance of the competition is perceived by the athlete to be neither extremely high nor extremely low. The chances of success are estimated as neither completely uncertain (50 percent) nor extremely high (100 percent) or low (0 percent).

Figure 2.1—which should look familiar—displays these three possible motivation states and how they affect performance. Just as with arousal, it is an inverted-U function.

Figure 2.2 expands on these states in the following table, exhibiting the relationships between the two motivating components (personal significance of the competition and perceived chance of success) and the three states or levels of motivation. Interestingly, you can also observe a hidden inverted U in the table, but of another kind (did you find it?).

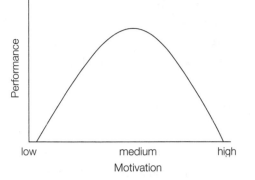

Figure 2.1 Motivational States versus Performance.

To sum up, there are two kinds of inverted Us exhibited here: the first, between the different motivational states and performance, and the second, between the two different components (personal significance and perceived chance of success) and the different levels of motivation (too high, too low, or optimal).

Gershon and I asked ourselves how top athletes perceived these three states in terms of their vulnerability to psychological performance crisis in competition. We studied twenty-eight elite German basketball players and forty-five elite Israeli team-handball players, having them fill out a

Perceived chance of success / Personal significance of competition	Extremely low chance (around 0%)		Extremely uncertain chance (about 50% to 50%)		Extremely high chance (around 100%)
Extremely high significance			Too high motivation		
		Optimal motivation		Optimal motivation	
Extremely low significance	Too low motivation				Too low motivation

Figure 2.2 Components and Levels of Motivation.

questionnaire about crisis vulnerability. What did we find? You proba-bly guessed right: the too-high state was perceived by the athletes—both Germans and Israelis—as the most problematic (that is, most vulnerable to crisis), followed by the too-low state. Of course the optimal state was evaluated as the most positive.

These findings are perfectly in line with the idea of choking under pres-sure, as well as with Dan Ariely's findings. But more than that, they provide us with a great way of trying to help top athletes and employees by refram-ing either the perceived importance of a forthcoming event or the perceived chances of successful performance. For example, when speaking in front of an audience at work, if you recognize the fact that it is *only* a presentation, the significance of the event will decrease in your eyes, along with the self-imposed, subjectively experienced pressure. Similarly, coaches can reduce athletes' experienced pressure by reframing the perceived chances of suc-cess in the eyes of their athletes—for example, through emphasizing the athletes' own strengths or pointing out that the opponents are not in their best shape that day, while insisting that their players are.

Nonoptimal motivation states can produce detrimental effects. In par-ticular, overmotivation can hurt—it may cause unnecessary (often self-imposed) pressure, choking, increased probability of crisis, decreased performance, and in the end, burnout. Such overmotivation can become negative—as in the Beatles' notable song, "I Want You (She's So Heavy)," if you want something so bad, they sing, it may sometimes drive you mad.

SUMMARY

An increase in motivation can result in increased performance, but it's not such a simple equation (for example, it should not be *too* high). There are numerous types of motivation, both for individuals and groups, and understanding the best way to motivate yourself and your team can be dif-ficult. It is necessary to take into account employees' and athletes' intrinsic motivation, which will make them more dedicated and industrious. As an individual, try to do something in your life for which you have intrinsic motivation—simply put, if you can, do something that you love, and you will find more success and happiness.

Overmotivation by coaches and bosses, in which they provide the wrong incentives by motivating the athletes too much, can lead to buckling under pressure and eventual burnout. When bosses misunderstand how to motivate their workforce, they may find their values are out of whack with those of their employees.

One's psychological ability to reframe the perceived importance of a task or project, and the perceived chances of success, is crucial. Motivation will increase when the perceived significance of the competition increases, along with the uncertainty of the perceived chances of success; however, these two elements can be reframed to optimize motivation. Finding ways to properly motivate yourself and your team will help everyone involved overcome choking, not only responding better to motivation tactics, but also in reframing the situation to help you cope, providing a sense of meaning in your personal life and career.

DAILY PRACTICES

As an Individual

- Ask yourself if what you're doing is intrinsically rewarding, not "just a paycheck." If necessary, consider what changes you potentially could make to create a more satisfying career.
- Don't put extra pressure on yourself—when you do so, you subjectively create a highly stressful situation under which you are more likely to choke.
- Incorporate reframing techniques to change your perspective and boost your motivation.

As a Leader

- Help your employees reframe perceived tasks by discussing their importance and the related planned goals.

- Get to know your team members so you understand what motivates them and how you can appropriately reward them for their work (remember: money isn't always the best motivator).
- Avoid overmotivation, in which you are likely to tip employees' balance of stress from positive to negative.

NOTES

1. Jeff Weiner, "From Vision to Values: The Importance of Defining Your Core," *LinkedIn*, October 28, 2012, www.linkedin.com/pulse/20121029044359-22330283-to-manage-hyper-growth-get-your-launch-trajectory-right.
2. David Sturt and Todd Nordstrom, "Do What You Love? Or, Love What You Do?" *Forbes*, March 13, 2015, www.forbes.com/sites/davidsturt/2015/03/13/do-what-you-love-or-love-what-you-do/#52e352e1628a.
3. Nicole Fallon Taylor, "12 Reasons to Do What You Love for a Living," *Business News Daily*, May 21, 2015, www.businessnewsdaily.com/7995-reasons-to-do-what-you-love.html.
4. Y. Galily and M. Bar-Eli, "From Tal Brody to European Champions: Americanization and the 'Golden Age' of Israeli Basketball, 1965–1979," *Journal of Sport History* 32 (January 2005): 303–327.
5. Scooby Axson, "Gregg Popovich Rips Spurs for 'Going Through Motions' in Loss to Bulls," *SI WIRE*, December 9, 2016, www.si.com/nba/2016/12/09/san-antonio-spurs-gregg-popovich-criticizes-team.
6. Elysha Ames, "Five Reasons Non Monetary Recognition is Better than Cash," *TemboSocial*, July 8, 2015, www.tembosocial.com/blog/five-reasons-non-monetary-recognition-is-better-than-cash.
7. M. Bar-Eli, "On the Use of Paradoxical Interventions in Counseling and Coaching in Sport," *The Sport Psychologist* 5 (March 1991): 61–72; M. Bar-Eli, G. Tenenbaum, and G. Elbaz, "Pre-Start Susceptibility to Psychological Crises in Competitive Sport: Theory and Research," *International Journal of Sport Psychology* 20 (1989): 13–30.

3

Aspiration

Enhancing Performance through Goal Setting

You are never too old to set another goal or to dream another dream.

—C. S. LEWIS

In the winter of 1971, I was a newly minted recruit in basic training in the Israeli Defense Forces (IDF), where my fellow soldiers and I had a sports instructor—what today is called a "combat fitness instructor"—named Eliezer Halfin. At the time, Halfin (1948–1972) was an impressive lightweight wrestler who was about to fulfill his greatest dream: he had been selected for the Israeli Olympic team at the Twentieth Olympic games, the 1972 Summer Olympics in Munich. (The event would have been the highlight of his career, but unfortunately, Eliezer came back from the games in a coffin: along with ten other Israeli athletes and coaches, he was taken hostage by Palestinian Black September terrorists and was later killed during a rescue attempt conducted by the German police.)

While Halfin was still with us, he was in charge of our daily fitness training. Among other drills, we had a 3,000 meter run (1.86 miles) that he required we complete in less than twelve minutes. He gave us time to build up to this speed with several training runs, preparing us for the "great day" when the money would be on the line. In training, among the 120 soldiers in our company, I was always one of the last to complete the run. Honestly, I didn't want to invest too much effort in vain or, in my mind at the time, when it didn't "really count"—basic training was hard enough already! This caused the commanders in charge of my group to become angry with me. So angry, in fact, that a few days before the final run, one of them disciplined me with two extra hours of nighttime guard duty—a terrible punishment for a recruit who had had almost no sleep over the last three months. I always had chutzpah, though, so I proposed a deal with the commander: if I completed the final run in less than twelve minutes, he would cancel my extra guard duty, but if I exceeded twelve minutes, my punishment would be doubled (four hours of nighttime duty is an eternity). Being sure of himself, he agreed—which was his big mistake.

Not only did I believe in myself, but I also had a plan. During all these training runs, I had observed that the company usually ended up in the following rank order:

1. Haim Avitan, a soldier who was "swift of foot, like a gazelle in the open field."[1] Haim was always way ahead of the rest of the pack.
2. Four soldiers who always finished behind Haim, in one order or another.
3. The majority of the company.
4. The laggards: ten to fifteen soldiers, including yours truly, who were always way behind all the others (and made the commanders furious).

My plan was simply to leach onto the first five runners from the beginning of the run as much as I possibly could. I knew that about three-quarters of the way through the course there was a steep hill (a real killer!) at which point Haim usually zoomed off while the four in group 2 left the rest of the company behind. If I managed to stay with Haim and group 2 until that uphill climb, I'd achieve my goal of staying below twelve minutes (my ranking did not matter, only my time).

During the run, the magnificent five gave me looks that said, "What are *you* doing *here* instead of lagging behind?" The commander who had planned on instituting my punishment was more than astonished to see me running down the hill for the last 400 meters (1,312 feet), finishing in sixth place and way below the magical twelve-minute barrier. My plan succeeded! The commander was fair enough not only to cancel my punishment but also to praise me time and again during the rest of basic training for what he considered my unbelievable achievement.

Though I was proud of my accomplishment (and happy to avoid the punishment), if you break down what occurred, it shouldn't seem unbelievable at all. I had no motivation to run faster until I faced potential discipline. At that point, I knew if I came up with a plan and developed an appropriate strategy with a specific goal, I could increase my performance even without any additional physical training. Once I had a clear goal—stay with the leading group until the steep hill—I pushed myself to anchor to the lead runner. In doing so I reset my expectations, my motivation increased, and I knew exactly what had to be done.

Simply put, human performance isn't always all about strength or ability—sometimes all that is necessary is the motivation to reach a clearly defined goal. People may be surprised to find that they can meet or rise above expectations (their own or others) through this process. Thinking about my experience in running the IDF drill more than forty-five years later, I believe I may have succeeded in this task because I actually followed advice offered by good old Aristotle, who said, "First, have a definite, clear practical ideal; a goal, an objective. Second, have the necessary means to achieve your ends . . . Third, adjust all your means to that end."

GOAL SETTING AS STRATEGY

> Miki, Bob Weinberg wants to visit Israel. Let's study goal-setting with him.
>   —GERSHON TENENBAUM

Today, goal setting is one of the most commonly used performance-enhancement strategies in the behavioral sciences. I believe part of the reason the subject has become so popular is the fact that goal setting has one unique characteristic, which is substantially different from most, if not all, studies on what motivates us to succeed: in goal setting *actual behavior*, not attitude, is measured. In essence, most of the research on motivation is attitudinal—the participants report verbally when we ask them to what extent they want something, intend to do something, and the like. However, in the goal-setting domain, we usually measure observable performance.

In the late 1960s, Professor Edwin A. Locke of the University of Maryland—later joined by fellow psychologist Professor Gary P. Latham, then of the University of Washington—proposed a theory of work motivation based on the concept of goal setting. From their theory, they derived goal-setting techniques that rely on a series of propositions that help explain, predict, and enhance human performance. Over the years, more than 90 percent of the studies investigating goal setting have demonstrated that goal setting does indeed have a powerful and consistent effect on human performance. However, it was only after the publication of Locke and Latham's seminal 1985 paper that such techniques were used in the sport and exercise domain on a more or less systematic, research-based way. This was a few years before I met Robert Steven (Bob) Weinberg, a professor of sport psychology at Miami University in Oxford, Ohio.

Bob was one of the first sport psychologists to study goal setting in sports. After meeting him in the late 1980s, my senior colleague Gershon Tenenbaum (already mentioned in chapter 2) suggested that he, Bob, and I write a research proposal together on the topic. Bob came to Israel and stayed with us at Wingate, and I was pumped into sports-related goal-setting research. Over time, as with many aspects of sports psychology, I saw that the concept of goal setting, examined through a sports lens, could be applied to many other areas.

Specificity and Proximity

The most important goal-setting principle is goal specificity: specific goals are much more effective than nonspecific goals in producing change in one's behavior and increasing performance. For example, if a sales manager were to tell her staff that each member of the team had to sell a certain number of products per month to reach a company-wide revenue or profits goal (specific), the employees are more likely to hit that target than if the sales manager simply said, "Go out there and do your best!" (nonspecific).

Why do specific goals work so much more effectively? First and foremost, because they regulate performance, helping you in planning, focusing, and directing your activity. They also elicit your effort, perseverance, and dedication, and accurately measure your actions and success in performing your task. The ability to effectively evaluate performance means that it is possible to then receive feedback, which will eventually help in making corrections to increase your later performance. However, there are different kinds of specificity.

Toward the end of the 1980s, almost no sport research existed about goal proximity—that is, the time range in which a person plans to reach a goal. Therefore my colleagues and I decided to study goal proximity in a sports setting. In essence, goals can be set in the short run, in the long run, and in both. What we wanted to find out was whether using short-term goals *plus* long-term goals would indeed lead to better performance than using short- *or* long-term goals alone.

In a large field experiment, we took 214 Israeli high school students (ninth graders participating in physical education classes) and randomly assigned them to one of the following goal-setting conditions:

Specific
GROUP A: short-term goals;
GROUP B: long-term goals;
GROUP C: short- plus long-term goals.

Nonspecific
GROUP D: "do your best" goals;
GROUP E: no goals.

After a three-week baseline period, participants were tested once every two weeks on a three-minute sit-up task over the course of a ten-week experimental period. We found that all the specific groups progressed substantially through the ten weeks: the short- plus long-term group (group c) exhibited the greatest increase in performance (29.34 sit-ups on average, an increase of 29.43 percent). The short-term (group a) and the long-term (group b) groups also displayed significant improvements (18.83, 20.7 percent and 11.42, 10.5 percent, respectively). However, the "do your best" and the "no goals" groups did not progress significantly.

In other words, our results supported both principles: goal specificity (only specific conditions improved, but not nonspecific conditions such as "do your best" or "no goals") and goal proximity (the greatest increase was demonstrated in short- plus long-term goals, followed by short-term and then long-term improvements). To strengthen these conclusions, we ran a second field experiment with 102 participants, this time 11th- and 12th-grade students, but with only the long- plus short- term goal versus the "do your best" goal. Again, we found a significant improvement only in the specific combination condition (average improvement of 24.76 sit-ups, an increase of 24.3 percent).

In 1991, we published the article based on our findings.[2] We were honored when the great psychologist Albert Bandura referred to our article to demonstrate goal-proximity in his seminal 1997 book *Self-Efficacy: The Exercise of Control* and took it further by describing in a vivid example how John Naber, one of the greatest American swimmers of all times, prepared for the Olympics. Bandura explained that Naber came up with the specific goal of cutting four seconds off his best time, estimating that if he succeeded in doing so, he would win the gold.

The athlete trained himself by breaking this major goal down into small steps. That is, in order to achieve his specific long-term goal—shaving off those four seconds, leading him to the gold medal—he broke this time goal into smaller pieces, which he then achieved step by step. Thus, Naber actually combined long- and short-term goals to increase his performance, just as shown with the Israeli phys. ed. students.

Bandura's major notion was that short-term challenges serve to optimize performance, thereby facilitating the achievement of long-term goals. This idea was further demonstrated in a study my colleagues and I conducted in which we compared only two conditions—long-term versus short- plus long-term—trying to improve physical performance of adolescents with behavior disorders.

In a similar though not entirely identical procedure as the previous study, we measured the participants' performance on a one-minute sit-up task.[3] As predicted, we found that the short- plus long-term condition exhibited the greatest increase in performance, although the long-term group also displayed significant improvements (9.05 and 4.35 sit-ups respectively, small but statistically significant averages of progress). Thus, we provided further evidence for the goal-proximity principle. What was far more important, however, was that this was the first time ever that goal setting was used as a motivational technique for enhancing physical performance of any special population, in this case adolescents with behavior disorders.

Aside from solely physical performance, it is possible to see how such goal-setting techniques in relation to goal proximity can be effective in one's professional career, combining specific short- and long-term goals. Think of Naber again: he reached his long-term goal through mastering a series of short-term goals. As an individual, you can develop daily, weekly, monthly, and yearly goals (short-term) that will lead you to continual success in your career (long-term). Combining specific short-term ones (e.g., daily tasks) with long-term ones (e.g., career advancement) will lead to higher productivity.

For example, if you have a plan to be promoted to a certain level within the next five years, think of the specific steps you need to take in order to receive that promotion. Though you may have a general idea, it's imperative that you know the *specifics*, which may require feedback from bosses, managers, and even colleagues. What does your boss expect from you over the next few months? Over the next year? Though most companies institute quarterly, six-month, or annual reviews, you may want to check in with your boss or manager more regularly to make sure you are on track to reach your planned goals, short- and long-term.

As a boss or manager, your ability to create specific, short-term and long-term goals for your team, and yourself, will be necessary to maximize performance as well. However, as we will see in the following sections, you must make sure that the goals are also attainable, understandable, and acceptable.

GOAL DIFFICULTY AND ACCEPTANCE

> Stuff your stupid goals.
>
> *—our participants in the IDF goal difficulty study*

Toward the mid-1990s, evidence accumulated that supported the most central principle of goal setting, goal specificity. However, evidence was somewhat less decisive regarding the *kinds* of specificity. For example, Locke and Latham suggested a principle they called goal difficulty, which hypothesized that in order to maximize human performance, specific goals that are difficult, yet realistic and attainable, should be set. According to this idea, specific goals that are too easy or too difficult for the performer would be less effective (i.e., would result in smaller improvements in one's performance) than realistic and attainable goals. A problem existed in the sports and exercise domain, however, since only a few studies had tested this hypothesis; moreover, they failed to demonstrate any negative effects (i.e., lesser performance gains) of setting unreachable goals.

To deal with this problem, my colleagues and I conducted a huge field experiment that led to one of our best papers, published in 1997.[4] Similar to our earlier work on goal proximity and specificity, this was a pioneering study as it was the first in the sport and exercise domain to demonstrate that unattainable, improbable goals produced significantly lower performances than difficult but realistic ones.

In the study, we employed 346 male ninth- and tenth-grade Israeli high school students from fifteen schools as participants. The schools were randomly assigned to one of fifteen conditions, representing five levels of goal conditions and three levels of practice durations (four, six, and eight weeks). The five goal conditions were:

Nonspecific

1. "do" (no goals);
2. "do your best."

Specific

3. "improve by 10%" (easy);
4. "improve by 20%" (difficult and realistic);
5. "improve by 40%" (improbable or unattainable).

We found that across practice durations, the greatest gains in sit-ups (average of 25.84) were achieved by the "difficult and realistic" groups, followed by the "easy" groups (25.13). The "improbable and unattainable" groups demonstrated a smaller average gain (19.26) in sit-ups. The lowest gains were achieved by the "do" and "do your best" groups (10.15 and 7.75 respectively). Thus, all the specific groups (goal conditions 3, 4, and 5) performed much better than all the nonspecific groups (goal conditions 1 and 2), and across practice durations, the "difficult and realistic" groups (goal condition 4) exhibited the greatest increase in performance, followed by the "easy" groups (goal condition 3).

Most important, however, was the finding that performance gains of the "improbable and unattainable" groups (goal condition 5) were *substantially smaller* compared with the "difficult and realistic" groups (goal condition 4). Thus our study strongly supported not only goal specificity, but also, for the first time in the sports and exercise domain, Locke and Latham's goal-difficulty principle. In other words, our findings showed that goal specificity works, and that Locke and Latham's predictions concerning too easy and especially too difficult goals are of high validity also in the sport and exercise domain.

Why did we succeed in showing that setting specific, difficult, and realistic goals works and that the predictions made by Lock and Latham were valid in the sports domain, in particular with regard to the substantially smaller performance gains of the "too difficult" group, when so many others had tried to do so and failed? First of all, we carefully defined the specific improvement scores—percentage gains or the difficulty levels—based on three procedures:

(1) We used real data collected by Bob Weinberg and his colleagues in a previous study;[5]
(2) We validated these numbers with the help of two top experts in physical education, both of them high-ranking officers in the IDF Combat Fitness Center with extensive experience working with youth in this area;
(3) We asked our participants about their perceived levels of goal difficulty in each of the specific conditions.

We did not simply assume that something was easy, difficult, or too difficult—we also tested our assumptions. But there was a deeper, no less important reason: we learned from our own failure.

Prior to this study, in 1993 we had conducted another field experiment to test goal difficulty, but despite our best efforts, we failed to demonstrate the effects predicted by Locke and Latham.[6] We employed 184 IDF soldiers as participants, having them perform a number of athletic tasks, including an uphill run, maneuvers on a horizontal bar and parallel bars, an obstacle course, and the 3,000 meter (1.86 mile) run (exactly what I did when I was a soldier). The results? No significant effects whatsoever—a catastrophe for a researcher, but we did not give up. In fact, we learned what we should *not* do, which led us to the success of the 1997 study.

We encountered a few different problems in the IDF soldiers' goal-setting study, but one major issue we found was of particular significance both theoretically and practically: more than 50 percent of our participants in the different conditions *set goals for themselves*—they did not accept the goals *we set for them*! Essentially, they thought: "stuff your stupid goals, I'm setting my own."

We did not take into account the nature of our participants: they were soldiers who were voluntarily taking part in a physical fitness training camp. It is logical to assume that such participants would strive to excel when facing *any* physical challenge since they would perceive the challenge as an integral part of their daily training regime, which naturally entails striving to excel (otherwise they would not have volunteered). Accordingly, we came to the somewhat provocative conclusion that a formal setting with specific goals may be unnecessary for people who are always strongly motivated to excel in a particular area since such participants may successfully motivate themselves through spontaneous goal setting.

In other words, goal setting is a story of "on average": a particular group will be on average better than another group (depending on the goal conditions, of course), but there is also a variance reflecting individual differences. In the IDF study, for example, we did not take into account the unique characteristics of our participants. Contrary to its image, goal setting is not like a puppet-on-a-string situation—you don't simply set goals and expect your participants to jump accordingly. People must understand the goals set for them and accept them as their own, internalizing them, otherwise goal setting will not work.

The importance of goal acceptance becomes even higher when it comes to application in working with others. Keep in mind that you often work with *individuals*, so you must take into account their unique way of seeing things. In any professional or business setting, working with a group of people with disparate points of view, backgrounds, and talents can be difficult. Therefore, getting to know and understand your staff is necessary to ensuring that everyone internalizes their individual, team, and company goals. As the opening song in the old musical *The Music Man* put it, "you've got to know the territory."

Today's most successful organizations make a concerted effort to align their employees with the goals that will lead to the highest levels of performance. Keep in mind that this may not always mean looking solely at the "bottom line." For example, Apple's Chief Design Officer Sir Jonathan Ive—the designer behind the iMac, iPod, iPhone, iPad, Apple Watch, and many other Apple products—has been quoted as saying Apple's goal "isn't to make money," but to "try to make great products."[7] He believes that if the company attains this goal, people will like the products, and the revenue will follow. This concept is passed down throughout the company.

It's easy to see from Apple's simple, elegant products to how their employees at all levels—from the sales team on the floor, to the Genius Bar, and to current CEO Tim Cook—come together to create a consistent brand with a consistent overall goal: "enriching lives." These two words are actually included on the small Apple Retail credo card all employees are encouraged to carry. The idea behind such a motto is to bring a whole company together, to connect and become in synch around a common vision. When that vision is then broken down into goals, and goal-oriented actions, everyone from assistant to CEO knows what is expected and how they play a part in the company's overall performance and success.

Goals at Apple are considered "organization-centered."[8] When a specific organizational goal is set at Apple, it is fully explained to employees. Line managers discuss these goals with the members of their teams, along with the steps that need to be taken to reach them. Individual performance is measured compared to the set goals, and bosses and managers let employees know how they have helped achieve these company objectives through annual performance reviews.[9] Apple also uses 360 degree assessment—a type of feedback system that provides employees with confidential, anonymous feedback from the people they work with, including their peers.[10] In this way, Apple not only stresses the ultimate objective to make great products and enrich lives, but also gives their employees specific directives and goals on how to make this possible.

Apple cofounder Steve Jobs, however, was well known for setting seemingly impossible goals at a micro level. For example, there is the fabled story of the creation of the iPod. Supposedly during an early prototype meeting, engineers presented the new product to Jobs. He picked the iPod up, looked it over, and then flat-out told the engineers, surely to their chagrin, that it was too big. According to the tale, the engineers protested, saying there was no way to make it any smaller. Jobs listened to them attentively, then, after they finished talking, he walked over to a fish tank in the room, and dropped the brand new device in. Air bubbles began floating to the top once the iPod landed on the aquarium floor, at which point Jobs stated, "Those are air bubbles. That means there's space in there. Make it smaller."[11] Though it may be extreme, this story exemplifies the main elements of goal setting discussed throughout the chapter: specific, difficult, attainable, and accepted.

First, Jobs could not have been any more specific about the goal: make the device smaller. In regards to difficulty, the team of engineers thought it was an immense challenge—they were originally convinced the prototype was the smallest it could be. But Jobs knew better, and by dropping that iPod into the water, he showed that there was space for improvement: he knew it was attainable and he convinced his team that it was, too. They understood the goal—he couldn't have been clearer—and accepted the challenge. In the end, they made the iPod smaller, and over the years, they have continued to do so. The first iPod released to the public had a depth of 19.88 mm,[12] and the most recent version of the iPod touch is only 6.1 mm thick.[13] Jobs may have aimed high at times, but he always knew what was truly possible.

Leaders need to set attainable goals for their employees, and for themselves, and need to get the whole group on board by clarifying what is expected, what the goal is, and how to achieve it. Difficult but realistic goals help lead to success, but they need to be fully explained and accepted by those involved. Creating clear, acceptable goals for your team is instrumental. Still, disruptions are likely to occur, at which point goals need to be re-examined—if they've changed, they need to be reconsidered, rediscussed, and re-explained.

GOAL SPECIFICITY IN A NATURAL SETTING

> But Dad, it's obvious.
>
> —Asaph Bar-Eli

Is it more advantageous for a soccer team in a home-and-away set of games in a knock-out system to enjoy the home advantage in the first game, or the second? If we accept basic fairness principles, then a team's chances of winning when playing either the first or second game at home should be 50/50, right? My good friend and colleague Ronnie Lidor and I investigated this very question.

To make a long story short, we analyzed 398 soccer games (199 played at home and 199 played away): 220 games (110 home and 110 away) played in the European Football Association (UEFA) Champions League—the highest level of European play—and 178 games (89 home and 89 away) in the UEFA Cup, a lower level contest than the Champions League. What we found was astonishing.

Across both levels of contest, teams playing the second game at home had a substantially higher chance of advancing to the next round (61.8 percent) than teams playing the first game at home (38.2 percent). Digging deeper into the data, we looked at the number of goals scored. Here we found something even more interesting: The average number of goals scored increased from game 1 to game 2—but only for the home teams. In game 1, the home team scored 1.27 goals on average, and the away team 0.89. In game 2, however, the number of goals scored by the home team jumped to 1.68 on average, but the average score for the away team was similar to that of game 1 at 0.85 goals. In other words, it was not that the away teams became worse from game 1 to game 2, but that the home teams improved substantially.

It seemed that we had found something interesting, but what was it exactly and how could we explain it? To be honest, as clever and intelligent as we believe ourselves to be, sometimes even university professors with extensive research experience are blind to the obvious. Such was this case; Ronnie and I broke our heads trying to understand what had happened here, but it was all in vain.

One day, however, I told my son Asaph—who has a great interest in, and knowledge of, sports—about these results. He looked at me with a pitying "are you kidding me?" expression and without hesitation said, "But Dad, it's obvious: in the second game, they know *exactly* what they have to do!"

And then, the bell rang. I literally kissed Asaph on his head and then immediately rushed off to call Ronnie. I told him Asaph's idea, and that Ronnie and I were both idiots, especially me: How can a supposed expert on goal setting disregard this obvious difference between "do your best" and "goal specificity"?

In the first game, both teams strived for maximal performance, but in the second game, each team had a specific goal because they knew exactly where they stood and could therefore pursue that specific goal. Notice: across all 398 games, the average number of goals scored in the second game was 2.53, as compared to only 2.16 in the first game. In other words, at first sight, the overall total "production" of the teams in the second game seemed to increase substantially. However, taking a closer look at the source of this overall increase, it is clear that it comes only from the increase in goal production of the home teams (from 1.27 to 1.68) and not from any change in the scoring average of away teams (0.89 versus 0.85). In terms of goals scored, goal specificity seemed to substantially affect only the home teams because only their performances improved substantially under specific versus nonspecific conditions.

Although the motivational level and overall performance could have been greater in both teams in the second game, it was only the home team that was able to elevate performance due to the specific goals they set. We thought what happened there had something to do with the so-called home advantage, a well-documented phenomenon, which is, however, still somewhat ambiguous. We believe that when goal specificity exists, home advantage is amplified; when the home team knows exactly what to do, this team's performance will be substantially better than when it hosts the first game with no specific goals. The major effects result from the fact that in the first game, both teams attempt to achieve their best, whereas in the second game, goal specificity exists, amplifying the already existent home advantage. All in all, then, we were happy to see that we could demonstrate how goal conditions substantially affect performance in a "natural" rather than artificially planned experimental context, in line with the goal-specificity principle.

APPLYING THE GOAL-SETTING PRINCIPLES

A journey of a thousand miles begins with a single step.

—Lao-tzu

Levi Eshkol (1895–1969), Israel's third prime minister (serving from 1963–1969), was famous for his earthy wisdom, often expressed not in Hebrew, but rather in Yiddish. As the story goes, one day, labor union representatives came to Mr. Eshkol and requested that he shorten the working week from six days, which it was at the time, to five days. Mr. Eshkol listened carefully, and then responded with a very serious expression on his face: "You want to work five days? Fine with me, but do me a favor—start by first working *one*"—sarcastically implying that the union members weren't currently working *at all*. He was saying that they needed to start slowly and then work up to five days. Funny as it sounds, I often use the same notion (which I call "the Eshkol principle") when consulting athletes.

For example, a few years ago, I worked as a consultant to one of the top basketball teams in Israel. One young player suffered from a problem many basketball players face, which is a fear of "penetrating to the basket." The term, well known in basketball terminology, refers to the point when the offensive player breaks through the defense and drives toward the basket. Having a fear of doing so seriously limits the player's game because opponents who are aware of this limitation simply prevent the player from shooting from outside the key—the common alternative to penetration— thereby neutralizing him or her.

This young player, Yaacov ("Kobi") B.—not to be confused with Kobe Bryant—had precisely this problem: he was an excellent three-point shooter, but was afraid of driving the ball to the basket. As a result, if opponents prevented him from shooting threes, he wasn't a threat. This became quite an obstacle to the team's game plan, until the coach asked me to intervene to help "promote the player's aggressiveness in general and penetrations in particular." For this purpose, I used everything I know— and now you also know—about goal setting, specifically incorporating the Ekshol principle.

I started by asking Kobi how many penetrations he believed he could realistically make in the twenty minutes (on average) he usually played. He told me that six or seven would be an attainable challenge. Just as Ekshol told the union reps, I told Kobi that instead of going for seven, he should start smaller. Then we agreed that in his next game, he should commit to make only two penetrations (a specific goal). Every additional penetration would be considered a bonus. The immediate effect was that in the following game, he made more than the two obligated; he simply gained confidence in his own competence after successfully making these penetrations. Consequently, he started to penetrate more and more, giving me a thumbs up after every successful penetration as I sat on the bench and watched.

In the long run, Kobi became much more versatile in his game. His opponents started to take his penetration ability much more seriously; as a result, he also found himself free more often to shoot the three-pointers he liked so much. Over time not only was his problem solved, but slowly, he received more and more playing time as the coach continuously gained confidence in him. Kobi found that in order to be an efficient three-point shooter, he had to penetrate, because it was precisely penetration that paradoxically facilitated the opposite—the shooting.

This case was a successful application of all three principles discussed earlier:

1. The player had a specific goal ("aggressiveness" was translated into "number of penetrations");
2. The goal was set in the long term (six to seven penetrations) plus short-term (two penetrations);
3. The goal was difficult yet attainable (according to his own perception).

In addition, Kobi accepted the goal after he and I worked it out together. Taking his individual, subjective perspective into account was of crucial importance to the success of the entire process. Only then could he take his first single step to begin his journey of a thousand miles.

Wisdom versus Smarts

I'd like to take a moment to point out that even the most effective principles we've discussed here must be applied with great caution. I'll give you a somewhat grotesque example to demonstrate what I mean. Take the most

basic principle of goal setting, goal specificity. Goal specificity is usually connected with quantitative measurement so it's possible to examine results and
provide feedback, as mentioned. But wait a minute: What do you do with
a performance that is by nature not measurable? Do you evaluate painters
only by the number of paintings they draw? Or the Beatles by the number of
songs they composed? How about measuring philosophers by the number
of opinions they present?

A smart industrial engineer, setting specific goals according to the principles of organizational psychology or operational management, might
say: "O.K., my friend the philosopher, you are expected to invent 2 plus/
minus 0.5 opinions per day," or "If you invented 4 opinions yesterday, don't
bother working today, because you already invented enough for both days
combined." You get the point. As we say in Israel: "Smart people know
how to get out of troubles that wise guys know how to avoid in advance."
So don't be smart, be wise!

SUMMARY

As the quote from C. S. Lewis says, even if you are old—like me, for
example—you are advised to set goals, those that are often derived from
dreams (or as we say in the current organizational jargon—so-called
visions). Goal setting is effective, but only if you set the right goals, taking
individual differences into account, cooperatively setting goals among a
team, group, or whole company.

The most important goal-setting principle is goal specificity. Specific
goals regulate performance, helping in planning, focusing, and directing
a team's activities; eliciting their effort, perseverance, and dedication; and
measuring the results, receiving feedback, and making corrections to the
process.

A major component of goal specificity is goal proximity, the consideration of short-term and long-term goals. In your career, combining specific short-term goals (e.g., daily tasks) with long-term ones (e.g., career
advancement) will lead to higher productivity.

But even with goal specificity and proximity, there are still the questions of goal difficulty and acceptance—for example, improbable goals produce significantly lower performance gains than difficult but realistic ones. Leaders need to set attainable goals for their employees, and for themselves, and need to get the whole group on board by clarifying what is expected, what the goal is, and how to achieve it.

DAILY PRACTICES

As an Individual

- Set a combination of short-term and long-term *specific* goals for yourself. Include every day tasks that will help lead to your overall larger, long-term goal.
- Work with your manager or boss to make sure these goals are understandable and acceptable to both of you.
- Don't be smart, be wise!

As a Leader

- Set specific, short- and long-term goals for your team that are challenging but also attainable.
- Regularly provide feedback to employees and team members so they know whether or not they are on track to achieving set goals.
- Help foster a common work culture to make sure that, despite people's differences, everyone is on the same page in regards to your company's shared goals and values.

NOTES

1. 2 Sam. 2:18.
2. G. Tenenbaum, S. Pinchas, G. Elbaz, M. Bar-Eli, and R. Weinberg, "Effect of Goal Proximity and Goal Specificity on Muscular Endurance Performance: A Replication and Extension," *Journal of Sport and Exercise Psychology* 13 (1991): 174–187.

3. M. Bar-Eli, I. Hartman, and N. Levy-Kolker, "Using Goal Setting to Improve Physical Performance of Adolescents with Behavior Disorders: The Effect of Goal Proximity," *Adapted Physical Activity Quarterly* 11 (January 1994): 86–97.

4. M. Bar-Eli, G. Tenenbaum, J. S. Pie, Y. Btesh, and A. Almog, "Effect of Goal Difficulty, Goal Specificity and Duration of Practice Time Intervals on Muscular Endurance Performance," *Journal of Sports Sciences* 15 (April 1997): 125–135.

5. R. Weinberg, C. Fowler, A. Jackson, J. Bagnall, and L. Bruya, "Effect of Goal Difficulty on Motor Performance: A Replication across Tasks and Subjects," *Journal of Sport and Exercise Psychology* 13 (June 1991): 160–173.

6. M. Bar-Eli, N. Levy-Kolker, G. Tenenbaum, and R. S. Weinberg, "Effect of Goal Difficulty on Performance of Aerobic, Anaerobic, and Power Tasks in Laboratory and Field Settings," *Journal of Sport Behavior* 16 (1993): 17–32.

7. Katherine Rushton, "Apple Design Chief: 'Our Goal Isn't to Make Money,'" *Telegraph*, July 30, 2012, www.telegraph.co.uk/technology/apple/9438662/Apple-design-chief-Our-goal-isnt-to-make-money.html.

8. Adelina Chelniciuc, "Performance Management at Apple, Google, and Statoil," *Performance Magazine*, September 5, 2013, www.performancemagazine.org/performance-management-at-apple-google-and-statoil/.

9. Audi Cole, "The Usefulness of Performance Management in Aligning Individual and Organizational Goals for Successful Results," Academia.edu, 2011, www.academia.edu/1999551/The_usefulness_of_Performance_Management_in_Aligning_Individual_and_Organizational_goals_for_successful_results.

10. Chelniciuc, "Performance Management at Apple, Google, and Statoil."

11. Steven Tweedie, "Steve Jobs Dropped the First iPod Prototype into an Aquarium to Prove a Point," *Business Insider*, November 8, 2014, www.businessinsider.com/steve-jobs-threw-ipod-prototype-into-an-aquarium-to-prove-a-point-2014-11.

12. Ibid.

13. iPod Touch Product Specs, Apple, 2016, www.apple.com/ipod-touch/specs/.

PART II

Calibrating Your Behavior

Self-Confidence

Handling Expectations and Unexpected Obstacles

If I can take it, I can make it.
—Louis Zamperini, *US WWII veteran and Olympic distance runner*

In 2013 I won a scholarship through the Mercator foundation, which finances expert foreign (non-German) professors to visit Germany and work with local universities. Eberhard Karls University invited me to spend a semester in Tuebingen, a small, colorful city in the southwestern part of the country. There, I enjoyed the opportunity to quietly cooperate with my colleagues from the Institute of Sports Science, working on various problems related to the psychological side of sport management.

In my leisure time, I traveled around Tuebingen's beautiful environs, including the Black Forest. When traveling in this wooded mountain range, you will frequently see signs warning you about different kinds of animals. These included cows, gazelles, horses (with their riders, of course), toads, and ticks. Seeing these signs gave me a laugh since back in the Beer-Sheva region, where I live, you will find many such signs, but with pictures of only one animal: the camel.

So what would happen if you were visiting me in Beer-Sheva, and while driving in the city's surroundings, you suddenly encountered a donkey (with or without a rider)? Or a lamb? Or a goat? In fact there is a large Bedouin population, traditionally nomadic tribes, near Beer-Sheva, who frequently use such animals, so it's not entirely impossible. That being said, if you didn't know that fact and since no signs are posted about those animals (only camels), if a donkey ran out in front of you, you'd likely be quite surprised! Think for a moment then: why are such signs posted at all, whether in the Black Forest, in the desert next to Beer-Sheva, or anywhere else? To *avoid* surprises. If you are warned about camels and one actually appears on the road, you are not shocked. The signs therefore reduce the gap between what you expect and what happens in reality.

EXPECTATIONS AND PERFORMANCE

False expectations take away joy.

—SANDRA BULLOCK

The term "expectation" is almost as old as psychology itself, having been introduced to the field in the 1930s by the notable American psychologist Edward Chase Tolman (1886–1959). Tolman was one of the first psychologists to promote the cognitive approach, emphasizing the connection between human perception of environmental stimuli, individual expectations, and performance. In his seminal 1948 article "Cognitive Maps in Rats and Men," published in *Psychological Review*, he argued that expectations are embedded in a "cognitive map" that determines, for example, a person's anticipation about the performance of an upcoming task in a particular environment.

Prior to any athletic event, athletes form expectations about the competition. They define a goal, as discussed in chapter 3, and design a plan, which forms a basis for the effecting realization. A plan is designed to control our actions and regulate performance; it includes our expectations concerning not only the performance itself, but also the outcome or results of this performance. For example, athletes will not only consider how they expect to perform a drill the best way they can, but also what they expect as a result of that optimal performance, such as becoming a world champion. Similarly, in an office setting, you would likely expect that your positive performance would lead to new responsibilities, a potential raise or bonus, and an eventual promotion.

However, even if your plan is wonderful on both the strategic-tactical macro level and the tactical-operational micro level, there will always be some degree of uncertainty—paradoxically, that uncertainty is the only thing you can definitely count on. (For example, that promotion may go to a colleague.) To cope with this problem you must try to reduce uncertainty and increase the expected at the cost of the unexpected. People therefore need to adjust to the specific conditions of any contest or obstacle, obtaining continuous feedback about performance and its result, and adapting accordingly.

Adaptation to uncertainties in the environment is required of every living creature to ensure survival. To adapt, one must correctly anticipate future events or changes. If the weather forecast calls for rain later in the day, you'll want to have an umbrella. If you know a client of yours is quite erratic, you'll want to consider how he or she is likely to respond to bad news or delays on your end. Thus it is very beneficial to align your expectations with reality, otherwise you will be faced with the frequent need to adjust and change your initial plans.

Even if we're told to "expect the unexpected," surprises are likely to occur, and in my opinion, people generally hate surprises. "Stop right there, Mr. Wise Guy," you may be saying, "a surprise is something negative only if it's bad." You'd probably reason that a surprise could also be positive, like an unexpected birthday party or winning the lottery, which would likely be more than welcomed! However, I've always had a slightly different take on it when it came to performance, and I decided to test my theory.

I suspected that performers, such as top athletes, might feel more comfortable in a state where everything goes according to plan even in comparison to a state where things are *too good*. Contrary to our basic intuition, there could be a self-limiting effect at play: we may feel better with a lesser actual performance, which fits our mindset and planned goals, whereas a better performance, if it is too good to be true, may make us feel less comfortable, precisely because it is, to a great extent, unexpected.

My colleagues and I researched this idea, attempting to investigate what we called "perceived team performance" in competition. We believed that perceived team performance could be analyzed in terms of three factors:

(1) the direction of lead (one's own team or the opposing team);
(2) momentum (positive or negative);
(3) events expectancy (expected or unexpected events).

In order to understand how athletes in team sports perceive team performance, and to link these perceptions to the chances that these players would fall into a state of crisis or, alternatively, achieve optimal arousal conditions, we decided that it was not enough to focus only on the obvious factor: direction of lead (i.e., whether one's team or its opponent is leading in points). We reasoned that we should also investigate the hidden factor of momentum (which I will discuss in detail later in the chapter). In addition, we believed that the question of whether each of these factors was expected or not by the player would be highly important.

We conducted two studies: one with twenty-eight elite German basketball coaches and players and another with forty-five top Israeli team-handball coaches and players.[1] In both cases, contrary to what might be expected intuitively, we found that direction of lead had the weakest effect of all three, while momentum had the strongest. In other words, it doesn't matter so much where you are, but where you are going. Moreover, in regards to the question of expectations, we found that any unexpected event (be it negative or positive), as compared to any expected one, was much more associated with the probability of crisis. Expectations were even found to be more meaningful to the athletes than the momentary direction of lead, though less important than momentum. The combination found to be most problematic for athletes was negative momentum, an unexpected event, and a lead by the opposing team. Positive momentum, an expected event, and a lead by one's own team were considered least problematic.

We identified two game standings, which everyone would agree can be defined as positive for the players:

(1) the lead held by one's own team is being maintained or extended;
(2) the lead of the opposing team is decreasing.

However, if you add the word "expectedly" to each of these, they will be evaluated as *more favorable* than if you add "unexpectedly." In all cases, then, expected situations were judged as being more favorable by the coaches and players, even if an unexpected situation produced a positive result. Why, for heaven's sake, would an "*unexpectedly* good" state be judged as less favorable than an "*expectedly* good" state? You guessed it right: simply because people prefer things to happen according to their plans and in line with their expectations, even if the surprise is positive and things go "too well." Unexpected events have been found to be detrimental for athletes—at least in their own perception—in several investigations conducted on psychological performance crisis in competition.[2] What is most interesting, however, is that even positive unexpected events are less favorable than positive expected ones.

Many years ago, I consulted a German volleyball coach who had heard about my theories and was impressed by their uniqueness. As a consequence, he used to take time outs precisely when his team played *too* well. Fortunately, his team had a winning streak so that the press (I know these guys; I was once a sports journalist during my doctoral studies days in 1980–1984) kept wondering, "What's your secret?" He responded, "I take time outs when the team is playing too well to prevent crises." Talk about going against common sense.

I refer to the concept behind this coach's upward time-out strategy as the "Icarus effect." In Greek mythology, Icarus was the son of the master craftsman Daedalus, the creator of the Labyrinth. As the story goes, Icarus and his father needed to escape from Crete and attempted to do so by flying out of the city on wings that his father constructed from feathers and wax.

Icarus's father warned him first of complacency and then of hubris, asking that he fly neither too low nor too high, so that the sea's dampness would not clog his wings or the sun's heat melt them. Icarus ignored his father's instructions not to fly too close to the sun, causing the wax in his wings to melt and leading to him falling into the sea. This classic tale shows the tragic theme of failure at the hands of hubris.

While consulting the coach concerning his team's performance, I had Icarus on my mind—a story my late mother, Nurith, used to tell me time and again in my childhood. I realized that when athletes' performance on court is unexpectedly good they can then crash precisely because they are flying too high. In such a case, their performance is raised too much in comparison to expectations, leading to a potential downfall. Honestly, I cannot conclusively determine whether the coach was right or wrong; the fact is that his team won beyond expectations, exceeding its preseason goal. I also can't categorically state whether coaches should stop their teams when they are on a roll or to just let them go when they seem to have forward momentum. What I can tell you, however, is that no matter what, surprises are bound to happen. Sometimes they are quite sudden and at other times they may take a while to develop, but rest assured, major disruptions will continue to occur. This has been recently apparent, for example, in the contemporary music and healthcare industries—two industries that may seem miles apart, but are experiencing similar issues in changing technology and business environments.

Industry Disruption

In the 1960s and 1970s, there were records, followed by cassette tapes and CDs in the 1980s and 1990s—there was the eight-track tape, too, but it certainly was more of a footnote in the history of recorded music. CDs, however, took the technology away from analog devices and birthed the era of digital music. Today, the CD is nearly obsolete as fans have found new ways—ways no one could have ever expected in the good ol' days of the vinyl album—to listen to their favorite songs.

What started in the 1990s with peer-to-peer music file sharing by companies like Napster, which was shutdown due to a copyright infringement lawsuit brought by the Recording Industry Association of America (RIAA), has developed beyond anyone's imagination. The failure of the downloading, file-sharing model gave rise to new ideas on how to access and listen to music, while working with the industry instead of against it. In less than ten years, Swedish music-streaming mammoth Spotify has gone from a small startup touting an idea that music executives scoffed at—free or inexpensive access to a seemingly endless collection of music—to a worldwide service with over 100 million users (and available in more than fifty languages).

The concept of streaming songs, unable to download but essentially listenable at any time on any digital device, has become nearly synonymous with listening to music. Spotify's forward-thinking attitude put them at the head of this trend and though there has been some outcry and criticism in how bands and musicians are compensated, in 2015 the company paid its artists two billion dollars.[3] Spotify is also now working closely with record labels and executives, helping to contribute to the $42.39 billion global music industry revenue.[4]

As reported in *Statista*, revenue from music subscription and streaming went from $650 million to $1 billion between 2011 and 2012 in thanks to services like Spotify and Pandora, which have also contributed to lower instances of piracy due to the relatively inexpensive, legal, online streaming services. In the meantime, companies like YouTube, which until recently was mostly used to post videos but have now fully embraced streaming music and podcasts, are following suit. Spotify founders Daniel Ek and Martin Lorentzon saw the changing face of digital music and pursued their vision wholeheartedly. At times of disruption and rapid change, expectations may be dashed, but finding ways to work within a new paradigm will be essential.

Similarly, the US healthcare industry found itself amid a major disruption with the Affordable Care Act (ACA), signed into law in 2010 and going into effect in 2013. Though ideas about a new system had been posed for years, and states such as Massachusetts were experimenting with a similar universal system, many were still surprised by the passing of the ACA. Seen as a rapid disruption, healthcare providers had to quickly shift focus and in many ways transform their business models.

Today, however, more people in the United States are insured than ever before, and the industry has found new ways to provide better, low-cost, quality care. The US Department of Health and Human Services reported that 25 percent more insurance issuers joined the health insurance marketplace in the 2015 open enrollment, meaning that insurers are embracing the system and giving consumers more choices with more affordable premiums.[5] Both insurers and consumers win. Though widely touted as a success, the ACA continues to face opposition and could possibly be repealed—another potential disruption.

Despite people's fear of change and the concerns over unexpected events, these types of surprises push businesses, leaders, and entrepreneurs to find new ways to function and succeed. The word "disruption" may have a negative connotation, but when handled properly and effectively, both businesses and consumers can benefit. It may be difficult to constantly expect the unexpected, but there is a way to make sure you can continue forging ahead: have confidence in your product or service, team, company, and most importantly, in yourself.

HOW EXPECTATIONS AND SELF-CONFIDENCE SHAPE OUR PERFORMANCE

> Believe you can and you're halfway there.
>
> —THEODORE ROOSEVELT

Greek and Roman mythology tell us the story of Pygmalion and Galatea. Pygmalion was a sculptor who fell madly in love with a statue he had made. He offered the statue presents and eventually prayed to the goddess Venus to bring the statue to life. Venus took pity on Pygmalion and turned his prayers into reality. The statue came to life and Pygmalion named her Galatea. He then went on to marry her and together they had a son named Paphos.

This wonderful tale inspired many artists, including George Bernard Shaw (1856–1950), the Irish playwright, critic, and cofounder (in 1895) of the London School of Economics. Shaw—the only person to win both the Nobel Prize (1925) and an Oscar (1938)—wrote the famous play *Pygmalion* (1912) based loosely on the myth; later on, the play was rewritten as a musical and movie called *My Fair Lady* (1964), using the same old Greek–Roman motif.

In psychology, this motif has been used to describe a situation in which believing something can make it come true. This is called "self-fulfilling prophecy," which means that an individual's behavior may often be determined by other people's expectations. For example, recall legendary Israeli basketball coach Ralph Klein, whom I introduced in chapter 2. In 1992 Klein began to coach for the Tel-Aviv Hapoel team, much to the chagrin of Maccabi fans, who viewed his switch as nothing less than treason. An intense rivalry exists between the two teams and Klein himself was even once caught publicly muttering about the "stinking Hapoel" in the heat of a close intracity game. The Hapoel team, however, was an amalgam of mediocre players, who did so poorly that Klein was about a game or two from being fired.

At that point, he made a fateful decision and reshuffled the team, letting one player— who was slightly more talented than the others—do whatever he wanted on the court. The other players turned into aggressive "slaves" and the team began to play extremely ugly, low-scoring basketball: players pushed, charged, obstructed, and shoved opponents— sending fouls through the roof—provoking the opposing team and causing them to lose focus on the game and miss shots left and right. I believe that Klein was inspired to do so by the Detroit Pistons: in the late 1980s, the Pistons utilized aggressive behavior to their advantage with team captain Isaiah Thomas and Coach Chuck Daly at the helm, leading these "bad boys" to two back-to-back NBA championships. Through this aggressive style, though, Hapoel somehow finally began to do what every team should do: win! So successful was this unique tactic that the team almost won the Israeli championship, having an exceptional run and being stopped only in the final best-of-five series.

At the end of the season, a journalist asked Klein to explain how these players, who hadn't the foggiest notion of what defense was, became the best defenders in the league. Klein, a Holocaust survivor who had never had the chance to acquire much formal education but had deep intuitive human understanding, answered promptly: "I told them that they are the best defenders in the league, of course." Instead of berating, insulting, or disgracing his players, what many other coaches would have done, he decided to sell them a story: many years before Barack Obama, time and again he simply made them *believe* that together, "yes we can." Consequently, they could! In effect, Klein "artificially" boosted the players' self-confidence.

Thus, if the coach (in this case, Ralph Klein) communicates to the players that he expects big things from them (e.g., to be the best defenders in the league), they are not likely to let him down. Had he told them truth— that they really had no idea how to play defense—and expected them to play poorly, they would have met these low expectations. Instead, Klein created a new reality by planting expectations in his players' heads.

Actually, Ralph Klein—without knowing it—used the so-called Galatea effect, not to be confused with the "Pygmalion effect." In the Pygmalion effect, an individual's self-confidence and subsequent performance are *indirectly* increased through communicating to the individual's coach or supervisor that the person is of high ability. When coaches, bosses, or teachers believe that certain athletes, employees, or students are more talented or smarter than others, these leaders will spend more time with those individuals. During that process, they will also impose more challenging assignments and use a more enthusiastic tone of voice (or other forms of subtle nonverbal communication), thereby actually "sending" their high expectations. As a result, such beliefs will often lead to better performance, creating the Pygmalion effect.

By contrast, the Galatea effect occurs when high-performance expectations are communicated *directly* to the performer, be it a player or an employee. Klein developed this technique by himself. Aside from the one player who received carte blanche to do what he wanted on the court, Klein certainly didn't think any team member was more talented than the others. And he knew most of them were not as good as members of other teams in the league. But he sold them a bill of goods, creating a new reality by changing players' expectations and beliefs (i.e., using the self-fulfilling prophecy technique to artificially enhance their self-confidence). This technique was unique and original in Israeli coaching practices of the time and remains effective even today, when the term "placebo effect" is sometimes used to describe similar effects.

This phenomenon is certainly surprising because leaders are in fact praising performers who fail. This apparently paradoxical effect is also quite manipulative: these leaders are actually lying to these individuals, which may entail not only ethical questions but also practical consequences in the form of potential loss of credibility when the athletes find out they have been manipulated. But the more important issue, I think, is whether the problem is solved or not. In other words, there are certain situations where a leader has only two options:

(1) Be honest, tell the truth, and stay saddled with the problem;
(2) Manipulate with "stories" (as Ralph Klein did), and solve the problem.

Which is more moral? For example, would you tell your child who is learning an instrument, "You know what, you're right, you really are completely untalented," or would you try to boost her or his self-confidence and performance by implanting positive, albeit artificial, expectations as Klein did? Keep in mind, maybe tomorrow they will become a reality, just as with Hapoel. Thus, Klein produced players with confidence and belief in their ability to manage their environment and successfully control their own behavior.

From my own practical experience as a sports psychologist I have countless stories about athletes who came in complaining about loss of self-confidence, aspiring to restore it. For many years, self-confidence has been one of the most cited factors thought to affect athletic performance. It's therefore no surprise that self-confidence is also a major component to manager and employee performance. Just as a unique relationship exists between coaches and players, so does one between bosses and their employees. Instilling a sense of self-confidence, even if it's necessary to fudge the truth a bit at first, as Klein did with his Hapoel team members, may contribute to this sense of self-confidence. Equally as important is helping your team develop self-confidence through new skills, challenges, and opportunities.

According to *Harvard Business Review*, whether an entry-level assistant or a top-level executive, job seekers today believe that opportunities for learning and development are more important than any other aspect of a potential position. Related, up to 90 percent of this learning and development takes place on-the-job through new assignments, feedback, and conversations with bosses and mentors.[6] Helping others develop their skills will boost their confidence and, in return, create higher performance.

SELF-EFFICACY

> If you accept the expectations of others, especially the negative ones,
> then you never will change the outcome.
>
> — MICHAEL JORDAN

In practice, self-confidence has always been believed intuitively to play a critical role in determining success and failure; it has sometimes even been considered the most important factor that distinguishes successful athletes from unsuccessful ones. So it is quite surprising to learn that until the late 1980s, researchers lacked a reasonable theory to account for the precise nature of self-confidence in sport and exercise settings.

In 1988, Michigan State University sports psychologist Professor Deborah L. Feltz published a paper in *Exercise and Sport Science Reviews* titled "Self-Confidence and Sports Performance," specifically to clarify this issue. By "self-confidence," Feltz was referring to an individual's belief that he or she would "get the job done." To promote our understanding of the precise connection between self-confidence and performance in sport, Feltz imported several theories from outside sport-psychology, the most promising of which, in her opinion, was Albert Bandura's theory of self-efficacy.

Simply put, self-efficacy is our personal judgment or belief in our capability to successfully execute an activity. It reflects the extent to which we feel confident about performing a specific task in a particular situation (i.e., "I can" versus "I cannot"). In 1977 Bandura, the Stanford University professor and social cognitivist mentioned in the previous chapter, published an article that for the first time, presented the central aspects of "a unifying theory of behavioral change" (as the title says), which he labeled "self-efficacy." In short, his article said that if you want to change people's behavior, change their perception of self-efficacy: make them believe that they "can do."

Bandura actually developed the self-efficacy concept from his work with adults suffering from severe ophidiophobia, or fear of snakes. Considered from this perspective, it makes a lot of sense: if you are phobic, you want to gain more confidence when faced with snakes. In principle, a useful strategy for doing this would be to take a little step, approaching a snake for example, and then rest. You will have gained some confidence, feel better, and believe you can cope more effectively. Next, you approach the snake a little more; again, rest, enjoy your achievement, feel the enhanced confidence. You should now have higher expectations about your ability to successfully cope with snakes. Then you repeat the action again and again. (This should remind you of the goal proximity principle discussed in chapter 3.)

Bandura predicted that self-efficacy was generalizable beyond the domain of psychotherapy. He was right: soon enough, it was spreading like wildfire from clinical to other domains of psychology, such as organizations, education, health, and last but not least, athletic performance. In fact, today, efficacy is central to almost everything. Virtually all of us can identify goals we want to accomplish—things we would like to achieve or change—realizing at the same time that putting our plans into action is often not so simple. Self-efficacy expectations have a substantial impact on everything from psychological states to motivation and performance; since these expectations play a major role in how goals, tasks, and challenges are approached, they must be handled accordingly (that is, changed from "no, I cannot" to "yes I can"). As mentioned, sport- and exercise psychologists quickly embraced self-efficacy, first and foremost, to account for the intuitively popular yet somewhat elusive concept of "self-confidence."

Backward Generalizations: The Pharaoh Principle

One crucial issue still remains to be addressed: How can we change our efficacy expectations from "no, I cannot" to "yes, I can"? Here, Bandura speaks about four sources of self-efficacy information (later extended to nine in the sports area), each of which could be used to change self-efficacy beliefs concerning the task at hand. In what follows I'll shortly describe and exemplify the two most important, main sources of self-efficacy.

One important source is called "vicarious experiences." Here, people obtain efficacy information by observing or imagining others engaging in a task that the observers themselves do not perform. Vicarious sources of efficacy information (that is, witnessing others successfully completing a task) are weaker than performance accomplishments of the observers themselves, but they are still of substantial importance in enhancing one's self-efficacy.

A great example for this source comes from Major General Avihu Ben-Nun (born 1939), who was the eleventh commander of the Israeli Air Force from 1987 to 1992. In 1995 he too was diagnosed with Parkinson's disease. Unlike other celebrities with Parkinson's who often try to hide their disease, Ben-Nun announced it publicly, thereby serving as an inspiration for many others fighting the decease. I often use Ben-Nun's struggle against Parkinson's as a model; I tell myself that if he can handle it, evidently for so many years, I can, too!

The strongest source, and the most dependable foundation of self-efficacy judgments, however, is "performance accomplishments," also known as "enactive mastery experiences." Performance accomplishments refer to clear successes and failures, which provide the most influential source of efficacy information and the most authentic evidence on which we can build robust beliefs about personal efficacy. If such experiences are generally successful, they will raise the level of self-efficacy; repeated failure will result in lower-efficacy expectations.

For example, Parkinson's disturbs my daily activities and functions for a number of hours every day. I set a goal, however, to increase the number of Parkinson's-free hours per day (or at least keep this number stable) by regulating my body and mind through medication, rest, physical activity, and joyful intellectual activities, such as writing this book. Success in achieving this goal increases my confidence, not only in my ability to gain more Parkinson's-free hours, but also in my ability to successfully reduce the Parkinson's influence on my life in general.

The performance accomplishments source demonstrates not only that reality (i.e., one's performance) can foster one's expectations, but also that expectations (i.e., self-efficacy) can foster reality. This situation results in a "performance-efficacy cycle" that may account for our ability to cope with increasingly difficult problems: you wipe out a small problem, successfully coping with it; then you wipe out a somewhat bigger one, and so on. Over time people undergoing such a process increase their confidence in their ability to cope with difficult situations or obstacles, precisely because they continuously prove themselves successful in managing smaller problems. But what if something really big—and negative—suddenly falls on you? What do you do? Where do you draw the confidence in your ability to cope with it? For example, how could I cope with Parkinson's, a *huge* problem indeed, without handling smaller problems previously? The answer lies within what I call "backward generalizations."

In 1995 Noam Eyal—a masters student working under the supervision of Gershon Tenenbaum and me—conducted an interesting study in which he used Bandura's notions to create a so-called generalization slope.[7] He presented participants of the study with a primary, original task, followed by four additional tasks that, at least in the eyes of the participants, had a decreasing order of similarity to the first one. In this case, he used motor tasks with gradually increasing levels of execution difficulty, examining whether outcome expectations could be generalized from one defined task to other increasingly difficult ones in line with this generalization slope.

The main results were in line with Bandura's generalization idea: if you feel efficacious in performing task A, you will also feel efficacious with tasks B, C, and onward, in a decreasing order of generalization and increasing order of difficulty. More interestingly, a substantial generalization effect was revealed not only with regard to outcome expectations, but also with regard to actual performance, meaning that expectations were once again affecting performance.

In principle, this concept implies that when you are faced with a major problem, you should take a "from light to heavy" approach. In our paper, Noam brought in a nice example from his experience as a psychological consultant in soccer. He described a player who developed a fear of kicking penalties—a common phenomenon discussed in detail in chapter 5—and was treated by Noam using the "generalization-of-confidence" principle: using a clinical procedure called "systematic desensitization," they began with relatively unfrightening kicks (e.g., from the corners), proceeded to more frightening kicks (e.g., kicks from outside the penalty area), and terminated with the most frightening of them all—the penalty kick itself. But what happens if we are obliged to do this entire process backward? Consider the soccer player that Noam treated: in the future, if he has one difficulty or another, he can be told, "But you already overcame your greatest problem—your fear of penalties; therefore, the present problem should be a piece of cake for you to handle." I call this idea "the Pharaoh principle."

In the biblical story of Exodus, Pharaoh (seemingly Ramses II) is described as a demonic opponent of the Jewish people. In 1990, the late Meir Ariel—an Israeli Bob Dylan—released a song in which he lists a series of troubles he undergoes, which increase in their order of difficulty. At the end of each stanza, he repeats: "We survived Pharaoh, we will get through this too!" Over the years, that line became a widespread expression in Israel to describe such "backward generalizations."

In my case, when coping with Parkinson's or any other major issues in my life, I generalize backward, considering all of the other serious obstacles I have already overcome in the past. Who or what fills that role which enables me to say to myself: "Miki, you survived Pharaoh, you'll survive this, too"? We should probably keep that a secret for now, but I'll give you just one small hint: it is associated with one of my 2.5 divorces (of which I'll say no more).

Throughout your working life, you will be faced with increasingly difficult challenges. The concept of backward generalizations, however, can help you handle these obstacles as you think about them in an incremental way. For example, when you find yourself rushing around the office like a madman trying to meet a last-minute deadline, it might be helpful to take a step back. Think about other deadlines you've met in the past, those that may have also seemed impossible at the time. Or consider larger issues you've faced and overcome—maybe you've had the unfortunate experience of being laid off and forced into a new position or even new career. These types of major issues that you've successfully tackled will make a deadline seem like child's play in comparison, a simple task that you know you can complete. If you've survived one hurdle, you can survive the next. Keeping the Pharaoh's principle in mind will keep you on task and confident in your performance.

THE POWER OF ATTITUDE

> Two years ago . . . we were very happy that we made it to the title game. Tomorrow, we will arrive . . . to win the gold.
>
> —TONY PARKER

In this book so far, we have seen that expectations may significantly shape and foster performance. A performer's social environment is highly important in this context, because it may transmit expectations that can substantially affect performance. For example, we already saw how a coach may affect an athlete's performance by forming expectations and behaving in a way that affects the athlete's performance (which, in turn, may confirm the coach's expectations). But an athlete's social environment contains other influential factors in addition to the coach; most notable among them are teammates, referees, spectators, and the media, each of which can potentially have a substantial affect on athletes' perceived efficacy and their attitudes toward upcoming contests.[8]

If you want to change people's behavior, you must change their perception of self-efficacy, their belief in their ability to execute behaviors integral to reaching specific goals, or their attitude toward the task they are performing. Sometimes this might mean entirely altering expectations, such as the French national basketball team did in the 2013 EuroBasket.

On September 22, 2013, for the first time in history, the French national basketball team won the EuroBasket contest, the European championship of national teams. Two years earlier, France lost to Spain in the final game of the championship with a final score of 98 to 85. Although the French team had more EuroBasket appearances than any other national team in Europe, the 2011 final was its first ever appearance in a title game. On September 21, 2013, just before the game, Tony Parker, the team's superstar (regularly playing for the San Antonio Spurs), was interviewed on TV and said: "We learned a lesson from 2011. Two years ago we were in the same situation. Then, however, we were very happy that we made it to the title game. Tomorrow, we will arrive very differently. We should stay focused on the final; the most important goal is to win the gold and the entire championship." And they did. After having lost to Lithuania 76 to 62 in the early stages of the 2013 EuroBasket only eleven days earlier, France won the contest, humiliating Lithuania with an 80 to 66 win that gave the French team its first ever European championship.

In France's case, it was all about their attitude: despite the odds, they were positive and came to win. In the workplace, having such an attitude can be more difficult than it seems. According to *Gallup*'s "Employee Engagement in U.S. Stagnant in 2015," only 32 percent of US workers were considered "engaged," whereas 50.8 percent were "not engaged" and 17.2 percent were "actively disengaged," and similar percentages have been recorded every year since 2011.[9] Gallup categorizers employees as "engaged" based on how they rate key workplace factors, including "having an opportunity to do what they do best each day, having someone at work who encourages their development, and believing their opinions count at work." Such elements are considered to predict performance outcomes by a company or organization.

Also according to *Gallup*, in Germany, 84 percent of employees are not engaged or are actively *dis*engaged at work, costing the German economy up to 287.1 billion euros per year in lost productivity.[10] Furthermore, disengaged employees feel greater levels of stress, have less fun at work, feel burnt out, and miss work more often (one of the highest contributors to the economic loss in productivity). It's easy to say "stay positive" to yourself or others, but it's possible to fall prey to overwhelming negativity, especially during major changes at a company, such as a round of layoffs, or when faced with economic uncertainties on the world stage, for example, during a recession.

Leaders must therefore help instill a positive, can-do attitude, especially at times when morale is low and risks are high, helping employees become more engaged at work. Employing techniques discussed in the previous chapters—for example, reframing the perceived importance of a task and setting specific, attainable goals—will go a long way in fostering engagement and better attitudes. Open feedback and discussion with your employees is important as well. Find ways to keep morale high and people engaged, and you will see a marked increase in performance.

MOMENTUM: SOME LIKE IT HOT

> I am a hot-hand player. After a run of successful baskets, I feel good and I know that any shot will go in, so I keep shooting.
>
> —GIANLUCA BASILE, *inventor of the "ignorant shot"*

As in the title of Billy Wilder's wonderful 1959 comedy, many people "like it hot" and believe in the concept of a "successful streak"—a time when some type of momentum exists in their own or in others' actions and the resulting outcomes, even if no such "hotness" is truly there. The late

Amos Tversky (1937–1996), who first observed this phenomenon, vividly described what happened when he tried to show people that the hotness they see is actually *quasi*-hotness—or, more simply, an illusion. As science and technology journalist Kevin McKean reported in his 1987 *Discover* article "The Orderly Pursuit of Pure Disorder," Tversky stated:

> I've been in an endless number of arguments since then . . . I've won them all, and yet I didn't convince a soul . . . I had philosophers at Berkeley jumping up and down on tables, red in the face. *USA Today* ran an article in which they asked all sorts of basketball greats, Red Auerbach, Jerry West—all the heroes of my childhood, what they think of this, and it was headlined, "High-Handed Professor's Comments Called Hot Air." I couldn't believe the intensity of the reaction.

Why was this study considered *so* provocative? Because all basketball coaches, players, and even fans are momentum addicts, convinced that hot streaks exist and are essential to the game. Tversky went on to say that "the more basketball you see, the more you're convinced. Nobody can tell you otherwise. You know it in your bones."

Indeed, athletes and coaches, in general, firmly believe that being able to produce positive momentum or reverse negative momentum is an important asset. But what is "momentum"? David Lehman and Jungpil Hahn provided a nice, updated, strictly scientific definition in their excellent 2013 paper "Momentum and Organizational Risk Taking" in *Management Science*, which states that momentum is a "sustained and systematic trajectory in performance over time, and . . . such trends impact interpretations of current performance as well as expectations of future performance." In its common usage (e.g., "our campaign is gaining momentum"), "momentum" is a sort of slang adapted from physics. It comes from Latin, comprised of "mo-" from "movere" and "-mentum," and first meant "moving power." In short, "momentum" refers to something that is in motion, moving in one way or another.

"Game momentum" can be conceived as a substantial source of feedback for athletes concerning their own competitive performance. When one team (let's say, in basketball) is rapidly gaining an advantage over the other, this team is in a state of positive momentum, while the opposing team is in a state of negative momentum. When a team comes from behind, quickly closing the gap in points scored, that team is also considered to be in a state of positive momentum, while the team about to lose the lead is then in a state of negative momentum. In other words, momentum, both positive and negative, can be conceived as a major determinant of an athlete's psychological state, regardless of the direction of the lead. So it is the *perceived* direction of movement that matters most. To determine whether we see a particular situation optimistically or pessimistically— the question of whether we see the glass half full or half empty—is actually much less important than the question of whether we believe that the glass is being filled up . . . or emptied out.

In a classic 1985 article, Tversky, along with Tomas D. Gilovich and Robert Vallone, analyzed the probability of a basketball player making a successful shot after having previously made several successful shots in a row. Simply put, they discovered that a player was just as likely to *miss* the next basket as to make the next basket. This was of course a frontal attack on the traditional belief in the hot-hand phenomenon in basketball— because there was no evidence whatsoever found in support of the hot hand in any of the researchers' data sets! A real "scandal."

To be honest, it feels quite unbelievable. When I first started to work as a psychological consultant to elite basketball players, many of them would say that in order to get into the zone, they would take a few throws at the beginning of the game. "If I hit," the player would say, "I'll be confident in my playing going forward." But if Gilovich and his colleagues are right, then this strategy is grounded in an extremely common but basically false assumption: that our past performance must predict our future performance, or in other words, that "success breeds success" (and "failure breeds failure"). This actually means that we are in fact victims of a cognitive error, which is responsible for the hot-hand illusion.

This fallacy has meanwhile become one of the most well-known riddles in sports. On a much deeper level, however, I think that Gilovich et al. challenged the very idea that if we succeed at something, we have a better chance of succeeding in subsequent attempts—the deep, highly influential belief in psychological momentum. Indeed, it is quite hard to believe that just as one coin toss coming up heads doesn't statistically alter the probability of the next one coming up tails, that one sunk basket or, if we generalize—as Kahneman did in his 2011 book—one well-chosen stock pick, or one correct answer on an exam doesn't have any impact on the outcome of the one immediately following.

Hot Hand and Self-Efficacy

At the beginning of the 2000s, I had the opportunity to further research the hot-hand topic, which for some strange reason had found no appropriate echo in sport psychology. Despite the high interest in Gilovich et al.'s provocative, counterintuitive findings, and the almost two decades that had passed since publication of their paper, nobody had bothered to review all the studies conducted on this fascinating subject. My colleagues (an excellent doctoral student at the time, Simcha Avugos, today Dr. Simcha Avugos of the Wingate Academic College, and Professor Markus Raab, today of both the German Sport University in Cologne and the London South Bank University) and I set to work, resulting in the first review ever written on this issue, published in 2006 in *Psychology of Sport and Exercise*.

What did we find? We did not want to be too blunt, so we formulated our findings delicately, but the long and the short of it was that there simply was no hot hand. However, some people challenged our review, which gave us a reason to write another article on the topic, again published in the same journal, this time led by Simcha.[11] We used a sophisticated statistical review method (called "meta-analysis") to try and detect hotness, but our results were even more disastrous for the "it-is-impossible-that-there-is-no-hot-hand" supporters: even the use of this supposedly more sensitive review method found no solid evidence whatsoever for either the existence of a general hot-hand effect, or for any moderating variables that can explain the extent of a hot hand (or "hot foot" in soccer) effect.

Then, I realized there was a hitch: these findings may have some severe and unpleasant consequences for one important theory that you, dear reader, should already be acquainted with. Take, for example, statistician Robert Hooke's 1989 paper "Basketball, Baseball and the Null Hypothesis," published in *Chance*:

> In almost every competitive activity in which I've ever engaged (baseball, basketball, golf, tennis, even duplicate bridge), a little success generates for me a feeling of confidence which, as long as it lasts, makes me do better than usual. Even more obviously, a few failures can destroy this confidence, after which for a while I can't do anything right.

The belief in performance accomplishments leading to greater ones is so deep that even a notable statistician such as Hooke falls victim to disregarding any contradicting data. But wait a minute: couldn't Bandura have written the same thing in regards to performance-efficacy cycles? If the general picture shows no hot hand, dismissing it as a mere illusion, then shouldn't the theory of self-efficacy be in big trouble?

To further elaborate on my argument: Bandura says that efficacy predicts success. As if we need further evidence, in her well-known book *Confidence*, Rosabeth Moss Kanter quotes the legendary coach of Duke University's men's basketball team, Mike Krzyzewski, on how confidence (which, as we saw, is very close to efficacy) affects performance:

> Confidence motivates people to put in extra effort, to stretch beyond their previous limits, to rebound from setbacks, or to play through injuries anyway. People with confidence stay in the game no matter what.[12]

For me, Bandura could not express the "yes we can" idea hidden here any better! Time and again, Bandura emphasized the cyclical nature of the efficacy–performance relationship, which implies a positive association between sequences of attempted actions. Moreover, Bandura claims that such associations should be even higher for sport activities in which the same routine is performed over and over again in the same isolated setting. But at least at face value, I thought, how could Bandura's self-efficacy theory peacefully live together with the hot-hand literature if these performance accomplishments were actually independent from each other?

Then I had an idea: what if we simply plant self-efficacy estimations into Gilovich et al.'s paradigm? In other words, take Gilovich et al.'s classic controlled shooting field experiment, replicate it, and then extend it to *directly* examine efficacy–performance cycles according to the conditions outlined by Bandura. I needed a crazy student like Simcha, who was ready to take up this challenge.

Can you imagine what it takes to get the entire male Israeli National Olympic Basketball team to cooperate in such a controlled shooting experiment? In line with the original study, we wanted all our participants to be experts—that is, professional basketball players—and they were all currently playing in Israel's top basketball division, the so-called Super League. Thanks to Simcha's endless devotion and to help from my good friend, head coach Yoram Haroush and his entire dedicated team (thank you, Yoram!), all the twenty-six players on the squad willingly cooperated.

What did we find? When efficacy beliefs are measured immediately before each upcoming shot, the efficacy–performance relationship is not likely to be reciprocal.[13] The average correlation between shooters' efficacy judgments and their performance was nearly zero. Yet the players' judgments were affected by the outcome of the previous shot, and these associations were considerably higher. Under invariant conditions, then, where adjacent performances of closed-skill, routine tasks (as the one conducted here) are expected to correlate highly, they don't end up doing so.

Then another idea came to mind: maybe no cycles were revealed, since our participants were experts; it is possible that proficient athletes have a relatively stable sense of efficacy, which has been developed through repeated success and is not affected to any great extent by momentary fluctuations in performance. We reasoned that nonprofessional players (that is, novices) could be affected more strongly than experts by immediate, momentary success or failure, which could then have a stronger influence on their sense of efficacy (thereby affecting their performance). Therefore we thought that positive associations, as predicted by Bandura, could probably be revealed among novices.

We conducted a second field experiment, basically the same as the first one but this time with thirty-two recreational basketball players as participants. Again, no correlation was found between shooters' efficacy judgments and their performance, but a significant correlation was found between efficacy expectations and the outcome of the previous shot.

Oddly enough, you *see* these cycles, but they don't exist (according to the statistics, at least). Practically speaking, however, even if the hot-hand phenomenon isn't real, who cares? That may be surprising to hear from a psychologist like myself, but after all, if sinking a few test shots before the game builds confidence and confidence boosts overall performance in other tasks on the court as well, then what does it matter? For a practicing sport psychologist, the existence of even an illusory cycle is important for understanding what is going on in the players' and coaches' minds and predicting their behavior on court.

As a psychological consultant to elite athletes, I've recommended many of these tactics myself. For example, I used to advise basketball players to conduct two or three other successful actions (let's say, steals on defense) right at the beginning of the game to boost their confidence on court—and believe me, it works. When players go into a game feeling better about themselves or pull off a successful action early on, they play better all around, not just in scoring baskets. Indeed, it seems that this is the case in many types of challenging situations, not just sports: if we believe ourselves to be smart and capable—and are willing to work hard—we will perform better and rise to meet our own high expectations.

SUMMARY

Humans prefer things to happen according to their plans, in line with their expectations. Through my colleagues' and my own research, we surprisingly found that positive, expected events are often perceived as more favorable than equally positive—or even better—*unexpected* ones.

But surprises happen! To combat these surprises, confidence in your product, company, staff, and self is necessary to forge ahead.

As a leader, you need to first develop self-confidence, and then instill that same feeling in your team. If you want to change people's behavior, you must change their perception of self-efficacy, their belief in their ability to execute behaviors integral to reaching specific goals.

In this chapter, we saw how expectations and performance are interrelated. Reality fosters performance, in the sense that we hate surprises (that is, our expectations should preferably be as realistic as possible). Then we learned how expectations foster performance. Finally, we focused on hot-hand research and its implications for the so-important theory of self-efficacy. At the end of the day, if we believe ourselves to be smart and capable, we will perform better.

DAILY PRACTICES

As an Individual

- Stay on top of industry trends, both your industry and others that may be seemingly unrelated, by attending events and conferences, reading about the latest developments, and understanding how such changes could potentially affect your job and work life.
- Take advantage of advice from mentors, bosses, and experienced colleagues, while developing new skills and embracing new opportunities.
- When faced with a daunting task, utilize the concept of backward generalization—you've overcome larger obstacles in the past, so this one should be a piece of cake.

As a Leader

- Help your employees and team members develop new on-the-job skills through everyday mentoring, increased responsibilities, and informal learning opportunities.

- Provide feedback, support, and compliments on a job well-done (or even a job that may need some improvement) to help boost employees' self-confidence and increase their performance.
- Support your staff by instilling a positive "we came to win" attitude, keeping up general morale and engagement.

NOTES

1. M. Bar-Eli and G. Tenenbaum, "Game Standing and Psychological Crisis in Sport: Theory and Research Findings," *Canadian Journal of Sport Sciences* 14 (April 1989): 31–37; M. Bar-Eli, G. Tenenbaum, and G. Elbaz, "A Three-Dimensional Crisis-Related Analysis of Perceived Team Performance," *Journal of Applied Sport Psychology* 3 (1991): 160–175.
2. I reviewed these studies in M. Bar-Eli, "Psychological Performance Crisis in Competition, 1984–1996: A Review," *European Yearbook of Sport Psychology* 1 (1997): 73–112. A more recent review—though with a rather methodological emphasis—can be found in my book chapter with Gershon Tenenbaum: M. Bar-Eli and G. Tenenbaum, "Bayesian Approach of Measuring Competitive Crisis," in *Measurement in Sport and Exercise Psychology*, eds. G. Tenenbaum, R. C. Eklund, and A. Kamata (Champaign, IL: Human Kinetics, 2012), 367–379.
3. Sven Carlsson, Agence France-Presse, "Inside the Spotify Success Story," *ABS-CBN News*, March 14, 2015, http://news.abs-cbn.com/business/03/14/15/inside-spotify-success-story.
4. Statista, "Statistics and Facts about Music Industry in the U.S.," *Statista: The Statistics Portal*, www.statista.com/topics/1639/music/.
5. Assistant Secretary for Public Affairs, "The Affordable Care Act is Working," *HHS. gov*, June 24, 2015, www.hhs.gov/healthcare/facts-and-features/fact-sheets/aca-is-working/index.html.
6. Monique Valcour, "If You're Not Helping People Develop, You're Not Management Material," *Harvard Business Review*, January 23, 2014, https://hbr.org/2014/01/if-youre-not-helping-people-develop-youre-not-management-material.
7. N. Eyal, M. Bar-Eli, G. Tenenbaum, and J. S. Pie, "Manipulated Outcome Expectations and Competitive Performance in Motor Tasks with Gradually Increasing Difficulty," *The Sport Psychologist* 9 (1995): 188–200.
8. I explore this idea further in my paper "Psychological Performance Crisis in Competition, 1984–1996: A Review."
9. Gallup Poll, "Employee Engagement in U.S. Stagnant in 2015," *Gallup*, January 13, 2016, www.gallup.com/poll/188144/employee-engagement-stagnant-2015.aspx.
10. Marco Nink, "The Negative Impact of Disengaged Employees on Germany," *Gallup*, April 5, 2016, www.gallup.com/businessjournal/190445/negative-impact-disengaged-employees-germany.aspx?g_source=work%20attitudes&g_medium=search&g_campaign=tiles.

11. S. Avugos, J. Köppen, U. Csienskowski, M. Raaab, and M. Bar-Eli, "The 'Hot Hand' Reconsidered: A Meta-Analytic Approach," *Psychology of Sport and Exercise* 14 (January 2013): 21–27.
12. R. M. Kanter, *Confidence: How Winning Streaks and Losing Streaks Begin and End* (New York: Crown Business, 2004).
13. S. Avugos M. Bar-Eli, I. Ritov, and E. Sher, "The Elusive Reality of Efficacy-Performance Cycles in Basketball Shooting: An Analysis of Players' Performance Under Invariant Conditions," *International Journal of Sport and Exercise Psychology* 11 (February 2013): 184–202.

5

Action

To Do or Not To Do?

Well, Miki, if what you say is accurate, and if I understood you correctly, then maybe, if we look at it very carefully, there is the possibility that there could eventually be something in what you say.

—Ilana Ritov

In the summer of 2013, Israel was flooded by a wave of hysteria caused by an outbreak of the polio virus. Two such waves preceded this one: the first in 1949–1953 and the second in 1988. This time the Ministry of Health decided on a large-scale vaccination campaign for children throughout the country, in which even President Shimon Peres actively took part. The campaign, however, stimulated some public objection.

Many Israelis believed in a conspiracy theory, claiming that there was no real justification for such a large vaccination operation and that the whole campaign was a pharmaceutical industry ploy for its own financial gain. Not only were concerns raised about the effectiveness of the vaccine, but some also suspected that the vaccine actively harmed children. In fact, to me at least, such a response was no surprise because similar phenomena had already been intensively investigated and demonstrated in the context of the so-called omission bias, although in cases of other diseases.

The omission bias states that people consistently tend to judge harmful actions, relative to alternative options, as worse than inactions that are equally harmful, or even more harmful, than the alternatives. In the 1990s Professor David A. Asch, from the Perelman School of Medicine at the University of Pennsylvania, and his colleagues investigated the omission bias regarding pertussis vaccination.[1] Their rationale was based on several previous studies that had suggested that many people favor potentially harmful inactions, or omissions, over less harmful actions. In this study, Asch investigated the role of omission bias in parents' decisions whether to vaccinate their children against pertussis (the action) or not (the omission or inaction). A large survey was conducted in which participants were asked about their beliefs concerning the vaccine and the disease, and whether they had vaccinated their own children or planned to; they were also given test items to identify omission bias in their reasoning. The results clearly indicated that omission bias played a major role in the decision not to vaccinate against pertussis, much beyond the role played by one's belief about the risk of vaccination.

To give you a simple but clear numerical illustration of this kind of bias, let's say you are the head of your country's medication licensing authority, and you have to decide whether or not to approve a new medication for patients who are defined as terminally ill. The medication will save the lives of 80 percent of those patients in the short run, but it has strong side effects—it immediately kills the other 20 percent of patients. What would you do? Intuitively, most of us would *not* approve the medication, perceiving the immediate death of every fifth patient as worse than the immediate alleviation of suffering and short-run extension of life for 80 percent of the patients. This of course goes against the principle of utility maximization, because we would not end up with the best decision possible from an economically rational point of view.

Similarly, parents sometimes hesitate about vaccinating their children, despite the obvious and substantial decrease in the risk of becoming ill if the child is vaccinated. In an earlier study psychology professors Ilana

Ritov, of the Hebrew University of Jerusalem, and Jonathan Baron, of the University of Pennsylvania, investigated the reluctance to vaccinate using an idea similar to the 80 percent to 20 percent example. They found their participants reluctant to vaccinate a (hypothetical) child when the vaccination itself could cause death, even when this was much less likely than death from the disease prevented; this effect was even greater when there was a mortality risk group. All in all, several investigations conducted by Ritov and Baron in the early 1990s showed that people consistently tend to judge acts that are harmful as worse than omissions that are equally harmful, or even more harmful.[2]

In 1995 I got my professorship at Ben-Gurion University in the newly established school (today faculty) of management. The founding dean, the late Professor Abraham Mehrez (a real soccer freak) tried to help me find research partners; among others he suggested that I should meet Ilana Ritov, who at the time was a senior lecturer at Ben-Gurion University. I didn't know who she was, but as a newcomer in the university, I wanted to follow the advice of my dean, so I knocked on her door.

Ilana was very polite to me; she said, "Yes, I heard about you," and added that "sport is not my domain, but rather my husband's" (Ya'acov, a notable professor of statistics at the Hebrew University). I made it clear to her that I didn't want to bother her too much but perhaps we could conduct some "cheap" research if she could find the time. I suggested that she could provide me with a problem, study, or research paradigm she was well acquainted with, or was currently researching, and I'd review it to see if we could conduct research on the topic without investing too much effort. Ilana gave me all her then-recent articles on omission bias.

To be honest, I didn't follow every detail and complexity (Ilana was originally a mathematician), but one major point stood out: I saw a theoretical framework that was possibly suitable for an old problem I had wanted to deal with for years: penalty kicks. As you may recall, my interest in the topic dated back twenty-one years to 1974 (I am a real long-distance runner where research is concerned). What intrigued me so much? Very simple: Ilana's vaccination studies dealt with two options—"act" (vaccinate) or "omit the act" (don't vaccinate)—which were similar to my penalty problem: the goalkeeper can, in principle, "act" (jump) or "omit the act" (not jump).

But there was a basic, crucial difference: the inaction or omissions in Ilana's vaccine studies had harmful consequences (e.g., a child becoming sick), but in my problem, the consequences could be wonderful (i.e., a goalie stopping a ball). My reasoning was that the mother who must decide whether to vaccinate or not focuses on something negative, which may lead to omission bias. If we could turn it upside down and take the case of goalkeepers as an example of focusing on something positive—their chances of stopping the ball—we could reveal an "opposite bias," namely, that of *too much action.*

In addition to being a great scientist and world-class professional, Ilana is one of the most modest people I know, as well as one of the most cautious. Her first response to my idea of conceiving penalties as the opposite to her omission bias is quoted in the epigraph of this chapter (or, at least, this is the spirit of what I remember). Nevertheless, we started to search for an "action bias."

OPPOSITES

> Half the world is composed of people who have something to say and can't, and the other half who have nothing to say and keep on saying it.
>
> —ROBERT FROST

Generally speaking, people tend to see the world in black and white, one of opposites. A very funny example of this comes from the most enduring spaghetti Western ever made, *The Good, the Bad and the Ugly*, released in 1966. In one of the last scenes, Blondie (the "Good," played by Clint Eastwood) says to Tuco (the "Ugly," played by Eli Wallach): "You see, in this world there's two kinds of people, my friend: Those with loaded guns and those who dig" (needless to say, he adds: "You dig"). In fact, the movie provides a number of picturesque instances reflecting such a dual or binary way of thinking. For example, earlier in the film, Tuco—a wise, fast-talking bandit—divides mankind into "those with a rope around the neck, and those who have the job of doing the cutting," and "those that come in by the door, and those that come in by the window." Unknowingly, I suppose, Tuco and Blondie were practicing dialectical philosophy.

"Dialectics" is a term derived from ancient Greek philosophy, referring to the art of discussion based on two contradictory affirmations. Similar ideas can be found in other cultures, such as with the "yin" and "yang" in traditional Chinese philosophy; in Judaism, where the term *zugot*— meaning "pairs" or "couples" in Hebrew—refers to the time period (515 B.C.E.–70 C.E.) when the spiritual leadership of the Jewish people was in the hands of polemical pairs of religious teachers; and in German philosophy, in which giant philosopher Georg Wilhelm Friedrich Hegel (1770–1831) developed his own version of dialectics.

Such ideas are also evident from the beautiful graphic work of the Dutch artist Maurits Cornelis Escher (1898–1972), for example his "Day and Night" (1938), "Sky and Water" (I and II, 1938), and the "Swans" (1956), as well as from the Beatles' classic "Hello Goodbye" (released in 1967); from Literature Nobel Prize Winner Isaac Bashevis Singer's (1902–1991) "Enemies, a Love Story" (1966); and last but not least, from Robert Frost's (1874–1963) famous poem "The Road Not Taken" (1916). Our penalty kick studies dealt with another interesting pair of opposites: "do" and "not do," or "action" and "inaction."

My late mother, Nurith, was an expert in English and American literature (and a great fan of Robert Frost, by the way). In her memory, let's use the best-known line from Shakespeare's *Hamlet*, "To be or not to be?" as another example. While I will not attempt to answer this existential question, the point is that we are often confronted with the similar, albeit far less metaphysical, dilemma of "to do or not to do?" For example, a doctor might have to decide whether or not to perform a risky operation on a terminal patient. A homeowner might have to decide whether or not to sell their house or condo in a declining market. A politician might have to decide whether to respond to the provocations of a bitter opponent or to follow the principle that silence is golden. And so on. Ilana's studies show that generally speaking, we opt *not* to act in some of these situations, even when all the information we have tells us we'd be better off acting.

Our penalty kick research, however, demonstrated the opposite: namely that sometimes we opt to *act,* even when the information available tells us that we'd actually be better off doing nothing. This is precisely the basic dilemma of soccer goalkeepers in our study: "to jump or not to jump?" You may have already guessed the answer—most of the time, goalkeepers exhibit this action bias and jump when they should not. This action bias is relevant in countless realms outside of soccer. Understanding why so many of us fall prey to this bias in a wide range of situations will help us make better decisions at work, at home, and throughout the rest of our lives.

EVERYTHING YOU ALWAYS WANTED TO KNOW ABOUT PENALTIES (BUT WERE AFRAID TO ASK), PART 1: THE GOALKEEPERS

> I have discovered that all human evil comes from man's being unable to sit still in a room.
>
> —BLAISE PASCAL

What's in a penalty kick? That's a question I often ask my students. For me the answer is evident: everything.

In our most well-known penalty kick study, we collected video footage of 286 penalty kicks from actual games in top male soccer leagues and championships worldwide (our students Yael Keidar-Levin and Galit Schein were an invaluable help in this process). Using a 3 x 3 diagram of the goal area, we then asked three judges to determine the following:

1. which part of the goal the ball was kicked to;
2. in which direction the goalkeeper jumped (if at all);
3. whether he stopped the ball or not.

The main outcomes are summarized in Table 5.1 in the form of simple percentages. The data is divided according to the direction of jumps and

TABLE 5.1   PENALTY KICK OUTCOMES

	Left	Center	Right
Goalkeeper's choice[a]	49.3%	6.3%	44.4%
Goalkeeper's chance to stop the kick overall[b]	14.2%	33.3%	12.6%
Goalkeeper's chance to stop if the goalkeeper and kicker choose the same direction[c]	29.6%	60.0%	25.4%
Kicker's choice[d]	32.2%	28.7%	39.2%

[a] Presents the percentage of cases in which the goalkeeper chose to jump left, right, or stay in the center.
[b] Presents the fraction of kick that were stopped following each of the goalkeeper's possible actions, regardless or the kick's direction.
[c] Presents the fraction of kick that were stopped when both the goalkeeper and the kicker choose the direction (i.e., the goalkeeper chose the correct direction—the one that matched the kick direction).
[d] Presents the distribution of the kick's direction.

kicks, left, right and center (Note: when we refer to right or left, it is from the goalkeeper's perspective; therefore, a kick shot to his left actually means that the kicker shot the ball to *his* right, and vice versa.)

As Table 5.1 shows, 28.7 percent of the kicks went to the central third of the goal, but the goalkeeper chose to stay in the center during only 6.3 *percent* of the total kicks. This behavior is even more puzzling when we take into account that a goalkeeper's chances of stopping a kick when his choice matches the direction of the kick is much higher in the center than on the sides—60.0 percent (center) to 25.4 percent (right) to 29.6 percent (left). Consequently, the chances of stopping a kick are much higher when the goalkeeper stays in the center than when he jumps to one of the sides. Nevertheless, goalkeepers almost always (i.e., in 93.7 percent of the kicks) jump to the right (44.4 percent) or left (49.3 percent) instead of staying in the center.

In our 2007 article, chosen by the *New York Times Magazine* as one of the significant highlights and most innovative research breakthroughs of 2008, we suggested that the reason for this obviously nonoptimal behavior by goalkeepers was an "action bias."[3] Utilizing the so-called norm theory (first proposed by Daniel Kahneman in his 1986 article, with Dale T. Miller, "Norm Theory: Comparing Reality to Its Alternatives," published in the *Psychological Review*) we argued that because the norm, or expected response, is that goalkeepers should "do something" during penalty kicks (i.e., jump), the goalkeeper will feel worse if a goal is scored following inaction (i.e., staying in the center) than following action (i.e., jumping). Such a feeling would therefore lead to a bias in favor of action. A survey conducted among thirty-two top professional goalkeepers strongly supported this claim.

Traditional economic theory would imply that the goalkeeper's behavior is optimal when it maximizes the chances of stopping the ball. This would mean that as long as the shooters' strategy is consistent, the goalie should stay in the center and not jump. However, we found that the utility function of goalkeepers includes not only score outcomes (i.e., a goal is scored or not), but other components as well, such as if he felt worse after a goal was scored when he had not jumped than when he had.

Paradoxically, these nonoptimal considerations nonetheless seem to be rational from an economic point of view after all: it is also possible that people observing the goalkeeper—such as the owner or president of the club, the manager, the coach, the fans, or the media—are also biased in favor of action in their evaluation of the goalie's performance, and reward him financially in line with this very evaluation.

Thus, a goalie who does not jump runs the danger of being perceived as less professional, or as somebody who does not give everything he can for his team. In addition, a jumping goalie who saves a penalty is more likely to be viewed by fans as a much more attractive player, a hero even, than one who just stands in the center and gets hit by a ball. From the goalie's perspective, this would still not refute the decision to almost always jump, even though such action does not necessarily maximize utility and minimize scoring chances. The goalies' behavior, economists would say, is affected by preferences that differ from merely minimizing the chances of a goal.

A striking example of this line of reasoning comes from the Germany–Netherlands final on July 7, 1974, which, to me, will always be the game of all games. On August 28, 2015, Dutch *De-Correspondent* journalist Michiel De Hoog published an article under the title "What Can Investors Learn from Goalkeeper Jan Joengbloed?" If you recall, the Netherlands scored in the first minutes of the game 1 to 0 through a penalty shot by Johan Neeskens, who bombed the ball directly to the middle of the goal—a penalty for which he became very famous.

Something I did not know until I read De Hoog's article, however, is related to the penalty Germany received later in the game: while conceding Breitner's flat penalty shot to his right, Dutch goalkeeper Joengbloed remained standing in the middle of the goal, something not unusual for him to do. However, whereas Neeskens was praised for and cheered on his shot to the middle, Joengbloed has been heavily criticized in the Dutch public for being crazy by just standing in the middle—the very same idea! In a way, De Hoog wanted to rehabilitate Joengbloed by arguing that he actually performed optimally, using our 2007 article as an argument.

By contrast, De Hoog mentions the Czech national goalkeeper Petr Cech who, at that time, played for Chelsea; Cech admitted that he never wanted to stay in the middle because he worried that the fans would think he was not doing his best. On another occasion, Germany's early 1980s national goalkeeper Harald ("Toni") Schumacher said that he never stayed in the middle because it would be against his honor. He also claimed that a player who shoots to the middle is "a wimp, who does not deserve to kick a penalty against me."

Joengbloed's inaction, however, has been vindicated over time, not only by DeHoog but also by one of the greatest soccer coaches ever, Manchester United's legendary Sir Alex Ferguson—who won an astonishing forty-nine trophies throughout his career. In a 2015 book he wrote with world-renowned venture capitalist, philanthropist, and author Sir Michael Moritz, *Leading*, Ferguson describes how his coaching staff pored over penalty kick footage for hours, analyzing the kicks in order to help goalkeepers jump to the "right" direction, even though he saw no use in doing so: "I always thought this was useless, and kept telling our goalkeepers to stay in the middle rather than go sprawling to one side"[4] Sir

Alex intuitively understood the concept, despite the fact that he had, in his own words, "no idea" that it had been proven correct. As *Leading* implies, he was glad to learn about our penalty kicks study with the goalkeepers, which provided scientific support to his view.

For years, as you can imagine, I've been collecting statements by top goalkeepers on the issue of whether to jump or not during a penalty shot. The first goalkeeper I saw on TV who claimed that from time to time he did *not* jump during penalty kicks was Bernard Lama, the national goalkeeper for France during most of the 1990s. Years later, in his 2010 book, Jens Lehmann (Germany's goalkeeper in the FIFA 2006 World Championship) referred to a particular instance of not jumping during a penalty, in which he said: "I stayed simply standing, because I knew that [Swedish player] Henrik Larsson likes to shoot into the middle of the goal."

On April 26, 2006, however, Lehman acted otherwise. That evening, his team, Arsenal FC of London, won narrowly against Spanish club Villareal CF on a 1 to 0 aggregate scoring in the European Champions League. In the 89th minute of the game, Lehman saved a penalty kick by Argentinian superstar Juan Roman Riquelme. When asked about this save by a reporter from the Israeli newspaper *Ha'Aretz*, Lehman said, "I don't remember at all what I did in the penalty; I wanted to stay in the middle, but intuition sent me to the left." I would argue that in the second event, in addition to Lehman's intuition, he was exhibiting an action bias due to social pressure—the possibility of looking dishonorable or unfavorable to the audience, team members, and coaches. In this instance, his action bias played to his advantage, but our research shows that there are many times when *inaction* is the right choice. So even when it's better *not* to perform that operation or sell that house, we find ourselves making decisions based on emotion or social mores.

Everyday Inaction

Take a seemingly simple thing like writing and responding to e-mails. A 2010 study conducted by electronics company Plantronics, titled *How*

We Work, found that between 2005 and 2010, the use of e-mail increased by 78 percent. As of 2010, approximately 83 percent of professionals surveyed use e-mail as a primary communication tool.[5] Having made its debut in work settings over two decades ago, not to mention its widespread use, you would think we would have mastered e-mail etiquette and best practices by now—of course, we have not.

One issue is that e-mail can be a poor communication tool if not used properly. Think about the short, curt e-mails you've received or the impersonal almost robot-like responses to a well thought-out, crafted message you've sent to someone. Though such e-mails may be perceived as slights, even if not intended to be so by the writer, they are nothing compared to receiving a rude or snide e-mail.

Most people's first reaction is to start furiously typing out an equally, if not more, toxic response, banging away on the keyboard and muttering curses under their breath. If they're enraged enough—some communication can be particularly nasty—they'll hit "send" before they've given it a second thought, typically setting off a bigger issue involving increasingly angry e-mails, phone calls, and even potential intervention by managers if necessary. So what should we do in such a situation?

I argue for this: do nothing. Step away from the computer or avoid your e-mail for a good hour or two—give yourself time to let the insult pass. Nine times out of ten, any response you give will only further exacerbate the situation. Your course of *inaction* will help you get along with your day, move on to other tasks, and stay productive. If you're still fuming, write a response on a piece of paper, getting every emotion out that you need to, bask in it for a moment, then throw the paper in the trash.

Just as on the court or field when one player insults another or a referee makes a bad call, not responding is better than a negative response, which will only distract you from your ultimate goals. We see a similar idea in politics. It's better not to respond to provocations in a debate when your opponent tries to get you to lose your focus—a strategy that was recommended on the basis of our goalkeepers' study to Barack Obama in the *Washington Post* (March 31, 2008) when he and Hillary Clinton were contenders for the candidacy of the Democratic party. Voluntary inaction can be incredibly powerful, giving you the upper hand, even at times when you feel like you must act.

As a boss, if your employees are underperforming, you may find that instead of hovering over them, and micromanaging their every move, providing them with enough space to complete their work can be fruitful. Many employees desire autonomy and find that their performance increases when left to their own devices. Take Nordstrom, for example: this idea was built into their corporate culture, which managers credited as the reason for one of the best retention rates in the retail world.[6] When employees feel empowered, they are likely to make better decisions with greater results.

Of course many managers have gotten to their level by following somewhat of a type-A pattern, in which they feel the need to be in control, so it may be hard to let go. *Harvard Business Review* writer Rebecca Knight suggests taking it one step at a time, a gradual reduction in your helicopter-boss actions and attitude: first reflect on your behavior, and then receive feedback from those around you. Talking to your team will build trust and without that trust you'll never feel comfortable taking a more hands-off approach.[7]

Of course, some people want, or need, more attention than others; knowing your team intimately will give you a better idea of those members who will be better off working independently and those that might need a bit more support. Still, support is different than micromanaging. Take the path of least resistance—in short, sometimes you just have to stay off their backs.

The concept of action bias can also be seen in the world of investing, in which many participants panic during a rough patch and end up selling stocks when they should really do nothing and wait it out. What many investors fail to realize, however, is that they should really be aiming for long-term investments—follow a straightforward asset allocation plan and check back in once every few months. Obsessing over market fluctuations will only lead to bad decisions. Well-known, classic fund managers and investors such as Peter Lynch, Benjamin Graham, and David Dodd recommend a similar approach—you have to be in it for the long haul.[8]

Furthermore, it's been demonstrated time and again that you can't beat the market, so you're better off sticking to low-cost index funds that will increase over time. As a regular investor—a nonprofessional—the "passive management" approach, more akin to hands-off than day trading, will lead you to more solid investments with higher earnings. If your portfolio performs just as well as the major indexes, then you're all set—no need to buy, sell, and swap on a daily basis. Stay strong, do nothing.

Now, you're probably saying, "I've had similar experiences in the stock market and at work, and I've found that taking action turned out to my advantage." Well, there may be something to that idea, too. The fact of the matter is that it's more about knowing when not to act and when to act—a sense which can only be developed through deep practice and a development of your anticipation skills, that which may enhance your level of expertise in successfully answering the Hamlet-like question "to act or not to act?"

EVERYTHING YOU ALWAYS WANTED TO KNOW ABOUT PENALTIES (BUT WERE AFRAID TO ASK), PART 2: THE SHOOTERS

> A penalty can often be the highlight of the game . . . It is always a tense and exciting moment—the modern-day equivalent of a duel, with one big difference: an old-fashioned duel with pistols or swords between antagonists was an equal competition.
>
> —PETER SHILTON, *Shilton on Goalkeeping*

I've told you time and again that my initial interest in this topic of inaction versus action lay primarily in the question of why goalkeepers jump too much. In order to investigate goalies' behavior, however, we had to first study the shooters. As unbelievable as it seems, when we started our search around 1995, there were no reliable data about penalty kicks, one of the most important events in soccer, but a lot of common wisdom. And you know how reliable common wisdom can be.

Ofer Azar—my colleague and friend from the Business Administration Department of Ben-Gurion University—and I used the same set of data to examine the optimal strategy for the *shooter* in penalty kicks. Here, we augmented the data reported in our 2007 study and considered not only the horizontal direction of the kick but also its height—a unique innovation in the research on penalties, as far as we could tell. In our 2009 article we reported that when height is considered, 12.9 percent of the kicks reach the upper third of the goal, 30.4 percent the central third of the goal, and 56.6 percent the lower third, as shown in Table 5.2.[9]

We also found that none of the kicks (0 percent) shot to the upper third of the goal were stopped, as compared to the 12.6 percent of the kicks that were stopped when shot to the central third and 19.8 percent to the lower third, as shown, again, in Table 5.2. We therefore concluded that the optimal strategy would be to aim the ball to the upper part, in particular to the upper two corners; with proper training, the miss rates should be low enough to justify applying such a shooting strategy.

The major factor that seems to deter kickers from shooting to the upper part of the goal is probably the increased perceived chances of completely missing the goal frame. However, according to our data, the goalie's chances of stopping a ball in the lowest third of the goal are 19.8 percent, which makes the chances of scoring on a flat kick—a kick shot on the ground with no height or lift—80.2 percent at the most (because this number does not take into account flat kicks that miss the goal altogether, or hit the goalpost, which would reduce these chances to below 80.2 percent). Therefore, we can argue, in an economically rational way, that if the chances of a kick to the upper third missing the goal frame are lower than 19.8 percent, this should be considered a better strategy than kicking to the lowest third. Is it not reasonable to assume that with proper training,

TABLE 5.2   DISTRIBUTION OF KICKS REACHED AND STOPPED

Third of goal	Kicks reached	Kicks stopped
Upper	12.9%	0%
Central	30.4%	12.6%
Lower	56.6%	19.8%

professional, highly paid top soccer players will be able to substantially reduce the miss rate to less than 19.8? Yet leaving out for a moment the central-third height option, to simplify the discussion, we see shooters kicking over four times (4.388 exactly) more frequently to the lowest third (56.6 percent) than to the upper third (12.9 percent).

These results are puzzling; we are talking about highly paid top professionals with every incentive on earth to perform penalties optimally in real games. For example, John Terry's missed penalty in the Champions League final of 2008 cost Chelsea about 170 million dollars.[10] These players also have every opportunity to practice, improve, and maximize their performance in real-time penalty kicks, and yet they rarely shoot to the upper part of the goal, where the goalkeeper's chances of stopping the ball are negligible. Why?

As in the goalies' case, I think the answer lies in the kickers' preferences: they do not necessarily strive to only maximize the chances of scoring. It is possible that shooters consider missing the goal frame completely as worse than having a ball stopped by the goalkeeper. In the first case, only the shooter can be faulted for missing (i.e., "I am the only idiot to bear any blame here"), while in the second case, the talents of the goalie come into play. Consequently, shooters might avoid kicking to the upper part; if their behavior is indeed motivated by preferences other than maximizing their chances of scoring, it is not surprising that they continue this seemingly nonoptimal behavior. Their utility function reflects their significant disutility of missing the goal frame, which is higher than their disutility from a no-goal resulting from a shot stopped by the goalkeeper.

Even the greatest players are in danger of choking under the immense pressure placed on penalty shooters; nobody wants to be remembered for such an event, especially when completely missing the goal frame. One of the most famous tragedies in this respect is Roberto Baggio's missed penalty in 1994. After leading Italy to the final of the FIFA World Championship, scoring five goals in the process, Baggio missed the deciding penalty in the shootout, kicking the ball over the crossbar, sky-high, and losing the trophy to Brazil. Despite his many achievements as one of the greatest players of all times, Baggio is remembered mainly due to this failure. No wonder then that he later said: "It affected me for years. It is the worst moment of my career. I still dream about it. If I could erase one moment, it would be that one."[11]

Avoiding looking Baggiolike is probably more important to penalty shooters than trying to maximize utility by increasing the scoring probability (which would mean shooting to the highest, not lowest, third of the goal). We can see that both goalkeepers and shooters exhibit behaviors that at first sight seem to be biased and nonoptimal. Despite the huge incentives and opportunities to improve and maximize performance (e.g., through training), they still don't optimize their behavior. The goalkeepers are not only interested in minimizing the chances of a goal being scored; their utility function also seems to depend on whether they have jumped or not—they want to look more professional, sportsmanlike, and more highly motivated ("trying harder"). The kickers are not only interested in maximizing the chances of scoring a goal; in plain English they simply don't want to look like fools, having the rest of their career (and even beyond) marked forever.

Strangely enough, however, high-level soccer professionals do not usually train or practice for penalty kicks at all, partly because they believe that penalties are untrainable. German expert and sport psychologist Dr. Georg Froese calls it "the myth of untrainability,"[12] and exemplifies the idea with a recent quote from ex-superstar Paul Breitner (presently, an advisor to Bayern Munich's management board), who bluntly stated: "To practice penalty kicks is bullshit, you cannot train that!" (his words, not mine).

However, sometimes when teams suspect that an upcoming cup or tournament may be decided in a penalty shootout, they will prepare. The most that will happen, however, is that they practice shooting penalties with the attitude "O.K., guys, let's shoot penalties a little bit, even if we don't really believe that they are trainable." At face value there is nothing wrong with this technique, but at a slightly deeper level this actually sends a message or hint that says, "Houston, we *will* probably have a problem." This situation is an excellent example of expectations sent (discussed in chapter 4), but in a negative sense, of course. In such practice the scoring rate is obviously high and everybody is happy because they trained for penalties successfully. The problem, however, is that they have *not*.

In training, the success rate is affected mainly by the fact that "the goal is big and the goalie is small," that is, by the a priori chances, or "base rates," of shooting a penalty successfully. There are many statistics according to which the success rate of penalty kicks for top male professional players—in places like Italy, France, Spain, Germany, and England, as well as European and World Championships—ranges between 75 percent and 85 percent. These percentages were of course calculated across all possible contest conditions, but can give us a rough estimation as to what will happen in training, where there is no competitive stress at all (and therefore, scoring percentages may be even higher). Let's go with the 75 percent rate (these are the numbers in our 2009 study, for example): this means that if you shoot penalties in training, any old way, without having any model to follow, and without any stress, you expect top professional players to score at least three out of four shots on average.

In game settings, however, especially crucial ones (such as cup final shootouts), you should take into account and add the debilitating effects of stress and anxiety, which act to decrease these base-rate scoring probabilities. But shooters don't truly train to face this problem if they just shoot penalties in a peaceful training atmosphere. What actually needs to be emphasized is the *preparatory* phase to help the shooter cope with the stress and anxiety experienced right *before* the shooting itself.

Simply put, players do not receive correct instructions on how to shoot penalty kicks, nor do they receive sufficient training in the skills needed to convert penalty kicks into goals. Moreover, they are typically not trained to deal with the extreme stress and anxiety associated with such situations either. So what do we expect? Why are we surprised when even top players time and again choke under pressure and miss penalty kicks?

Dr. Georg Froese identified two kinds of penalty shooters: "goalkeeper-dependent" and "goalkeeper-independent." In our terms, the first kind of shooter plays a game with the goalie; the second one does not. An ideal penalty shooter (in Froese's terms, an efficient "keeper-independent" shooter) should shoot where goalies are "out of the game"—that is, to the upper corners. Notice, the first strategic instruction is to "shoot high" (i.e., to the upper third of the goal), because even if a player hits the central part of the upper third, goalies will usually not be there since, as you may recall, they jump in 93.7 percent of the cases.

This recommendation is also supported by more recent statistics: for example, German sport statistician Dr. Roland Loy claims that kickers are advised "to shoot to the upper half" because his statistics show that 99 percent of the balls shot to the upper half are scored.[13] However, I ask, why not shoot to the upper *third* where the percentage is even greater than 99 percent? Based on recent British research data, Professor Tom Riley of Liverpool John Moores University, another notable researcher of penalty kicks, put it as such: "A well-placed ball, high to the corner, will not be stopped by the goalkeeper even if he anticipates it. There is not enough time to react, so a kick placed in this area would have 100 percent strike rate."[14]

Such a kick can and should be used as a *model* to follow when players deliberately practice penalty kicks. If we agree that we should train shooters to try and automatize their responses under pressure, then they must be provided with a model behavior to be automatized—and this is precisely what I suggest, and not just in sport. This approach then implies something that is for us sport scientists more than evident, namely that a penalty kick is indeed trainable! But how?

Penalty Kick Training: Deliberate Practice

I strongly believe in the principles of deliberate, or deep, practice, a concept explored, developed, investigated, and promoted for many years by Florida State University professor K. Anders Ericsson. In Ericsson's 2016 book *Peak*, he lays it out quite bluntly: just practice, practice, practice![15] I don't see why highly paid top professionals should not be instructed to shoot penalties from dusk till dawn, or how this would not improve their performance—it is impossible, against all logic and all learning curves derived from any simple learning principle. They must practice until they become ideal, goalkeeper-independent experts on shooting penalties to the upper corners without taking the goalkeeper's actions into account.

Appropriate application of the deliberate practice approach means that amounts matter; an idea that is most reflected by the popular "10,000 hours law," which states that top-notch experts must practice their expertise for no less than 10,000 hours in order to become experts. Equally important, however, is *what* is practiced, *how* it is practiced, and *when*. The main thing—relevant to all of us, be it in sports, business, or other pursuits—is to apply these techniques smartly, that is, with *seychel*. The Hebrew word *sechel* means "common sense" or "intelligence"; in Yiddish, *seychel* becomes somewhat more indefinable, but similar to "using your thinking cap," having smarts, or being wise.

A central principle in this framework would be the one put forward by Sian Beilock, the great choking expert we met earlier in this book: try to close the gap between practice and competition. This can be done by creating stress conditions in practice (let's say, by your friends and family watching you) and can help you adjust to real pressure when it occurs. In the case of penalty kicks, for example, this would work as follows. We already saw that shooters usually don't follow any motor model. Therefore, they should first be provided with an optimal model (shooting to the corners) and then practice, practice, and more practice. Assuming that they do this time and again, they must then build the stress element into the training.

This element should strategically focus on the psychological disturbances occurring *before* the kick itself. When I asked penalty kickers what they usually do before shooting, the frequent response was "nothing." As a matter of fact, however, there is *a lot* going on in shooters' minds, even if they aren't always conscious of it. In a series of investigations conducted by Dr. Geier Jordet, who was my student while I was a guest professor at the Sport University in Oslo back in 1995 and is now director of psychology at the Norwegian Center of Football Excellence, he documented the devastating processes which occur when players supposedly do nothing; in fact, they are strongly affected by disturbances such as negative thoughts and worries, which are typical of what psychologists call "cognitive anxiety."

In his fascinating 2014 book *Twelve Yards*, UK journalist and broadcaster Ben Lyttleton reviews these studies. He concludes that for penalty shooters it all "comes down to pure psychology," and that they must do something against the "nothing." I'll go into the idea of mental preparation techniques in more detail later in the book, but at this point it's enough to understand that strategically speaking, techniques must be employed to fight against negative processes such as stress and anxiety, which are typical of supposed "nothing" states. (One such technique to be discussed in detail is that of imagery—which always makes me think of Michael Ende's "Fantasia," the land of imagination, which is at odds with the "nothing" in the book *Never Ending Story*.) Even though the option of doing nothing can sometimes be the optimal solution, in the case of penalty kickers, doing nothing is devastating and should therefore be fought.

Goalkeepers' Training: Anticipation and Distraction in Penalty Kicks and Business Settings

In 2012, my good friend Professor Ronnie Lidor (the current president of the Academic College at Wingate, whom you already met in chapter 3) and his associates published a review of research conducted on the psychological preparation of goalkeepers for the 11-meter (36-foot) penalty kick in soccer (they found only eighteen studies on this issue).[16] As you may recall, Shilton recommended preparing by relaxing and concentrating; in the European final of 2001, Kahn successfully exhibited the "getting in the zone" technique. Ronnie, however, identified two other ways to prepare: increasing anticipation skills and creating confusion in the kickers by distracting them.

In our 2007 goalkeeper study, we found a match between the direction of the shooter's kick and the direction of the keeper's jump, which is somewhat beyond chance. In other words, the goalies don't simply "gamble"—they seem to know *something* so that their response to a penalty reflects some systematic (albeit limited) knowledge. (Indeed, even traditional goalkeeping instruction books, such as 1990's *Goalkeeping*, written by Alex Welsh, offered some advice to goalkeepers on how to gather such "hints" as to where the shooter is going to kick, as do Shilton and Lehman.) Ronnie and his associates suggest studying video clips of different penalty kickers for this purpose, to increase the effectiveness of goalkeepers' anticipation.

In regards to creating confusion in the shooters, Welsh recommends "trying to dummy the kicker" while Ronnie claims that distraction strategies (such as waving arms up and down) are particularly effective in impairing kickers' performances. Two famous examples of distraction come from two great goalkeepers of Liverpool FC: in the 1984 European Cup final shootout against AS Roma, Bruce Grobbelaar comically wobbled his legs to distract the kicker; in the 2005 Champions League final shootout against AC Milan, Jerzy Dudek distracted his opponents by waving his arms aloft and moving around on the line.

Just as Ronnie suggests studying competitors on the pitch, your team and overall company must keep astride of competitors' actions and anticipate their moves. "Competitor centricity" has gained popularity in the last few years, in which you become intimately familiar with how other companies in your industry work. Steve Krupp and Toomas Truumees suggest "walking in the competitors' shoes" by internal role-playing exercises to better understand the competitor and their strategies.[17] They also recommend the "Colin Powell 40–70 rule" when it comes to leveraging information on the competition. This rule states that to make an informed, positive decision based on competitor actions, you need between 40 and 70 percent of the information available—any less and you won't be able to analyze the situation fully; any more and you'll end up overanalyzing.

Your team must be prepared to execute on high-impact decisions when the time is right, but it can be difficult to decide on the right time. Take into consideration factors such as how prepared your team or company are to enter new markets—if your competitors are ahead of you, maybe you want to consider an alternate route or doubling down on what's working best for you. What if they plan to launch a product or service that your intelligence says is destined to fail? Consider what your company's strengths are and how you can use them to your advantage. Developing these anticipation skills will help you understand when to strike, but equally as important, they will show you when it's time to sit back, with your feet up on the desk, and stay the course.

Though you may not be able to distract your business competitors through waving your arms or shaking your legs, the concept still applies, most directly in your organization's performance and practices. As the old saying goes, "the best revenge is living well," but for our purposes we could say, "the best distraction is performing well." For example, consider surprising the competition with new products and services that fulfill overlooked niches. This is of course easier said than done, but it will certainly lead to a higher market share for your company and will throw competitors off their game. Try keeping the new product under wraps until shortly before its release. Apple cofounder Steve Jobs was famous for this method, even surprising his own staff when launching new "i" products, such as the original iPhone. Keep the competition guessing!

TURN, TURN, TURN

A time to keep silence, a time to speak.

—King Solomon[18]

In reality, I cannot tell you *for sure* whether in a given situation you should "do" or "not do," because the line dividing them is often unclear. Think of the goalkeepers once again: to maximize performance, they should do nothing (i.e., not jump). But it is also recommended that they do something (i.e., try to distract the shooter). Or think about my Parkinson's: when I was diagnosed as suffering from Parkinson's disease, a good friend of mine, Professor Gabriel ("Gabi") Schreiber, a notable Israeli psychiatrist and the former dean of the faculty of medicine at the Ben-Gurion University, advised me not to think about myself as a sick person. But am I healthy? Not really. Thank God, I am not "sick" in the common interpretation of the word, but on the other hand, I am also not really "healthy." It goes back to the idea of opposites discussed at the opening of the chapter: like the yin and yang, I am *both*.

In fact, I sincerely believe in the dialectical approach: two seemingly opposing or contradictory forces may often comprise the two sides of the same coin, complementing one another to create the whole. Think of Bashevis-Singer's "enemies," who are actually in love; of the Beatles' "Hello Goodbye" game; of Esher's buildings, which are at the same time possible yet impossible; or of Frost's road not taken. In chapter 6, we shall see how rationality and irrationality are often unclear and confusing entities—but at any rate, they are complementary. So are doing and not doing: sometimes it's certainly better not to do anything at all, and sometimes it's necessary to strike while the iron is hot—two complementary sides of one smart decision-making process.

Unconsciously, we acknowledge this state of affairs. For example, do you say "black and white" when describing opposites? Think for a moment—shouldn't it be "black *or* white" if the two are noncomplementary? You probably didn't notice that at the very beginning of the opposites section of this chapter, when I told you about Blondie and Tuco, I used the phrase "black *and* white," where in reality, it should actually be "black *or* white."

At the end of the day I believe whether to take action or not fully lies in a matter of timing. King Solomon, the wisest of all people, recognized this state of affairs a long time ago. In chapter 3 of the Book of Ecclesiastes the wise King says that there is "a time to be born, a time to die; a time to plant, and a time to pluck up that which is planted; a time to kill, and a time to heal." (You may also recognize this text as it was repurposed by folk singer Pete Seeger in his song "Turn! Turn! Turn!," later popularized in 1965 by the Byrds.) The wise King tells us that life is comprised of a list of seemingly opposites (including death, regarded by the King as part of life), and that in fact everything is a matter of *timing*. Following King Solomon's advice, I sincerely believe that to do or not to do is also a matter of timing—a time to do this and a time (not?) to do that—a notion I will return to in chapter 6.

SUMMARY

Sometimes the best course of action is *inaction*. In both sports and business, however, an action bias exists. It is imperative to understand where this action bias comes from, how it affects you, and how you can overcome it. Even when you're better off not acting, and you know it, you may still perform an action only to demonstrate that you did something. Still, there are times when action is necessary, and knowing the difference between the two will lead to increased performance.

Frequently, everything lies in a matter of timing—a time to do this, a time (not?) to do that—provided that the limits between this and that are more or less clear. Through deliberate practice, you can develop a better understanding of this timing and increase your anticipation skills and ability to confuse and distract competitors, along with your performance as well. Developing these skills will also help you understand when to strike, but just as importantly, they will show you when it's time to wait it out.

DAILY PRACTICES

As an Individual

- Don't follow the knee-jerk reaction to respond immediately to every snide or rude e-mail. In most cases, it will be better not to respond at all.
- In day-to-day activities and in your overall career, don't rush to simply do *something*: do your research, know your facts, and consider the outcomes of your actions.
- Study your competitors—take a walk in their shoes and understand the inner workings of their company the best you can.

As a Leader

- Try giving your employees some space and take a more hands-off leadership approach.

- Develop your and your team's anticipation skills, by working in line with your strengths and knowing how you can use them against competition.
- Don't let the action bias affect you—keep in mind that there will be many situations where it's better to take no action at all.

NOTES

1. D. A. Asch, J. Baron, J. C. Hershey, H. Kunreuther, J. Meszaros, I. Ritov, and M. Sprance, "Omission Bias and Pertussis Vaccination," *Medical Decision Making* 14 (April 1994): 118–123.
2. J. Baron, *Thinking and Deciding*, 4th ed. (New York: Cambridge University Press, 2008).
3. M. Bar-Eli, O. H. Azar, I. Ritov, Y. Keidar-Levin, and G. Schein, "Action Bias Among Elite Soccer Goalkeepers: The Case of Penalty Kicks," *Journal of Economic Psychology* 28 (2007): 606–621.
4. A. Ferguson and M. Moritz, *Leading* (London: Hodder, 2015).
5. Om Malik, "Is Email a Curse or a Boon?" *Gigaom.com*, September 22, 2010, https://gigaom.com/2010/09/22/is-email-a-curse-or-a-boon/.
6. Beverly Kaye, "Give Employees the Space They Need," *Fast Company*, April 10, 2006, www.fastcompany.com/919161/give-employees-space-they-need.
7. Rebecca Knight, "How to Stop Micromanaging Your Team," *Harvard Business Review*, August 21, 2015, https://hbr.org/2015/08/how-to-stop-micromanaging-your-team.
8. Benjamin Graham and David L. Dodd, *Security Analysis*, 6th ed. (New York: McGraw-Hill, 2008).
9. M. Bar-Eli and O.H. Azar, "Penalty Kicks in Soccer: An Empirical Analysis of Shooting Strategies and Goalkeepers' Preferences," *Soccer and Society* 10 (2) (March 2009): 183–191. See also Michael Bar Eli, Ofer H. Azar, and Yotam Lurie, "(Ir)rationality in Action: Do Soccer Players and Goalkeepers Fail to Learn How to Best Perform During a Penalty Kick?" *Progress in Brain Research* 174 (February 2009): 97–108.
10. This number is based on S. Kuper and S. Szymanski's *Soccernomics* (New York: Nation Books, 2009), 114.
11. Timothy Farrell, *Attacker, Defender, Goalkeeper*, 2008, www.theadgalternative.com/.
12. Froese was the winner of the 2013 scientific award of the DFB (German Football Association) for his dissertation on penalty kicks. G. Froese, "Sportpsychologische Einflussfaktoren der Leistung von Elfmeterschuetzen [Sport-Psychological Factors that Influence the Performance of Penalty Shooters]," doctoral dissertation, University of Heidelberg, 2012.
13. Cited in an article that included various soccer statistics: Manuel Lippert, "Elementarteilchen des Fussbals: Interview mit Statistiker Dr. Roland Loy" (Elementary Particles of Soccer: Interview with Statistician Dr. Roland Loy), 11Freunde—Magazin fuer Fussballkulture (11 Friends—Magazine for Soccer

Culture), December 25, 2006, www.11freunde.de/interview/interview-mit-statistiker-dr-roland-loy.

14. Cited in Dr. Chris Doyle's e-mail to me from July 7, 2010; see also Kurt Desender's report from December 1, 2011: "Science Discovers Secret of the Ideal Penalty," with data analyzing England's penalties at major tournaments since 1962.

15. K. A. Ericsson and R. Pool, *Peak: Secrets from the New Science of Expertise* (New York: Eamon Dolan/Houghton Mifflin Harcourt, 2016).

16. R. Lidor, G. Ziv, and G. Tenenbaum, "Psychological Preparation of Goalkeepers for the 11m Penalty Kick in Soccer—A Review," *The Sport Psychologist* 26 (September 2012): 375–389.

17. Steve Krupp and Toomas Truumees, "Competitive Anticipation: How to Enhance Leadership by Sharpening Your Competitive Edge," *Decision Strategies International*, April 22, 2014, http://decisionstrat.com/news/competitive-anticipation-how-to-enhance-leadership-by-sharpening-your-competitive-edge/.

18. Ecclesiastes 3:1–8, King James Version.

6

Creativity and Innovation

On Floppers and Vaulters

I've never tried to be a nonconformist; I just find different solutions.

—RICHARD DOUGLAS FOSBURY

I n 1968, Israeli television was in its infancy. The first event ever to be shown—needless to say, in black and white—was the Jerusalem IDF Independence Day parade that May. The first news broadcast was on August 20. Between October 12 to 27, the Olympic Games took place in Mexico, and I had a front-row seat at my family's new TV. I followed those games with all the excitement you would expect from a teenage sports fanatic.

That year, unknown Olympic high jumper Richard Douglas ("Dick") Fosbury unveiled one of the greatest sports innovations ever. Instead of attempting to excel in the high jump using the time-tested straddle roll, as all the other high jumpers did, Fosbury broke with tradition and premiered a radical new approach—a back-first "flop," which had never before been seen.

Fosbury's new style evoked skeptical and cynical reactions, bordering on mockery, among track and field experts. I remember one of Israel's best-known TV sports commentators at the time literally shouting, "You don't jump like that!" This new jump, however, sent Fosbury home with not only the Olympic gold medal, but also eternal fame and glory—the "Fosbury Flop" was eventually adopted by every high jumper and remains the standard high jump to this day.

"Innovation" is defined as a new idea applied to initiating or improving a product, process, or service. For many years, I have been fascinated by the psychology behind this creative process; I've pondered what actually goes on in inventors' minds when they come up with great new ideas—and what makes them so innovative and effective. The one answer I keep coming back to is this: the greatest ideas, inventions, and solutions are often the most unexpected, or considered the least rational, when they are first attempted.

If we consider "rationality" in terms of "being effective" or "instrumental," we're actually saying that when you act rationally, you solve problems or perform better according to existing norms and models. Those people who do not follow these standards are seen as acting "irrationally." But that's the funny thing about innovation—sometimes what first seems to be irrational turns out to be the *most* rational. And you may find that standard or orthodox methods, those considered rational, end up being the *least* rational once new, more effective ones are introduced.

Once Fosbury's coach Dean Benson—who had taught him to jump according to the standard straddle—realized Fosbury's numbers were improving with the flop technique, he did not object to his development of the new move. In fact, Benson encouraged and supported him wholeheartedly. Following Fosbury's great success, his "irrational" technique became the new standard.[1]

The question of the role of creativity in performance raises the issue of whether it is better to stick to well-practiced behaviors you know that you can execute, or search for new ways of doing things, even if they take time to learn and perfect. Understanding the psychological underpinnings of creativity can help you think outside of the box where necessary and boost your performance in various situations. This type of innovation process is found throughout sports and can be applied in numerous settings.

No matter the context or task, innovative thought processes tend to follow amazingly similar—but not always identical—patterns, and you can be trained to think in ways that will produce creative solutions to performance-related problems. Such cases raise the question: how rational or logical are thought and decision-making processes? And why do seemingly irrational creative processes often prove to be the most performance-enhancing ones? Let's take a look at two case studies that my colleagues and I conducted, the first with the famous Dick Fosbury, illustrating the steps that lead to performance-enhancing innovation.

THE FOSBURY FLOP

You don't jump like that!

—Nissim Kivity, *Israeli sports broadcaster*

Since I became interested in the topic of creative and innovative thinking back in the early 1990s, I had a dream of investigating a great sports inventor like Fosbury. I wanted to understand what went on in his mind that made him so incredible, and what caused his innovation to become so popular. In 1998, I had the opportunity to meet Fosbury at the First International Congress of Olympic Winners conference in Greece.

During the conference, we had many conversations in which Dick told me how he came up with the idea of the Fosbury Flop and how it spread. He said that he lectured about his story now and then, but at that time, he was unaware of any systematic scientific documentation of his move. I was amazed that nobody had yet scientifically investigated such a monumental feat. Dick and I sat together during a long bus trip in the Peloponnese, and we talked while everyone else slept. I learned that Dick and I had some personal things in common, which brought us even closer. We quickly became good friends, and I promised Dick that one day I would investigate his case and document it scientifically—and I never break my promises.

In 2002 my colleagues Oded Lowengart and Jacob Goldenberg and I began a study on Fosbury and his amazing innovation. Using a qualitative approach, we had him respond by e-mail to five questions derived from previous research on inventions and innovations, with minor adaptations to suit him personally. These open-ended questions were designed to capture the various dimensions to how Fosbury developed his technique.[2]

For Fosbury, the initial development took place during his years as a high school athlete. He wanted to excel in high jump, but had substantial difficulties using the straddle, the dominant high jump technique of the period. The straddle was a complex motion where an athlete went over the high jump bar facing down. Straddle jumpers—who had to get the upper part of their bodies above the bar—approached from the opposite side, so as to take off from the inner foot; throwing one leg into the air to straddle, they passed over the bar face down (see Figure 6.1).

The straddle roll was perfected by the great Soviet high jumper Valeriy Brumel (1942–2003), who became the best high jumper in history during the Cold War, and is still widely regarded as one of the greatest athletes ever to compete in the event. Even though Brumel was regarded as a model to follow by many high jumpers, Fosbury had a hard time coordinating all the motions involved in the straddle method. Therefore, he started experimenting with other ways of performing the high jump, specifically using an older "scissors technique," which many people considered inefficient. As he continued to work on it throughout high school, his new style developed.

The development of the innovation took place over time, as he started using a curved approach to the bar and intuitively turning his inside

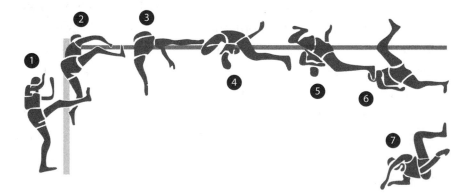

Figure 6.1 The Straddle Roll Jump.

shoulder away from the bar to get his head over the bar sooner. He began to go over the bar backward, headfirst, curving his body over and kicking his legs up in the air at the end of the jump. Slowly but surely, Fosbury fully evolved the technique whereby he cleared the bar with his back to it, first arching his hips over, then un-arching to kick his heels over and land on his back in the pit.

Prior to Fosbury's junior year, his high school had replaced its wood chip-landing pit with a softer material, which meant he was able to land safely on his back—a fortuitous event. Luckily for him, during the early 1960s foam rubber landing surfaces were becoming much more common across the United States, with high schools following colleges' lead. This development, which accelerated between 1964 and 1968, allowed for improvements in high jump results, because jumpers and vaulters could focus more on clearing the bar and less on landing.

Another crucial milestone was the attitude of Fosbury's coaches: after realizing he was doing better with his new move, they told him to do whatever he wanted—as long as it worked—instead of forcing him into the "right" model. (Not many coaches or bosses would have done so.) During the latter part of his sophomore year and the beginning of his junior year, the process began to produce results, with Fosbury gradually clearing increasingly higher bars. In his junior year, he broke his school record with a 6-foot-3-inch jump. By the next year, he was already second in the entire state with an impressive 6 feet, 5.5 inches. The technique was christened the Fosbury Flop after a Medford newspaper reporter poked fun at Fosbury, saying he looked "like a fish flopping in a boat." (I have a feeling the reporter ate those words after the 1968 Olympic games.)

In 1965, Fosbury went to Oregon State University in Corvallis and continued to refine various aspects of his technique. His most important discovery was that he had to adjust his takeoff point with increasing height: as the bar was raised, more "flight time" was required. The top of Fosbury's arc was attained when his hips passed over the bar, with his jump resembling a parabola. He moved his takeoff farther away from the bar and the pit, thereby increasing flight time and clearing the height (see Figure 6.2).

Figure 6.2 The Fosbury Flop.

The spread, or diffusion, of the innovation began at the Mexico Olympic Games, when Fosbury won the gold and set a new Olympic and US record: 7 feet, 4.25 inches. Even though he failed to break Brumel's five-year-old World Record of 7 feet, 5.67 inches, and despite the doubt, skepticism, and mockery from the high jump community, the Fosbury Flop gained acceptance over time. By the 1972 Summer Olympic Games in Munich most high jumpers had adopted the style, and within a decade, the move had practically become the standard approach to high jumping. Olympic medalists have used it almost exclusively since the early 1970s, and Olympic and World records have been improved substantially since its development, as shown in Figure 6.3.

The men's world record has improved by over 15cm since Fosbury's invention became the dominant style among high jumpers.[3] Figure 6.3 demonstrates that without the invention of the Fosbury Flop, the record would have been quite stagnant—it was the innovation that enabled a substantial "jump" in the record (Era 4 in Figure 6.3); currently, the world record is 2.45 meters (8 feet, 0.25 inches), set in 1993 by Javier Sotomayor of Cuba.

THE TSUKAHARA VAULT

> My original motivation . . . was just a desire to improve my gymnastics air sense.[4]
>
> —Mitsuo Tsukahara

While investigating the Fosbury case, we identified other sports innovators considered to be revolutionary, finding similar patterns in their creative

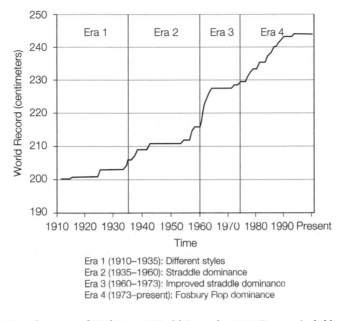

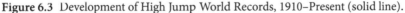

Era 1 (1910–1935): Different styles
Era 2 (1935–1960): Straddle dominance
Era 3 (1960–1973): Improved straddle dominance
Era 4 (1973–present): Fosbury Flop dominance

Figure 6.3 Development of High Jump World Records, 1910–Present (solid line).

processes. Mitsuo Tsukahara (born in 1947, like Fosbury) was a famous Japanese gymnast, Olympic medalist, and World Champion. Today, he is well known for inventing a technique called the "Tsukahara Vault" (or the "Tsukahara Twist"), which had a huge influence on the history of vaulting and has been used consistently since its introduction. His 1970 vault became universally recognized and used by both women and men all over the world.

We decided to compare these two great inventions, the Flop and the Vault. The idea was to investigate the similarities and differences in the evolution of these two moves, with respect to their stages of development, the inventor's motivation, the environmental conditions in which the inventions took place, and the effect each invention had on the athlete's own performance, as well as on the entire field. Keep in mind that even though the development of the moves took place in an almost parallel time period, they had entirely different cultural settings (late 1960s US and late 1960s Japan).

Using the same qualitative approach as we had with Fosbury, Tsukahara responded by e-mail to five questions derived from previous research on inventions and innovations, again with minor adaptations to suit him personally. As with Fosbury, these open-ended questions were designed to capture the various dimensions to discover how Tsukahara developed his move.

The major finding was that Tsukahara's innovation was similar to Fosbury's in many ways, though there was one main difference. Both of them were practitioners, who attempted to solve their own problems in order to improve their performances. However, whereas Fosbury's crucial turning point took place when he tried working with the supposedly less efficient scissors technique, Tsukahara's crucial eureka moment occurred when he creatively connected two originally unconnected things, taking an element from one domain—trampoline—and introducing it into another—gymnastics.

After adopting their respective new ideas, both Fosbury and Tsukahara needed a long, continuous, and relatively slow evolutionary process to fully develop them. Both innovations were quite similar in regards to their discovery, because they reflected an evolutionary and continuous, rather than revolutionary and discontinuous, process. Seemingly radical innovations are rarely a sudden stroke of ingenuity but rather gradual and incremental—a combination of converging abilities and the occurrence of complex, continuous development.

Both innovations were also based on the location of the jumper. In the Fosbury Flop, the combination of the angle in which the bar was approached and the direction the jumper faced (i.e., facing the bar in the straddle versus switching to the back in the Flop), resulted in the new style. In Tsukahara's case, a combination of rotating and twisting in one element was created in order to develop the new move. This innovation was based on existing rotating and twisting movements that were performed separately and were regarded by gymnasts as two different elements.

The stories of these great innovations also raise a question about the common belief that experts know best and are able to provide optimal solutions to any given problem. With Fosbury, the so-called experts were wrong. In Tsukahara's case, the experts simply didn't have the knowledge or insight to recognize the great potential of incorporating other methods from outside gymnastics. It seems the consensus that arises at a particular point in time among experts concerning optimal solutions is frequently transient or, even worse, reflects sheer ignorance.

THE STRUCTURE OF THE INNOVATIVE PROCESS

If you always do what you always did, you will always get what you
always got.

—ALBERT EINSTEIN

After closely comparing Fosbury's and Tsukarha's creative processes in
our 2008 study, four fairly distinct steps that contributed to the innovative
process emerged:

1. The innovator has a problem (e.g., wants to improve performance) and is looking for a solution;
2. The innovator has the creative idea of using a new, nondogmatic
   way of meeting this challenge;
3. The innovator begins to systematically improve the idea, and
   undertakes an evolutionary, incremental optimization
   process of the invention in order to maximize performance;
4. The innovation is diffused, adopted and applied by other
   potential users.

For example, in Fosbury's case, the first step occurred because he wanted
to remain competitive and increase the height of his jump but was experiencing trouble with the straddle roll. The second step took place when
he came up with the back-first movement to get higher up over the bar.
The consistent practice and development of the Flop was the third step.
Though he was essentially an unknown athlete at the Olympic Games,
the whole world had the opportunity to see him perform this strange
new feat—and as high jumpers found that the flop was effective, it spread
among the sport like wildfire, the final step to the process.

Breaking away from the mold led to Fosbury's and Tsukahara's success. We see such creativity and innovative thinking contributing to
individual and group performance throughout the business world, following the same pattern my colleagues and I identified in these studies.
Understanding the steps that lead to innovation will help you know how

and when you, your team, or your industry are ready for it. And when the time is right, if you properly implement innovation, following appropriate methods and thoughtful approaches, you'll experience new levels of higher performance: let's take a look at a company at the forefront of innovation, doing just that.

Tesla Motors

It wasn't that long ago that the Big Three automakers—General Motors, Ford, and Chrysler—experienced major setbacks around the time of the 2008 financial crisis. The early 2000s saw a trend of SUVs, trucks, and other low fuel-efficient vehicles, but as the price of oil went up and the US economy tanked, the Big Three had their own crisis on their hands, leading to a government rescue, or bailout, of both GM and Chrysler.

In 2003, however, a group of Silicon Valley engineers already had the foresight to quietly begin bucking the trend of extravagant gas-guzzlers. They believed they could create cars that would prove to be not only more environmentally friendly, but also increasingly affordable and overall superior to the status quo vehicle. Tesla Motors was on a mission to develop zero emission, all-electric cars and to accelerate the world's implementation of, and transition to, sustainable energy transportation.

In 2015, *Forbes Magazine* rated Tesla Motors as the world's #1 most innovative company, and understandably so. Not only did *Forbes* writers relish in the physical design of the new Model S, but also in the dedication that CEO and cofounder Elon Musk shows to his cause in the face of the complexity involved in such a high-end disruption.[5] The first Model S's were released in 2012 and they still carry a hefty price tag of $70,000, but in the ever-expanding plan to reach more consumers, that number is lowering every year. By 2017, a new model, Model 3, aims to retail for $35,000.[6]

And if radically changing the automotive industry wasn't enough, other industries are becoming interested in the power of Tesla's long-lasting batteries. Whether considering their implementation in the tech sector and military for portable devices or in energy production in general—showcasing both a cheaper and cleaner option over traditional oil—Tesla's innovations could potentially affect almost all facets of our lives, as its ideas and products continue to disperse throughout the world.

For Musk, the first step of the process was overcoming the problem of low-fuel efficient, high-priced, and environmentally unsustainable vehicles. The second step to meet this challenge was to focus on long-lasting electric battery-powered cars that produced no emissions. In the third step, we find Musk and Tesla improving on the idea by creating newer, cheaper models and longer-lasting lithium battery technology. In the fourth step, these cheaper models are designed to be more affordable for the general public, while other industries also begin to adapt and use these new technologies to change the way they function.

You may be saying, "Well that's great for Elon Musk and Tesla Motors, but how can I actually incorporate this four-step process into my daily work? How can I apply these ideas to my individual, team's, or organization's performance? What can I do to get my brain thinking creatively so I, too, can experience breakthrough innovations?"

I'm glad you asked.

TECHNIQUES FOR INNOVATION: UNDERSTANDING FIRST-ORDER VERSUS SECOND-ORDER CHANGES

> I don't like players who don't do what I say, and I don't like players who do exactly what I say.
>
> —LARRY BIRD[7]

The book of Proverbs is one of the most important traditional sources of Biblical wisdom. In part attributed to King Solomon, it discusses questions of values, moral behavior, the meaning of life, and appropriate conduct. In one section, the book illustrates how parents should educate their children. Probably the most famous, oft-cited, and debated pieces of advice included is, "spare the rod and spoil the child."

Of course, such language needs to be taken in context: in most of today's mainstream and popular religious thought, surely beating

children with sticks is not condoned, but the ideas of constructive criticism, limit-setting, and appropriate forms of punishment all play a
major role in child-rearing. Think about it: if you, as a parent, teacher,
army officer, boss, or coach avoid what is evidently necessary, you will
not be able to fully educate your child, pupil, apprentice, soldier, athlete, or student. If you fail to set limits and implement discipline when
needed, which are important for development, the "child" may become
spoiled.

All of us know cases in which a father deals with his son's chronic misbehavior by instituting increasingly severe punishments. In such situations,
the father is likely to consistently apply the old measures, becoming more
vigorous over time. The problem may be solved at one point or another,
but it may also resist resolution. So what can then be done? The answer
can be found in the work of the English anthropologist, social scientist,
linguist, and cyberneticist Gregory Bateson (1904–1980).[8]

Bateson differentiated between "first-order" and "second-order" change
processes. First-order change processes involve the assimilation of current
experiences into existing mental structures, whereas second-order change
processes reflect a fundamental, proactive change. In the first case, your
thinking is relatively simple and straightforward—when you have a problem, you may run the danger of being constrained in the range and nature
of solutions you can think of. As a result, you might end up doing more
of the same (e.g., the father punishing the son in the same way repeatedly
with increasing vigor).

In the second case, however, thinking about possible solutions to the
problem will transform into a more complex mode, because you're thinking "meta-cognitively"—that is, you will develop a completely alternate
perspective of the problem to be solved, which will challenge your mind's
current conceptual status. You will then decide to do something that is
fundamentally different from everything you have done in the past.

The father who uses the same tactics in punishing his son over and over
again without solving the problem is often actually worsening, or even
perpetuating, the situation, while frustration and anger accumulates on

both sides. He does not understand that the problem resists resolution because it does not stem from the son alone, but rather from the structure of the father–son relationship and interaction—this will remain constant, or become stronger, when using first-order solutions.

To really solve the problem, what must be changed is not the way one part works within the system, but rather the entire system. As a consequence, instead of using the same measures time and again, the father may have to try something radically different. He needs to start thinking about his own previous way of thinking (again, the idea of meta-cognition). By doing so, he will recognize the need to change the system instead of unsuccessfully trying to change only one element.

For example, on February 25, 1964, in Miami, Florida, boxer Mohammed Ali (Cassius Clay at the time) competed against world champion Sonny Liston for the title in one of the most famous fights in boxing history. Ali announced that he would "float like a butterfly and sting like a bee," which he successfully did. Ali, a heavyweight boxer, imported this style from the welterweight and middleweight categories, where it had been successfully practiced by boxers such as Sugar Ray Robinson (1921–1989). Sugar Ray was indeed Ali's hero and role model (Ali referred to Robinson as "the king, the master, my idol"). Thus, Ali—like Tsukahara—was creative in connecting previously unrelated things, introducing a whole new style of boxing from one domain into another. This is undoubtedly a second-order change process: Ali, just as Tsukahara, Fosbury, or Musk, didn't just change the means, but the entire concept.

Think about your own workplace environment and ask yourself the following:

- What obstacles are standing in your way toward innovation and a resulting increase in performance? Are these problems found throughout your organization or team?
- As a leader, what type of relationship have you fostered between employees and employers? Does this relationship need to be revamped or approached differently?

- Do you find that the standard operations set in place cause people to resist change? Or is your team open and ready for innovation?
- What have you done to break convention when necessary and apply outside-the-box thinking?

If you look at the New York City-based media company BuzzFeed, you'll see the power of second-order changes. When CEO Jonah Peretti started the website in 2006 it focused on viral content—you were likely to find humorous relationship quizzes, lists of "The 10 Songs Most Likely to Make a Dude Cry," and more photos of cute cats than you knew what to do with. Though all of this content is still available—some quite enjoyable— BuzzFeed has become much more than a place online to kill fifteen minutes of down time. As a "cross-platform, global network for news and entertainment," the site generates six billion views each month.[9] In 2016, *Fast Company* picked BuzzFeed as the world's most innovative company of the year.[10]

Instead of staying the same course, the company has evolved with reader interest and entered new platforms. In 2011, they began expanding the site to include more serious journalism, while taking advantage of social media channels such as Instagram, YouTube, Facebook, Twitter, SnapChat, Vine, and more. Evolving their product and processes, they have quickly reinvented themselves, attracting major investors like NBC Universal and garnering worldwide interest, with eleven international editions. They took what could have been a flash-in-the-pan entertainment site and innovated their way to being a major player in today's media landscape.

Some people may argue that a company like BuzzFeed has more room to innovate since it is a newer company dealing in the trendy media du jour of free Internet-based information and news coverage. But some of today's most innovative companies have actually been around for more than a century and sell what might be considered fairly boring products and services.

Whirlpool Corporation, for example, was first founded in 1911. Over one hundred years later, as a Fortune 500 company with annual revenue around $21 billion, 97,000 employees, and seventy manufacturing and technology research centers, it is internationally known for its dominance in the home appliances industry.[11] What many people don't know is how the company has interwoven innovation into its core business values and procedures. Whirlpool devotes a share of its yearly capital budget, typically around 20 percent, to projects that are deemed truly innovative and worthy by its board.[12] Their performance throughout the 2000s owes much to the 15,000 employees it has trained to be business innovators.[13] They supply unique products that are proven to be desirable by consumers and provide competitive advantage. Instead of just churning out washing machines—a first-order change—Whirlpool is developing new technologies, workarounds, and an in-house culture of continuous, evolutionary innovation.

Reframing and Paradoxical Interventions

First-order change processes seem rational because they rely on well-known, familiar, or habitual concepts, reflecting "means-end rationality": here, a failure to achieve an intended end leads to a search for more effective means within the same existing frame of thought. Such rational actions, however, may end up with a completely irrational outcome in which the problem has not been solved.

By contrast, when conducting a second-order change, you reflect on your own actions, questioning the very frame of thought that governs them. Second-order change processes focus on the framing of the setting of the problem; here, a failure to achieve intended consequences may lead to reflection on your original framing. Means-end deliberation occurs as a result of your particular frame of mind. When you focus on changing the frame (i.e., the way of constructing the problem), it may be seen as strange or irrational, but it is in fact rational. The point being, the use of seemingly irrational measures may lead you to solve the problem.

In their classic book *Change*, Watzlawik, Weakland, and Fisch explain how a logical solution can paradoxically perpetuate a problem: if we view event "A" as undesirable, we rationally tend to solve it by using the common sense solution of "not-A."[14] However, as long as the solution is sought within the A or not-A dichotomy, the participants are trapped in an illusion of alternatives, leading only to a reinforcement of the problem, not a solution. A solution based on a second-order change process may at first seem illogical, or paradoxical, but it is likely to lead us to a logical solution. Known as "paradoxical interventions,"[15] the idea is to change the structure of the entire system under consideration.

Reframing, in which the meaning attached to a problem is fundamentally altered, is the process by which paradoxical interventions work. If you've ever taken an issue with negative connotations and then thought about it in a different way, causing it to have subsequently positive connotations, then you are familiar with reframing. Reframing can help you recognize solutions to seemingly unsolvable problems.

While I was in charge of a team of sport psychologists supporting Olympic athletes at Israel's National Sport Institute, we identified and discussed three main paradoxical techniques—those that would help in reframing a negative or difficult situation—that applied to elite performance.

1. Symptom Prescription and Paradoxical Intention

Here, the athlete or employee is directed to intentionally carry out a problematic behavior. In the Israeli national rifle and pistol marksmanship team, for example, one athlete was occasionally bothered by the thought of missing the target. When shooting, if he thought about it too much, and became anxious or overly concerned, he indeed tended to miss more than usual. This anxiety was accompanied by statements such as: "I can't miss; if I miss, it will be a catastrophe; how will I look? What will everybody think of me? I must hit the bull's-eye!" These negative "if-then" thoughts are typical of cognitive anxiety. Under heightened, chronic pressure, they can lead to occasional choking.

The marksman was then advised to intentionally miss a few shots in training. The rationale was that instead of trying to avoid mistakes ("more of the same"), he would be better off if he tried to deliberately create them. He did this in order to exploit his wish to completely master the situation—this would be attained through successful, deliberate mastery of the smallest mistakes. In doing so, he was reframing through a positive definition of the problem. Paradoxically, the marksman was so busy performing his task of perfectly committing a few small mistakes daily, he had no time to be anxious about grave errors. His shots increasingly hit dead center.

2. Assenting to Pessimism

Here, the coach, leader, or consultant assents to a player's, employee's, or client's pessimistic viewpoint. One tennis coach, for example, complained that his player repeatedly expressed feelings of "not being good enough" or "totally untalented." Before every match, the player would say that he had "no chance at all." The coach's efforts to convince the player that he would do great, providing examples of his natural talents and incredible abilities,[16] were unsuccessful. So the coach was advised to agree with his player's pessimistic statements, even exaggerating them a bit.

Of course the player was more than a little surprised by this unexpected change in his coach's attitude. The coach would tell the player things like, "Don't bother training—there's no use! You're just going to fail again. Maybe you're not cut out for tennis anymore." After a while, the player stopped making so many negative comments, and the coach was convinced the player was out to prove him wrong and show his worth and skill. Similarly, I used this technique with an elite basketball player who used to complain that the whole world was against him (e.g., "whenever I start playing well, I end up injured"). I asked him if he would like to cry and mourn with me over his cruel fate. He began laughing and was immediately relieved.

3. Confusion

Here, confusion is created to trigger someone else's cognitive reorganization. Toward the end of the volleyball season, a top team in the Israeli first division had to play an opponent who was also contending for the championship. Tensions ran high prior to the game and led to a blowout argument between two central players during practice. After the argument, the psychologist went to these players, shook hands with each of them, and said: "Thank you for taking the responsibility for all the rubbish within the team."

Such an unusual and unexpected comment confused the players, but also gave them quite a laugh. Through this statement, the psychologist showed them how ridiculous their actions and perceptions were at the time. Their quarrel quickly deflated and they got back to cooperating like team members. Both players understood the psychologist's point and played together excellently in the game, beating their rival and later winning the national championship.

Net Reframing

Though reframing can be achieved through all three of these techniques, it can also be used directly. For example, the point guard of one of Israel's best basketball teams came to my office one day and complained about a continuous decline in his performance, which had led to a loss of his self-confidence. He specified two major problems: a fear of taking risky shots, especially from long distances, and a fear of penetrating the opponent's defense. In situations where he should either shoot or penetrate, he would pass the ball instead.

This became a problem when his opponents realized they could therefore leave him free while pressing his teammates, preventing them from getting the ball. A vicious cycle developed, as the player became increasingly anxious, stressed, and unconfident, further contributing to his performance slump. As a result, he was released from the national team—which is what brought him to my office. I decided to help him reframe the situation.

I first told him I was impressed by his outstanding ability to manipulate his environment. I explained that through the very process he had described, he had single-handedly managed to create a wonderful situation where none of his opponents were watching him. Without their prodding eyes, he was free to play without disturbance—if no one's watching, what's the problem? I insisted that he was so talented that this way of manipulating the environment was necessary; if he didn't, his opponents would put extra pressure on him. At first, the player was surprised by my reasoning, but soon understood the point.

"Net reframing" was used as a key for successful treatment in this situation: the player regained his self-confidence; improved his shooting, ability to penetrate the defense, and overall performance; and had his best season ever. As a result, he was recalled to the national team.

There is no standard guide for the appropriate use of paradoxical techniques. You can learn the principles of reframing first and foremost, but no two interventions are exactly alike. Can you teach somebody to cook? Or to paint? Or to compose music? You would probably say yes, but in fact, you can only teach the components and the technique—not the art of appropriately combining them.

A well-timed, precisely targeted paradoxical intervention hooks the employee, athlete, or client because it communicates the leader's real understanding of the problem, even if it does not necessarily comment on it directly. Therefore, before intervening paradoxically, it is essential to accurately diagnose the individual's idiosyncratic frame of reference regarding the problem to be solved. For this to happen, we have to tell a good story. Without telling the right story, no reframing, no second-order change, and no creative processes can take place.

CREATIVITY ENHANCEMENT AND OPTIMIZATION: COMBINING FIRST- AND SECOND-ORDER CHANGES

> To everything there is a season, and a time to every purpose under heaven.
> —KING SOLOMON[17]

Having praised and endorsed the concept of second-order changes throughout the chapter, I want to emphasize that in reality great innovators should be able to apply both first- and second-order change processes.

High-level sport practitioners are advised to use creative, or irrational, interventions in order to cope with problems that resist common wisdom solutions. Thus, critical assessment of one's thoughts and actions is rational in that it enables a break with tradition and supports the invention of new, creative, nondogmatic ways of meeting old challenges successfully. By doing so, however, the idea of instrumental rationality cannot, and should not, be abandoned. The previously mentioned principle of maximization through optimization (see chapter 1) should also be encouraged.

The radical innovator Pablo Picasso (1881–1973), cocreator of cubism and one of the most influential artists in history, claimed that both inspiration and hard, Sisyphean work combine to produce creative genius.[18] Fosbury and Tsukahara both underwent an evolutionary process in which they tried first-order solutions before developing their famous innovations. They then took the time required to improve their respective inventions (after all, Anders Ericsson's deliberate practice, discussed in chapter 5, is also a type of first-order change). As evident from Larry Bird's quote earlier in the chapter, the best players are those who integrate and synthesize both seemingly contradictory opposites. In other words, it's perfectly okay to produce innovations even if they are unexpected or crazy at face value—many times these are the best ones. But keep in mind that innovation should only take place when necessary.

In order to develop peak performance, the principles of optimization and creativity enhancement should be seen as complementary, not antagonistic. For example, BuzzFeed still provides its time-tested soft content and Whirlpool still makes their bread and butter products (first-order changes), but they also continue to innovate. It's necessary to be both creative and instrumental in order to succeed. Applying a time to be creative and a time to be instrumental will lead to great innovation.[19]

Excessive Innovation

I don't believe that creativity should be encouraged at all costs. I always tell my students that before they start reflecting on the material I'm teaching, they should first learn what they're talking about—which is hard and "dirty" work. I also regularly convey the following message to players and teams I work with: "Don't be creative where you don't have to be!" Sometimes just shooting the ball to the right spot is enough (as we saw in the penalty kick example in chapter 5). When considering overcreativity or excessive innovation in business performance, numerous factors come into play.

For example, the timing of innovation is imperative. Many tech start-ups have learned this the hard way when they enter the market either too early—experiencing a failure to attract audiences or demand for a product or service—or too late—finding that an app competing with the Instagrams and Facebooks of the tech industry will quickly become the next Friendster. There is also the question of infrastructure (physical, digital, or otherwise) and the ability for an innovative idea to be supported in the proper way. Without a proliferation of mobile devices and WiFi, you could have the best new app known to humankind, but no one is going to be interested in it. Think of the early days of the Internet: where it was first seen more as a novelty, it is now interconnected with almost every facet of our lives.

As a CEO, middle manager, or director, understanding costs and risks before trying to implement a creative new idea is also imperative. Sure, something simple like moving around meeting times or providing flexible hours for employees is less likely to incur major financial losses, but launching a brand new product that your team has spent the good part of a year or more on can be risky business. Larger companies also may innovate less due to a need for stability since they are answering to stockholders or other investors. Even Google, known for its emphasis on innovation, officially phased out its open innovation program, as they grew from a small tech startup to a more orthodox, established company.[20]

Formula One racing has exhibited timing, size, and structure issues when trying to innovate. An international team of researchers, led by Jaideep Anand of Ohio State University, found that even though there are changes every year in the sport, radical innovations proved to be the least successful, even at times that business leaders thought were optimal. The researchers pointed out that just like many businesses, Formula One cars have interconnected systems: "If you change one part of the system, you risk changing other parts of the system that you want to stay the same."[21] More subtle changes over time proved to have more positive effects.

SUMMARY

Every day, we make decisions in uncertain environments, although we hardly know for sure if our actions are rational or not. Moreover, it is our irrational thoughts, deeds, or developments that can lead us to new levels of creativity and the greatest innovations. Whether looking at famous sports innovators like Fosbury, Tsukahara, and Ali, or considering contemporary business leaders like Elon Musk and his company Tesla Motors, strikingly similar patterns and processes of innovation emerge. In following this process, it's often necessary to think outside the box, reframe the situation, and employ seemingly paradoxical interventions.

Of course, the timing and market must be right. Innovation should, and can, only occur when appropriate. Much of the time it will still be necessary to follow routine, well-practiced procedures. Without the right conditions, your creative performance may actually decrease, or you'll find that your invention is a total flop (and not the good kind like Fosbury's). Innovation for innovation's sake can be disastrous. In order to develop and sustain peak performance, the principles of optimization (a first-order change) and innovation (a second-order change) should not be seen as in conflict, but as complementary of one another.

When attempting to innovate, make sure to:

- Follow the four-step process of innovation;
- Understand and incorporate second-order change processes;
- Utilize reframing, both directly and through paradoxical techniques;

- See the principles of optimization and creativity enhancement as complementary, not antagonistic, and implement them accordingly;
- Don't overdo it!

Great inventors and innovators are able to identify opportunities and possibilities that other people simply don't see. These creative minds that push the envelope and improve their personal, team, or company performance are, as we say in Israel, smart enough to "jump on the train when it passes by them." Even more importantly, they were smart enough to be there to begin with, waiting for the train to come.

DAILY PRACTICES

As an Individual

- Try out a small innovation every day, including slight changes to your daily activities that may lead to greater productivity.
- Consider the four-step innovation process before suggesting new ideas to your boss or other employees—make sure the problem is one that can be solved through the entire lifecycle of the process.
- Understand the difference between first-order and second-order changes—sometimes you'll need to overhaul the whole system, but you don't always need to throw the baby out with the bath water.

As a Manager

- Apply outside-the-box thinking to help yourself and your team overcome everyday obstacles or larger roadblocks.

- Incorporate first-order *and* second-order changes into the workplace—don't be afraid to break convention and try something new.
- Don't overinnovate: understand the costs and risks and make sure the time is right before implementation.

NOTES

1. M. Bar-Eli, O. Lowengart, M. Tsukahara, and R. D. Fosbury, "Tsukahara's Vault and Fosbury's Flop: A Comparative Analysis of Two Great Inventions," *International Journal of Innovation Management* 12 (March 2008): 21–39.
2. J. Goldenberg, O. Lowengart, S. Oreg, M. Bar-Eli, S. Epstein, and R. D. Fosbury, "Innovation: The Case of the Fosbury Flop," *Marketing Science Institute (MSI) Reports, working papers series*, Issue 1 (Report No. 04-106) (2004): 153–155; J. Goldenberg, O. Lowengart, S. Oreg, and M. Bar-Eli, "How Do Revolutions Emerge? Lessons from the Fosbury Flop," *International Studies of Management and Organization* 40 (December 2010): 30–51.
3. M. Bar-Eli, O. Lowengart, M. Master-Barak, S. Oreg, J. Goldenberg, S. Epstein, and R. D. Fosbury, "Developing Peak Performers in Sport: Optimization Versus Creativity," in *Essential Processes for Attaining Peak Performance*, eds. D. Hackfort and G. Tenenbaum (New York: Meyer & Meyer, 2006), 158–177. The improvement of the high-jump world record for men is presented in Goldenberg et.al., "Innovation."
4. See Bar-Eli et al., "Tsukahara's Vault and Fosbury's Flop."
5. Jeff Dyer, Hal Gregersen, and Nathan Furr, "Decoding Tesla's Secret Formula," *Forbes*, August 19, 2015, www.forbes.com/sites/innovatorsdna/2015/08/19/teslas-secret-formula/#1e8300cb59f8.
6. Dyer, Gregersen, and Furr, "Decoding Tesla's Secret Formula."
7. M. Bar-Eli, Y. Lurie, and G. Breivik, "Rationality in Sport: A Psychophilosophical Approach," in *Sport Psychology: Linking Theory and Practice*, eds. R. Lidor and M. Bar-Eli (Morgantown, WV: Fitness Information Technology, 1999), 35.
8. Especially in his two masterpiece books, *Steps to an Ecology of Mind* (New York: Ballantine, 1972) and *Mind and Nature: A Necessary Unity* (New York: Bantam, 1979).
9. BuzzFeed: About, BuzzFeed.com, 2016, www.buzzfeed.com/about.
10. Fast Company, "The Most Innovative Companies of 2016," *Fast Company*, 2016, www.fastcompany.com/most-innovative-companies.
11. Whirlpool Corporation, "Our Company: More than 100 Years of Delivering Value One Moment at a Time," 2016, www.whirlpoolcorp.com/our-company/.
12. Gary Hamel and Nancy Tennant, "The 5 Requirements of a Truly Innovative Company," *Harvard Business Review*, April 27, 2015, https://hbr.org/2015/04/the-5-requirements-of-a-truly-innovative-company.

13. Hamel and Tennant, "The 5 Requirements of a Truly Innovative Company."

14. P. Watzlawick, J. H. Weakland, and R. Fisch, *Change: Principles of Problem Formation and Problem Resolution* (New York: Norton, 1974).

15. To the best of my knowledge, I was the first person to suggest the use of such interventions in applied sport psychology back in 1991: "On the Use of Paradoxical Interventions in Counseling and Coaching in Sport," *The Sport Psychologist* 5 (March 1991): 61–72.

16. According to the principle of rationality as "good evidence," see Bar-Eli, Lurie and Breivik, "Rationality in Sport," 38.

17. Ecclesiastes 3:1–8, King James Version.

18. Matthew Syed, *Bounce* (New York: Harper, 2010), 98–99.

19. M. Bar-Eli, O. Lowengart, M. Master-Barak, S. Oreg, J. Goldenberg, S. Epstein, and R. D. Fosbury, "Developing Peak Performers in Sport: Optimization Versus Creativity," in *Essential Processes for Attaining Peak Performance*, eds. D. Hackfort and G. Tenenbaum (New York: Meyer & Meyer, 2006), 158–177.

20. Jana Kasperkevic, "Google Secretly Phases Out '20% Time'," *Inc.*, August 16, 2013, www.inc.com/jana-kasperkevic/google-secretly-phases-out-20-percent-time.html.

21. Brian Amble, "Too Much Innovation Doesn't Pay Dividends," *Management Issues*, August 25, 2015, www.management-issues.com/news/7092/too-much-innovation-doesnt-pay-dividends/.

PART III

Working Together

7

Cohesion

All for One, and One for All!

Tous pour un, un pour tous.

—ALEXANDRE DUMAS, *Les Trois Mousquetaires*

Whether in the workplace or on the soccer field, in many situations we are called upon to perform in groups, which are in turn part of organizations. For example, soccer players are part of their "work team," which in turn is a kind of "department" within any modern professional club. In highly successful sports organizations, professional athletes work together under the supervision of the general manager or the head coach, whose goal is to provide services and support to the players.

Consider FC Bayern Munich's 2012–2013 season, in which they won the Quadruple—consisting of the German soccer championship, Cup, Super Cup, and European Champions League. The team included a squad of twenty-seven players, a staff of twenty-four professionals, and a fourteen-person board. Even in individual sports such as marksmanship, judo, or swimming, efficient teamwork is required at the elite level: mutual cooperation among the athlete's support group is vital for one's success in top events such as the Olympic Games.

Any companies or businesses that have more than a handful of staff members are likely further broken down into teams or groups as well. It's not uncommon to have numerous departments between sales, customer service, public relations, marketing, advertising, research and development—the list goes on and on. Members within each group or department are expected to work together to meet deadlines, complete projects, and, overall, contribute to the success of the company.

The terms "group" and "team" are often used interchangeably. Despite their similarities, however, they are quite different. All teams are groups, but not all groups are teams. The crucial factor to success is frequently that of groups *becoming* teams. The key issue in a group transforming into a team is effective interaction among its members, in particular toward the achievement of a shared, common goal. One of the world's leading social sport psychologists, the late Albert V. Carron of the University of Western Ontario, defined a "real athletic team" in the second edition of his book *Group Dynamic in Sports*:

> A collective of two or more individuals who possess a common identity, have consensus on a shared purpose, share a common fate, exhibit structured patterns of interaction and communication, hold common perceptions about group structure, are personally and instrumentally interdependent, reciprocate interpersonal attraction, and consider themselves to be a group.

This definition actually describes an ideal team, because Carron refers to both the group's *task* dimension (reaching a common goal) and the *social* dimension (getting along with one another). Such was the case in the German national men's handball team at the beginning of 2004, when it participated in the European championships and celebrated one of its greatest achievements ever: winning the gold medal for the first time.

Analyzing the reasons for this unprecedented victory, coach Heiner Brand and his players repeatedly mentioned the team's *zusammenhalt* (cohesion) on both the task and social levels. They believed that "sticking together" enabled them to overcome not only an unsuccessful start of the tournament but also injuries to key players, as they marched to victory in the championship. In other words, the feeling of being a cohesive group—whose members were ready to work together on task performance and who also connected on an emotional level—was considered one of the major reasons for the team's success, if not the most important one (after talent). But the issue is more complicated than it may first appear.

TASK COHESION VERSUS SOCIAL COHESION

> Do you really believe you can solve the faculty's problems with quiche parties?
>
> —*the author*

In 1994, I served as the sport psychologist of one of Israel's top basketball clubs. Prior to the season, the club spent a small fortune locating and recruiting the best players possible (and a very expensive head coach) in order to improve their chances of winning the national championship. After some unexpected losses at the beginning of the season, the club's president decided, on his own volition, to send the team to a quiet village in the Netherlands for one week. He wanted the players to escape the pressures of the local scene, while also getting the chance to socialize and play a few scrimmages together in a relaxed setting. The president's intention was to improve team cohesion, thereby positively affecting the team's future performance.

When the team returned to Israel, they seemed to be quite cohesive; however, after only a few days, under the pressure of real competition, their cohesiveness vanished and the team fell apart on the court. After a few weeks the coach was fired (as well as the psychologist), and the team finished the season in the middle of the league, far below its initial goal and expectations.

What happened here?

Traditionally, cohesion has been considered the most important group variable in sport,[1] with much effort being invested to produce cohesive teams. The belief that cohesiveness is a positive determinant of success is widespread among sport managers, coaches, athletes, and commentators, not to mention bosses and directors. Interestingly, however, groups are not always in the need of the same kind of cohesion; furthermore, there are some cases in which they don't need cohesion at all. Seems strange, doesn't it?

Essentially, there are two types of cohesion, social and task. "Social cohesion" refers to the level of interpersonal attraction among group members, that is, to the nature and quality of emotional bonds of friendship, liking, caring, and closeness among them. When people in a group rely on other members for feelings of connectedness, socioemotional rewards, and a positive social identity, that group displays high social cohesion: its members like each other, prefer to spend their social time together, enjoy each other's company, and feel emotionally close to one another.

"Task cohesion," however, refers to the shared commitment among members of the group to achieve a goal that requires its collective, coordinated efforts. This is actually the degree to which group members are ready to work together to achieve common goals and objectives. Task cohesion is high when group members rely on each other for mastery of material outcomes arising from that group's performance of the task. Group members share a common goal and are motivated to coordinate their efforts as a team to achieve that goal.

Evidently, the Israeli basketball team's president tried to solve a task-related problem by working on the social elements, wrongly assuming that if people love each other, they will also produce better results. But our president seems to have confused these two dimensions of cohesion. It's no wonder the group members enjoyed each other's company after returning from a nice, relaxing training camp in the Netherlands. Who wouldn't! But they were not ready to coordinate their efforts and work as a team in order to achieve a common objective—which was their major problem to begin with.

Commitment to the Task

As you can probably tell by now, I learned a great deal from my war-time experiences, much of which turned out to be relevant for my future professional career. For years I kept asking myself why I was willing to do so much, to the point of sacrificing my own life if necessary, for a bunch of people who were not always my cup of tea. In fact, I lost contact with almost all of them over the years, until October 2013, when one of my former battery members decided to celebrate the forty years that had passed since the war by establishing a WhatsApp group. It began with the names and telephone numbers of the few veterans with whom he had contact, but soon enough, through the friend-brings-a-friend grapevine method, the group snowballed.

In 1973, my comrades were probably the most important people in the world to me. I knew, for example, that my late mother Nurith, a Holocaust survivor and a widow who had raised me, her only son, single-handedly from infancy, was in real danger of committing suicide if I died in the war (she actually later told me that she had prepared some razors just in case)—and still, I never thought of leaving my comrades.

These feelings of loyalty led me to two deep insights:

1. A soldier is usually prepared to die not so much for his flag and country, as often assumed, but first and foremost, for his *fellow soldiers*;
2. What brings comrades together is not so much friendship, but some sense of deep, sincere commitment to the *task* they have to fulfill.

In his epic novel *War and Peace*, Leo Tolstoy (1828–1910) delineated, in graphic, detailed language, the events surrounding the French invasion of Russia in 1812. Among other factors, Tolstoy mentioned "an unknown X," which is necessary to determine the force of an army; he later referred to this "X-factor" as the army's "spirit." But what is it exactly?

Military literature, going back to the Ancient Greeks (e.g., Xenophon of Athens, the great Greek historian, soldier, and philosopher, ca. 430–354 B.C.) uses similar terms, such as "esprit de corps" or "morale," all of which refer to the enthusiasm and persistence with which soldiers carry out their prescribed activities. To do so, however, a great deal of task cohesion is required. For example, the US Army Chief of Staff from 1979 to 1983, General Edward C. Meyer, wrote in a 1982 article for *Defense*, "The Unit," that in order to succeed, an army needs "unit cohesion"—a military concept which dates back at least to Carl von Clausewitz (1780–1831), the noted German Prussian officer and military theorist. General Meyer defines unit cohesion as "the bonding together of soldiers in such a way as to sustain their will and commitment to each other, the unit, and mission accomplishment, despite combat or mission stress."

In other words, it is the *mission to be accomplished*, or the "prescribed activities" of the unit that matters above all. You know me by now: I always try to question conventional wisdom. As I grew up and became a psychologist, I saw that one of the most common assumptions in the business world was that social cohesion among groups of employees or workers not only improves the performance of these individuals but also makes the organization more successful as a whole. That's why we so often see companies pouring money into activities like company picnics, holiday parties, and corporate retreats: it's assumed that when employees have a chance to have a good time together and to bond socially, they'll be more motivated and productive in terms of performance.

Social group cohesion, however, can have its drawbacks; and in fact there are certain tasks and situations in which it is actually even *un*desirable. For example, when I served as an Israeli Defense Force (IDF) psychologist in the mid-1980s, a colleague of mine who was working in a huge induction base told me that the most problematic company he dealt with was also the most cohesive one. Why? Because the soldiers liked each other so much that they united against their commander, who they saw as an outsider; as a result they were impervious to his orders and he couldn't get anything done.

A study by Sean Wise of Ryerson University explored this idea in the workplace, and in 2014 he published his findings in the *European Management Journal*, in an article titled "Can a Team Have Too Much Cohesion? The Dark Side to Network Density." Wise found that there is an inverse curvilinear relationship between social interaction or bonding and team performance (another inverted U). Even though an initial amount of social cohesion resulted in increased performance, too much led to a decrease in performance. He suggested that interpersonal bonds that were too strong could potentially lead to a lack of innovation, since you don't want to shoot down your friends' ideas or rock your buddies' boats. Employees may also just be spending too much time chit-chatting and e-mailing one another in an attempt to create stronger social connections, when they should actually be concentrating on the task at hand.

As for the beloved corporate retreats—keep in mind that they come with their own baggage and may not produce the intended results, especially for the price your company is probably shelling out. In a relaxed setting, employees are willing to let their guards down, but sometimes they go that extra step—whether it's a few more drinks than advisable or ending up in a less-than-work-appropriate relationship with a coworker for the night, too much socialization can be too much of a good thing.

Many times, I have wondered why psychologists so often try the "I love you, you love me" route, assuming that such feelings will lead to an increase in task performance. Don't they realize that not everything can be solved with techniques intended for "soft," socioemotional problems? Why do they continue to seek them first and avoid dealing with "hard material" such as different structural factors (e.g., the size of the organization, its technology, the characteristics of the task to be performed, the environmental conditions under which it should be performed, and the like) which have a substantial effect on human behavior in organizations? I have seen, time and again—first in the army and later in the world of sport—that being cohesive or united on a personal level doesn't necessarily improve a group's performance. However, being united toward a common goal often does.

I had many disagreements concerning this issue with my colleague and friend, our late Dean of the Faculty Ayala Malach-Pines (1945–2012). As a psychologist, an expert on such issues as burnout, gender, and romantic love, Ayala firmly believed that she should promote good atmosphere (i.e., social cohesion) in the faculty. Cynic that I sometimes am, I used to ask her: "Do you really believe you can solve the faculty's problems with quiche parties?" Of course, I had no objection to quiche, but I didn't believe eating a nice meal on a summer evening in a beautiful garden would solve the faculty's functional, task-related problems.

In actuality, task cohesion may be achieved without social cohesion—a fact that surprises many people. In the late 1970s, the New York Yankees won several pennants and World Series, despite some major ongoing personal conflicts within its top managerial staff, as well as between players and management. The key to the team's success was its high task cohesion (i.e., strong desire to win and readiness to do everything required to achieve the set goal), which overcame its low social cohesion.

I learned this lesson for the first time in the late 1980s, when, as a young sports psychologist, I was invited to consult a basketball team in the Israeli second division. It was nearly the middle of the season, and the team was performing far below its initial professional expectations (in fact, it was in serious danger of relegation, in which the team would be moved into a lower-level league). In evaluating the team's level of cohesion (using sociometry as a springboard; see Figures 8.1 through 8.6), I found that the players were highly cohesive, but only in the social dimension. Furthermore, as sometimes happens in teams with low productivity, social cohesion was precisely the reason the players rejected the coach's productivity-related directions or disregarded the potential task-related leader within the group. As a matter of fact, this situation reminded me very much of the induction base of the IDF, in which the soldiers' high social cohesion made them unite against the commander, who therefore couldn't get anything done.

In other words, the team had a strong *negative* socioemotional leadership in the group, which conflicted with a potentially strong task-related leadership. A social leader emerged, who controlled the team through two other players, both of whom had a very strong social status. The group also had a potentially acceptable task-related leader: he was a player who was not socially popular, even though he wasn't *un*popular either; the team was simply indifferent toward him when it came to the social dimension. He was almost unanimously recognized as the one person everybody would be ready to follow from a professional, task-related point of view, but he could not express and realize his potential task leadership status due to the existing negative social leadership.

The social leader that emerged was perceived as something of a trouble-maker—goofing off, acting childishly, showing little signs of discipline—and his teammates therefore expected him to play this role; he was happy to oblige. It was obvious to me that his first and foremost objective was to gain the attention of his teammates and spectators by fulfilling his troublemaker status. In doing so, he reinforced his reputation, creating a cyclical effect: the more he was expected to play this role, the more he followed suit, and the more he followed suit, the more people expected him to play the role. His two buddies on the team essentially egged him on, only making the problem worse. The coach objected to removing this problematic player since he was considered integral to their rebounding game. Accordingly, he had time and again tried to convince the social leader to improve his behavior, but to no avail. (As a matter of fact, I told the coach: "If you continue like this, you'll probably have rebound, but no team.")

To address the problem, as a first step, instead of removing the problem-atic player, I recommended breaking up the social cohesion of the team, thereby enabling actualization of task cohesion. My major strategy was to dissolve the clique around the problematic player in order to reduce his social control of the team. To do so, the two players that helped him maintain social control had to be removed, separated, or otherwise mar-ginalized to isolate the social leader. Somewhat fortuitously for us, though potentially unfortunate for the two individuals, one of the social leader's buddies on court was injured and had to sit out the rest of the season, while the other was drafted into the Army and had to report for duty. In this way, the first goal was achieved—the troublemaker had become isolated.

Only after he was isolated was the second step of intervention possi-ble: we had to convince the social leader that the success of the team relied almost solely on him. We pumped him up with positive messages, forcing him to realize his importance. In doing so, we were employing the par-adoxical technique of reframing (discussed in chapter 6) to reverse the player's expectations in regards to his attitude and role. In this way, we drafted him into the process of task fulfillment.

As a result of this two-step intervention (i.e., isolation of the negative social leader and then employing reframing to draft him into the task-related process), negative social cohesion was broken, and an emphasis returned to task cohesion. The troublemaker had been blocking the potential task leader from expressing and realizing his role. As soon as we isolated the negative social leader and reframed his attitude, the potential task leader was able to become the task leader that we knew he could be. The group became a team again, which continued to increasingly gain task-related cohesiveness, mainly because the task-related leadership was substantially strengthened. As the season progressed, the team played better and better. The individual players worked hard together to achieve their common goal; indeed, later in the season, this team went on a winning streak, turning them into the season's surprise, finally placing them in the upper part of their division.

Our ability to remove the emphasis on social interaction made it possible to focus on the task at hand. If a team's members are coming together and bonding over elements that are unlikely to contribute to the team's success—such as the attention the two players were giving the troublemaker—then it's necessary to find a way to rework this relationship and direct it toward more constructive ends. As shown by the socioemotional leader in this story, social cohesion may be dysfunctional to performance. The player was negatively influencing others on his team, who were in turn negatively influencing him. It's not all that unlike class clowns in elementary school—once they get attention for bad behavior, they will continue to goof off or act out!

It can therefore be necessary at times to try to dissolve cliques that work against turning your group into a team (more on building teams in chapter 8). If you can get rid of the negative social element, you can help your team members work together on a shared task. Sometimes that may mean moving disruptive elements from one team to another or having them work on different projects. Understanding the makeup of a team's personalities will help you in this process as it will be necessary to figure out who will work together positively and productively, and who might end up working together to simply spin their wheels and pass the time away.

Cooperation versus Competition

Counter to common wisdom, however, task cohesion isn't always completely necessary either; it depends on the tasks. For example, tasks that don't require cooperation—like a player on a basketball team taking a free throw, or a cellist in an orchestra performing a solo, or a member of a sales team making a personal pitch to a long-time client—need not entail task cohesion. But even this idea becomes more complicated: while being united toward a goal is usually good for the success of the team (when the task requires it, of course), it doesn't always work out so well for each individual within that team. Think about the baseball player who is told to bunt, sacrificing his at-bat so that his teammate can advance a base, or the assistants made to take the blame for their superiors' screw-ups so the department can save face with management. Many times the success of a team depends on certain members making sacrifices that keep them from being their very best. In other words, often, there is a built-in tension between the individual's interest and the team's interest. These differing interests may lead to an environment of competition.

But is competition, as opposed to cooperation, always so bad? Not necessarily—competition is an essential part of many human activities. Although at first glance, the two might seem to be at odds, both can have similar effects on group performance. Just as cooperation, or task cohesion, can improve overall group performance, so can a certain amount of healthy competition among individuals within a particular group.

In 1898 Norman Triplett, an enthusiastic bicycle racing fan, who also happened to be a research psychologist at Indiana University, demonstrated this in what is considered the first research experiment ever conducted in both social and sport psychology.[2] Interested in why cyclists sometimes ride faster when they race in pairs or groups than when they ride alone, he concluded that it was because competition, even against one's own teammate, can push people to try harder. Later on, studies showed that this effect depends first and foremost on the nature of the task to be performed; sometimes, cooperation between group members, such as in soccer or basketball, is more important than competition, sometimes less.

Friendly competition in the office can provide similar opportunities to maximize participants' performance. As with many of the topics discussed in this book, however, you need to make sure not to overdo it. Too much competition between employees is likely to lead to resentment or a hostile work environment. A small amount of competition, however, can motivate workers to reach their potential. As a boss, think what it's like when you hire a new employee—it's likely that current employees will want to see how they match up to the the new kid on the block and may give them an incentive to work harder (and the new employee is likely to reciprocate). As mentioned earlier in the book, providing incentives can help increase performance—the right incentives in fostering competition are likely to have similar effects. Such intraoffice competition may also keep employees focused on their goals and therefore improve productivity.

CIRCULAR COHESION–PERFORMANCE RELATIONSHIP

Which came first: the chicken or the egg?

—PLUTARCH, *"Moralia"*

It is often assumed that teams exhibiting conflict and dissention fail to realize their potential, but those that are cohesive, as mentioned, will perform at high levels. To examine this intuitive belief, Brian Mullen and Carolyn Copper, from the department of psychology in Syracuse University, conducted a meta-analysis of forty-nine studies that produced sixty-six tests of the cohesiveness–performance effect relationship in a wide variety of settings such as work and social groups, army crews, laboratory groups, and sport teams.[3] Of the sixty-six tests, 92 percent reported a small but highly significant positive effect for the cohesion–performance relationship.

Mullen and Copper found that the direction of the cohesion–performance effect was stronger from performance to cohesion than from cohesion to performance. This finding, however, by no means negates the argument that cohesion may cause increases in performance. It only suggests that the changes in cohesion brought about by increases in performance are probably even stronger than changes in performance that can be brought about by increases in cohesion.

It seems, then, that the relationship between cohesion and performance is circular: like the old chicken or egg causality dilemma, where chickens and eggs are trapped in a circular feedback loop, so are cohesion and performance. Performance success leads to increased cohesion, which in turn leads to increased performance. The crucial point is that the commitment to a task emerges as the most critical component of cohesion in the cohesion–performance relationship. Mullen and Copper found that, again, commitment to task was the best predictor of group success. Their results showed that only task cohesion was related to success, whereas social cohesion was not. It seems, then, that coaches should not waste too much time on developing social cohesion unless they are simply interested in the feel-good benefits of everyone getting along. According to Mullen and Copper, these feel-good benefits do not lead to better team performance.

But of course the story is somewhat more complex: in the early days of sport's cohesion research, Carron and his associates promoted the idea that task type may serve as a moderator in the cohesion–performance relationship. In Carron's classic book from 1980, *Social Psychology of Sport*, sports were classified into the following four categories:

1. Teams with independently acting members;
2. Coacting teams;
3. Reacting/pro-acting teams;
4. Interacting teams.

As to the first category, think of our friends Dick Fosbury and Mitsuo Tsukahara: although each athlete is part of a team in the sense of a national Olympic delegation, let's say, they do not have to work with others in order to achieve their goals. Such athletes compete at their own specialty; as long as these individuals do their best, how well they get along with others does not really matter to team performance. (Other examples are archery, bowling, or golf.)

As to the second category, think of rowers in the Olympic Games. They coact, where boats include two, four, or eight person crews, who must act together effectively in order to win the regatta.

As to the third category, a good example would be a relay team of runners or swimmers: one athlete "pro-acts" for the other, while the second "reacts" to the first one. Similar pro-action/reaction chains are also typical of sports such as American football or baseball, where one athlete "prepares" and the other "completes." These sports are sometimes also referred to as "mixed coacting/interacting," because they contain a mixture of elements, such as hitting or catching a fly ball versus making a double play or hitting the cutoff man in baseball.

As to the fourth category, here the task requires team members to work together and coordinate their actions in order to succeed, seen in sports such as basketball, field hockey, or soccer. For example, players on a soccer team have to constantly pass the ball to each other, maintain certain positions, devise defensive strategies to stop opponents from scoring, and coordinate offensive attacks. Similarly, a smooth basketball offense requires passes, movement without the ball, screens away from the ball, and proper spacing among teammates, whereas an efficient basketball team's defense requires switching assignments, calling out screens, or blocking out for rebounds. All these maneuvers require team members to work together, while effectively coordinating their actions to achieve common goals. They require ongoing, close teamwork, with members understanding and fulfilling their different roles in the dynamic game environment.

These four categories require ascending levels of coordination, with interactive sports requiring the highest readiness among athletes to work together in order to succeed. Accordingly, task cohesion may be more closely related to team success for the interactive category of sports but would be progressively less associated with success in the other categories. This means that:

(1) Social cohesion is quite irrelevant for performance (i.e., if at all, mainly task cohesion is necessary);

(2) In some tasks (such as bowling), lower task cohesion is sometimes even better for performance (i.e., the competition between individuals may enhance performance).

In general, these nonintuitive ideas are supported by a substantial body of empirical research. For example, Mullen and Copper's meta-analysis found that the cohesion–performance relationship was indeed greater for groups with high interaction requirements. Carron et al. observed that positive cohesion–performance relations are reported in the literature more often for sports that require extensive interaction, coordination and cooperation.[4]

The same is true for the Musketeers, I think: they were ready to do everything for each other, perhaps because their task was interactive in nature. Did they like each other? It seems that they did. However, their sense of togetherness, their readiness to do "all for one, one for all," was evident primarily in the battlefield, where they had to fulfill complex, interactive tasks such as working together to defend members of the French royal family.

STICK TO THE TASK

I believe in good passers.

—Arsene Wenger[5]

Sports practitioners and business leaders still have an enduring fascination with developing team cohesion because they believe it determines success. The truth, however, is that they should spend less time and energy on developing team cohesion, but if they insist on doing so, they should do so accurately, with a focus on task cohesion over social cohesion. Moreover, task cohesion is much more relevant in teams with high interdependence; that is, I would recommend task cohesion particularly in highly professional, interactive teams where high achievements depend on teamwork. For example, an IT department that needs to work together to provide tech solutions throughout an office, or an advertising or marketing team that collaborates on a company's new product launch.

In regards to social cohesion, I tend to agree with Arsenal's coach Arsene Wenger who, like me, seems not to believe in emotional cohesion and leadership. Instead, as evidenced by his quote, he seems to believe in task-related cohesion and leadership. Without a doubt, one of the greatest soccer teams of all time was FC Bayern Munich in the early to mid-1970s. Among other titles, the team won the European Championship three times in a row (1974–1976). In a YouTube video series from 2014, "Football's Greatest Teams," midfield Rainer Zobel raises my precise argument in the film devoted to that "golden team." "We were not friends," says Zobel. "We really weren't; well, maybe one or two of us were, but when we were together on the pitch, we knew exactly what we wanted."

That being said, it seems that social cohesion may increase as result of success in whatever you do (that is, even a group of bowlers or rifle shooters would feel better together if they always win). Moreover, it is, of course, much more pleasant to be in the company of people who like each other than in a group of persons who are constantly bickering and rife with personal conflicts. In an office environment, no one wants to be stuck with a bunch of people they can't stand and with whom they feel a constant, excessive level of competition, which would likely lead to burnout or simply finding another job. So, ideally, both social and task cohesion should be considered, and a combination of both dimensions developed in an optimal manner, based on the individuals within the group. It can be hard enough getting up everyday to head into the office, onto the job-site, or out into the field, a little bit of social interaction certainly won't hurt . . . but first and foremost, let's make sure you keep everyone on task.

SUMMARY

The concept of cohesion, or the effects of social dynamics on the performance of the group as a whole unit, is multifaceted. To succeed as a group, leaders must promote cohesion while considering the effects of competition and cooperation, and reconciling the goals of the group with the goals of each of its individual members.

There are two types of cohesion, task and social, and many times leaders focus on the wrong one—observing sports teams sent away for some R & R and bonding, or a company who has a weeklong retreat of team-building exercises, it's possible to see that social cohesion is not as imperative as task cohesion.

Task cohesion will improve team performance, as shown through the soldier prepared to die not so much for his flag and country, but first and foremost, for his fellow soldiers. What brings them together is not so much friendship, but rather comradeship, a sense of deep, sincere commitment to the task they have to fulfill together. It's possible to find an immense amount of social cohesion within a team, but little task cohesion—in which case it is imperative to refocus on the set goals through enhanced task cohesion, even at the expense of social cohesion.

Cooperation and competition go hand in hand, too, such as in a team bicycle race, where one rider pushes himself not only against opponents, but also against teammates. Besides cooperation, then, friendly competition in the office can provide similar opportunities to maximize performance.

DAILY PRACTICES

As an Individual

- Though it's good to build relationships, staying focused on your tasks at work will lead to higher performance.

- If you find yourself on a corporate retreat, make sure to keep the party G-rated and avoid any actions that you'll regret when you're back in the office Monday morning.
- Intraoffice competition can be enjoyable and give you the opportunity for the occasional bragging right, but always be a gracious winner, or loser, and remember that it's all in good fun.

As a Leader

- When your team is working toward a common goal in which they must interact together, make sure to emphasize task cohesion.
- Consider additional ways to developing cohesion aside from typical company retreats or holiday parties.
- Foster a sense of friendly competition to motivate yourself and your employees—but don't overdo it!

NOTES

1. Even though coaching style (i.e., leadership), roles (i.e., clarity and acceptance), and norms (or team culture, as it is sometimes called) should also not be neglected.
2. N. Triplett, "The Dynamogenic Factors in Pacemaking and Competition," *American Journal of Psychology* 9 (1898): 507–553.
3. B. Mullen and C. Copper, "The Relation between Group Cohesiveness and Performance: An Integration," *Psychological Bulletin* 115 (March 1994): 210–227.
4. A.V. Carron, M.A. Eys, and L.J. Martin, "Cohesion," in *Measurement in Sport and Exercise Psychology*, eds. G. Tenenbaum, R.C. Eklund, and A. Kamata (Champaign, IL: Human Kinetics, 2012), 411–421.
5. J. Lehmann and C. Siemes, *Der Wahsinn liegt auf dem Platz* [The Madness Lies on the Pitch] (Cologne: Kiepenheuer & Witsch, 2010), 100.

8

Team-Building

Finding the Right People for the Right System

One thing is going against the Dutch . . . they have become a group of individuals playing for their own causes.

—*ESPN reporter*[1]

The Chicago Bulls drafted Michael Jordan in 1984 with the intention of building a winning team around this incredible athlete. Though Jordan would go on to be one of the most legendary players in the game, and despite his outstanding performance in the 1980s, Chicago did *not* really succeed: in 1985–1986 and 1986–1987, for example, they were swept by the Boston Celtics (even though Celtics forward Larry Bird referred to Jordan as "God disguised as Michael Jordan").

In 1987 the Bulls addressed their lack of depth by several drafts and trades, acquiring rookies Horace Grant and Scottie Pippen. But in 1987–1988 they were swept again, this time by the Detroit Pistons. In 1988–1989 and 1989–1990 they continued to beef up the team through a series of off-season moves, including additional trades and drafts and the replacement of Coach Doug Collins with former assistant Phil Jackson. Meanwhile, Pippen—who had remained under the shadow of Jordan—was promoted to the starting five and chosen to the all-star squad in 1989–1990 for the first time.

The so-called Bulls Dynasty lasted for most of the 1990s, in two different periods: 1991–1993 and 1996–1998. In each of these periods the Bulls won a "three-peat," coached by Phil Jackson and led by superstar Jordan, but strongly supported by Scottie Pippen, and later on by Denis Rodman. For example, in the first of these championships, Pippen played a major role by destroying the Lakers' point guard, and iconic athlete in his own right, Magic Johnson on defense.

However, when Jordan retired (temporarily, as it turned out) and the Bulls had to play without him for two successive seasons, Pippen did not succeed in leading the Bulls to the NBA championship, even though he had established himself as one of the top players in the league by winning the 1994 All-Star MVP. The Bulls were first beaten in 1993–1994 by the Knicks. In 1994–1995 the situation became even worse, with some important players, including Horace Grant, Bill Cartwright, Scott Williams, and John Paxson, leaving the team. Even though Jordan returned from his retirement in midseason (March 1995), it was not enough to take them all the way and Chicago was beaten again, this time by the Orlando Magic.

In the off-season, the Bulls brought on Denis Rodman to further strengthen the team. This controversial player was exactly what the Bulls urgently needed: an aggressive rebounding specialist and a relic from the highly successful Detroit Pistons' "Bad Boys" squad. In fact, it was the Jordan-Pippen-Rodman trio that led the team to a second three-peat. Although Pippen and Jordan were the only two players involved in winning all six of the Bulls Dynasty titles between 1991 and 1998, the dynasty was not solely attributed to their performance. Horace Grant, Bill Cartwright, and John Paxson, along with B. J. Armstrong and others, were major factors in the success of the Bulls' first three-peat. Players such as Jud Buechler, Randy Brown, Bill Wennington, Ron Harper, and Luc Longley may not have put a huge number of points on the board, but without their expertise on the court, the Bulls likely would have not won their second three-peat—and of course Rodman's performance was a deciding factor as well. Coach Jackson also played a major role, keeping the team together and leading them forward throughout the six titles.

We can learn from this example that even a god like Jordan had to have two vice-gods at his side (Pippen and Rodman), and many more angels, such as Tony Kukoc, who won the NBA Sixth Man of the Year Award for 1995–1996, to achieve the great successes of the Bulls Dynasty. It seems that every successful team needs not only big stars but also "servants" and good "number twos"; even the brightest stars need a team around them, whether it's Jordan on the court, Brazilian soccer legend Pele on the field, or business magnate and investor Warren Buffett in the board room.

This point was excellently made by my former graduate student and current colleague, clinical and sport psychologist Noam Eyal: while the Chicago Bulls were at their peak, with Jordan outshining all other players, Noam hung the picture of Scottie Pippen on the wall of the room where he consulted and treated his athletes. Every Israeli basketball fan admired Jordan, and every kid wanted to imitate him, but in Noam's opinion, it was Pippen who perfectly demonstrated the point that even the best players need a supportive, talented team; strictly speaking, *without Pippen, there probably would not have been Jordan.*

It is well known that when told that "There is no 'I' in 'team,'" Jordan promptly responded: "But there's an 'I' in WIN." Or as University of Chicago behavioral economist Tobias J. Moskowitz and *Sports Illustrated* writer L. Jon Wertheim say in their 2011 book *Scorecasting*: "There's no 'I' in TEAM, but there is an M and an E." They define this seemingly contradictory state of affairs as a "delicate balance" to be kept between these two seeming opposites. In my opinion, we see here again a reflection of a dialectical state of affairs, as discussed in chapters 5 and 6, in which a synthesis of both thesis and antithesis is required.

Former coach and current team President of Miami Heat Pat Riley hints at this somewhat paradoxical state of affairs (even if he does not mention it explicitly) when he talks about Michael Jordan, who is, in his opinion, "simply the greatest player probably to ever play this game."[2] However, even Jordan's greatness could not come out without the team around him. Says Riley: "He went to a team and was the whole team . . . he was doing superman kind of feats . . . And it wasn't until they made some trades and they brought Scottie Pippen in . . . that they developed."[3] To show his individual greatness, Jordan *needed* the team around him; otherwise, he would have remained a superman—or even a god—but without his greatest achievements.

Similar evidence is shown time and again throughout the world of team sports. For example, one of the most famous positions in the history of soccer is the "sweeper," which is often referred to as "libero" (from the Italian word "free"). This highly specialized defensive position, especially popular in Europe from the 1960s through the 1990s, is usually placed between the goalkeeper and the defensive line. The notable German soccer Captain Franz Beckenbauer is widely recognized as the inventor of the libero in its broader sense; that is, the "attacking sweeper." He added a substantial offensive component to the role—not to mention performing it perfectly—literally revolutionizing soccer at that time. However, when "Kaiser Franz" was on his offensive forays, somebody had to cover for him, and this someone was Hans-Georg ("Katsche") Schwarzenbeck.

In a 2010 interview, Schwarzenbeck was described as a player who for eleven years was "the assistant of Libero Beckenbauer," or his "shadow-man."[4] Schwarzenbeck, however, did not take offense to this description, saying, "I was only a defender and had the task of protecting him [Beckenbauer]. There was wordless communication; Franz did not have to worry."

If you look at Schwarzenbeck's CV, it is very impressive; with Bayern Munich he has six German Championships and three Cups, three European Championships and one Cup Winners Cup. With the German National team he was a World and European champion. Each and every achievement came from his perfect coordination with the Kaiser and his readiness to be a servant to somebody else. You might ask what Schwarzenbeck would have been without Franz, but it's important to realize that you could likewise ask what Beckenbauer would have been without Schwarzenbeck. Schwarzenbeck was an expert on reading and reacting to Beckenbauer, wordlessly and seamlessly covering and protecting him.

He was surely not a *brilliant* soccer player, but he was an outstanding expert on *precisely* what the team needed at that time.

The same holds for Beckenbauer, who wouldn't have become Kaiser Franz without his Katsche. To build a team, then, you need the Beckenbauers and the Schwarzenbecks, the Jordans, Pippens and the Kukocs. And most importantly, you need them to understand that they *all* have an important and respected place under the sun.

There is almost unanimous consensus among experts that a successful team needs a clear hierarchy among its players—the superstar leaders, the number twos, and the other helping hands. The process in building such a team is not necessarily an easy one; it can take time to find the right people to successfully work together toward a common goal. Talent plays a role, but so does ego. Members of the team have to be willing to accept their hierarchical roles, knowing that they are contributing to the overall performance of the team. When it comes to the world of business, the same holds true.

THE BUSINESS HIERARCHY

> To take responsibility has nothing to do with blowing up a hierarchy.
>
> —PAUL BREITNER[5]

Research has shown that office hierarchies improve business performance. A study conducted by Richard Ronay, K. Greenaway, Eric M. Anicich, and Adam Galinsky—researchers from the Northwestern and Columbia business schools, along with the University of Queensland, Australia—found that in tasks requiring teamwork, if leaders and followers are defined, teams will get more work done.[6] As April Joyner of *Inc.* explains in an analysis of the study, "Without a clear chain of command, members often become sidetracked with grabbing power and lose focus on the task at hand."[7] As with Michael Jordan and the Bulls, major projects or initiatives require a balance between leaders and followers, but leaders are imperative to success.

Too many people trying to fulfill a leadership role within the same team—typically individuals with dominant personalities—could potentially lead to a negative work environment, in which performance is likely to suffer. To avoid this fate, a mix of different personalities should be sought after, not just the type-A overachievers. So hierarchies are good in a workplace setting, but what's the best hierarchy for your company or team?

Two main hierarchies that are implemented in offices today are "flat," also known as "horizontal," and "tall," also known as "vertical." Vertical hierarchies are those that most people consider the typical corporate hierarchal structure, in which there are many layers and every person, except one, is subordinate to someone above them. More recently, flat hierarchies have emerged in the business world, exhibiting few levels of middle management between staff and executives, such as in startups or other organizations with smaller staffs.

Neither way is necessarily better, but in building a business or developing a team, it's important to consider what kind of structure will likely work best for your organization. If you believe your company's culture is more entrepreneurial in nature, the horizontal style might work just fine—some argue that it empowers employees and provides greater independence. However, in other large companies, the vertical hierarchy may be more conducive to a structured, top-down environment.

In his 2015 *Entrepreneur* article "4 Considerations When Determining the Best Leadership Structure for Your Business," Andre Lavoie—an entrepreneur, CEO, and cofounder of the talent management platform ClearCompany—described four considerations you'll want to keep in mind when developing a team or business:[8]

1. Will your company perform better in a top-down or "side by side" manner? Keep in mind, top-down will typically be more efficient, but side by side will take everyone's suggestions and thoughts into account (which can certainly be time consuming).
2. Should roles be more defined, from the CEO on down, or flexible? With the vertical hierarchy, you always know who to

report to, but you may lose some ability to be involved at all levels of a process or project.

3. How much do you value transparency? In the horizontal setup, transparency is key throughout the business, whereas the vertical hierarchy may fall back on sharing information with staff only on a "need to know" basis.

4. How much of a division is acceptable between the "higher ups" and the "worker bees"? The standard hierarchy tends to create an "us versus them" or "management versus employees" mindset, while the horizontal hierarchy tends to help people feel that they are all on the same cooperative level.

No matter the hierarchy you decide on, you need to make sure you have chosen the right people to work with. For example, they should be ready to take responsibility—that is, to be a "big head" (as opposed to a "pin's head," as we say in Hebrew)—regardless of their position in the hierarchy (at last, something I can agree on with Paul Breitner, as opposed to other statements of his, e.g., concerning the "untrainability" of penalties; see chapter 5). The process can be an arduous one, but it's worth the trouble to increase team and business performance.

CHOOSING THE RIGHT TEAM MEMBERS—AND TRUSTING THEM

> Don't tell people how to do things, tell them what to do and let them surprise you with their results.
>
> — General George S. Patton

No matter the shape of the hierarchy, in order to build a high-performing team, you've got to choose the right individual members. As discussed in chapter 7, what starts as a group must often end up as a team. There are two main approaches to doing so:

1. Select good players and build a team—and an entire
   system—around them.
2. Choose a system in which you believe and select players who fit
   into this system.

The Chicago Bulls, for example, followed the first method—drafting Michael Jordan in and trying to build the future team around him. French soccer manager Arsene Wenger (mentioned in chapter 7) follows the alternate approach, and has done so for many years. In his 2010 book, Jens Lehmann, whom I mentioned in chapter 5, indicates: "In Arsenal, the system makes the players successful, and not the other way round." But what exactly is a system?

If you want the "heavy" version, you can read my 2013 academic book with Felix Lebed, *Complexity and Control in Team Sports,* but for simplicity's sake, I'd like to explain the idea through a funny, but completely true, story from my university, Ben-Gurion University (BGU). One day, a few good souls who simply loved animals approached the university management and asked them to approve a "feeding corner" for stray cats—a place where food could be left for these hungry animals. After some discussion, the university approved the idea and a few areas were officially set up for this purpose. I have no doubt that these people's intentions were good, but the results were mixed:

1. BGU turned into a pilgrimage destination for all the cats in the
   Beer-Sheva region. Not so terrible, right?
2. The gutters, however, were soon rife with rats—the cats became
   simply too spoiled and lazy to chase them—and, in the
   end, the university had to pay a pretty penny to bring in
   exterminators and dispose of them (needless to say, instead of
   the satiated cats).

In this example, both the cats and rats must be seen as parts of one whole system in order to understand the connections. (There was also a conspiracy theory that the whole affair was a sophisticated plot hatched by the city's exterminators—piecework laborers—who sent the good souls to give the cats food, so that the exterminators would have more work and earn more money).

Another example of system thinking would be the throwing of a football: the quarterback doesn't throw where the receiver is now, but to where the receiver will be. In essence, teamwork is exactly such an interplay, a reciprocal and cooperative interaction between all elements participating in the game, whether you're talking about football, the stray cats, or the inner workings of an office.

Whether building a system around selected players or choosing a system before selecting them, there are numerous ways to create a team. One example from the world of sports comes from the sports-finance point of view, which suggests a few interesting ways of effectively choosing players. My colleague Haim Kedar-Levy and I wrote an article together on this topic, specifically related to how owners and managers of teams in general, such as in football, soccer, or basketball, are advised to choose players for a team.[9]

The main idea of this paper reflected the motivation or desire of club owners to hire the best athletes and coaches in order to maximize team performance. Although one of the largest expenses in the budgets of professional sport teams is players' and coaches' salaries, this investment yields an uncertain future income. This is because team profitability depends on the uncertain performance of each player as well as the uncertain synchronization of players—both of which are affected by the coach.

Our model accounted for:

1. a team of homogenous players (admittedly, a somewhat simplistic and hypothetical case);
2. a team with star players who are compensated differentially (such a heterogeneous team reflects reality more accurately, in which not all of us are equal);
3. team synchronization (which essentially reflects task cohesion);
4. the value of the coach.

We found that players who are well synchronized with other team members receive a higher share of payroll budgets. We also tried to determine whether players are fairly paid, overpaid, or underpaid given the expected rate of return they earn for the team; the correlation between their performance and team performance; and the preferences of the team owner.

The key point is that payments made for professional players and coaches represent a financial investment made by the team owner, for which the rate of return is uncertain. When you own a club and want to hire, the model enables you to estimate the reasonable compensation for a star player or a successful coach, in order to try to optimize your choice process (of players and coaches) in interactive sports such as basketball.

This process is similar to hiring leaders (bosses and managers) and team members (employees). When businesses look to bring in the right talent they need to take many factors into consideration. First and foremost, hiring managers need to decide whether they are hiring someone for a new position or an existing one—this is the same idea as hiring to fit a system or hiring someone to build a system around. For example, in today's rapidly expanding technological landscape, new positions within companies are being created all the time. Five years ago, the title "social media manager" didn't even exist, but at larger companies today, these positions can fetch a salary of $50,0000 or more.[10]

Of course the job candidate's background and experience are paramount. Simply put, the applicants must match up with what a company is looking for. Equally as important, however, is something that can't typically be gleaned from a resume—how will this person fit into the organization's overall culture and environment? Similarly, is this a person that others feel can be trusted? It's not unusual to have three or four people interview the same applicants to get a feel for their personality, character, and other traits.

At the end of the day, from a sports-finance perspective, when selecting members of a team, the main concern is the return on investment (ROI). In measuring the overall performance of a company, the equation is quite simple: ROI = Company Earnings (total profit)/Company Investments x 100), and will show you the percentage increase or decrease of an investment over a year. This same equation will help you figure out new employees' worth over the past year if you take into account their salary and any onboarding or hiring costs you incurred in hiring them. Once you have those numbers, you'll be able to see what the employee has contributed monetarily and whether or not you made a good investment.

Of course, just like in football and other team sports, there is uncertainty in how any one team player will pan out. That's why the initial stages of the hiring process are so imperative. Obviously the point of building a high-performing team of individuals is to produce better results, but questions remain on how the team will work together or gel. As we discussed in chapter 7, focusing on task-oriented cohesion will help interactive teams in which working together is necessary. Let's return to that subject for a moment to see how task cohesion can lead to higher team performance.

BUILDING A MORE TASK-COHESIVE TEAM

You don't have to go to bed together, just play basketball together.

—*the author*

Choosing the coach and players is only the beginning of the team-building process. To overcome barriers to group cohesion—such as clashes of personalities in the group, conflicts, individual members struggling for power, disagreement on group goals, and breakdowns in communication—the late Professor Albert V. Carron and his associates suggested the five following major steps in team-building:[11]

1. Profile the team's performance;
2. Set team goals;
3. Foster mutual respect;
4. Develop role clarity and role acceptance;
5. Promote effective communication.

You will also want to focus on the team structure (including task-related leadership); team environment (feelings of togetherness, uniqueness, and distinctiveness in task fulfillment); and team processes (such as cooperative behavior in light of competitive pressures inside the group). From my experience as an army organizational psychologist and a former soldier and officer (major), the following five tips to reinforce unit cohesion closely mimic these steps and actions:

1. Prepare your unit to deploy;
2. Spend time developing camaraderie;
3. Allow your unit to grow as a team;
4. Strive for effective leadership;
5. Pay attention to and address stressors.

Following these steps and tips will help during the team-building process, but there is also a way to measure the success of developing a group of people, working on a task, into a cohesive team. To do this, I have often employed "sociometry," which has its origins in sociology. Sociometry is a quantitative method to study and measure social relationships within a group, particularly in a small one (which corresponds to the number of athletes in most interactive team sports). This method is a valuable tool for understanding team cohesion and providing insight into the internal structure of a (small) group. I have used sociometry time and again in interactive sports—including basketball, soccer, and water polo. I often compare working with sociometry to peeling an onion: layer by layer, asking questions, getting answers, you slowly reach the heart of the problem.

Sociometry is frequently used in military settings as well, not only for mapping small groups (e.g., special units), but also as an effective tool for identifying and predicting future leaders (i.e., officers). In larger units, however, such as in a platoon (30 to 65 soldiers in the IDF infantry) or a company (100 to 250 soldiers in the IDF infantry) mapping is impossible. In a larger group, however, we can simply ask the soldiers to rate their comrades in the platoon or company, for example, in terms of their suitability for an officer's role. Or even simpler, we could have soldiers fill out questionnaires that ask them to name three or four comrades within the platoon or company that they believe would best fit the role of an officer. In this way, we actually measure a person's "sociometric status" in the platoon or the company.

From my experience as an Army psychologist, I can tell you for sure that this sociometric status is indicative of the soldiers' task-related effectiveness and social standing within that group (depending on the exact question you ask: e.g., does it refer to the task or to the social dimension?). Equally as important, the information about this status substantially improves the psychologist's ability to successfully identify and predict a person's future leadership behavior. Sociometry can be of great help in building a team, including in the processes of identifying, building, nurturing, developing, and preparing future leaders, whether they are on the battlefield, on the court, or in the office.

As a sports psychologist, I regularly employ sociometry techniques in working with teams to help them improve task cohesion. An example that also illustrates many of the issues we've discussed so far is of the time I was once called to assist a basketball team that was going through a critical period marked by a series of losses before the playoffs. Using sociometric measures and other information-gathering methods, I diagnosed issues such as a lack of team cohesion and leadership, as well as destroyed relations between the coach and players. More specifically, I found three major problems in the team:

1. Player X, the captain of the team, was not accepted as a leader by the majority of the players.
2. Player Y, however, was diagnosed as the most accepted, charismatic person with a substantial influence on the team.
3. The majority of players didn't rely on the coach anymore (today we would say "the coach lost the locker room") as he was more social-oriented as compared to task-oriented. The players felt that he was a nice guy and played the politics of the leader well, but when under pressure, the coach was unable to perform successfully and they could therefore not

trust him in decisive moments; instead, they preferred to be led by Y (if not by another coach) during the forthcoming decisive matches.

I confidentially brought these findings to the team's executive manager who immediately panicked—the playoffs were only two weeks away and he hadn't recognized how serious the situation had become. I also forwarded my conclusions to the chairman of the board personally and discreetly. My recommendations offered two major strategies:

1. Replace the coach immediately, which was the chairman's task;
2. Try to reconcile X and Y so they could get over their egos and cooperate in fulfilling their required duties together, which was my task.

Applying strategy number one was critical, not to mention urgent, in order to calm the situation down and create a quieter, more task-related team climate. As there was no time to work on improving coach-player relations—which I would have probably suggested had I been called in earlier in the season—I unfortunately saw no other solution than to fire the coach immediately and replace him with another one (which was of course the chairman's task, not mine).

As for strategy number two, if I could have, I would have recommended replacing the captain (player X) with player Y, the natural leader. However, X was an important player from a purely professional point of view—plus, he had a big ego, so we could have run the risk of losing him if he felt his prestige had been besmirched. I therefore undertook the responsibility of reconciling players X and Y, a supposed mission impossible, which I nevertheless successfully accomplished.

I began this process by talking to each one of them separately, appealing to their more mature or adult sensibilities. For example, instead of focusing on the type of childish back and forth that can rear its ugly head in the locker room (or in the office)—the "he said this/he said that" or "he did this/he did that" complaints and whining—I stressed the great responsibility that lies on the shoulders of each one of them in that particular situation. I wanted them to both understand that they were extremely important to the success of the team.

Next, I explained that they would get nowhere by insisting on the socio-emotional mutual dislike they had developed for one another. In this case, I appealed to their pride, their sense of ego, and, well, what their wives would say. Part of their salary was comprised of achievement-related bonuses, such as winning a title, so I asked them what was more important: that they bring home more money or that when their wives asked why they failed to win despite the financial incentive, they would have to explain that they couldn't play nice with their own team members?

After having a series of talks with each one of them individually, I brought them together so we could all discuss the situation. In this manner, I acted as a mediator. I started our first group discussion by saying "you don't have to go to bed together—just play basketball together." This got a chuckle, but it reflected, quite bluntly, but also quite effectively, that they needed to focus and cooperate on the *task* dimension only—the social dimension was irrelevant. Then, we agreed to talk *only* about how to accomplish the task, not their petty interpersonal conflicts. From there, they agreed to cooperate in order to save the situation—and did so very effectively.

This agreement enabled them to cooperate on task fulfillment, removing their ego and the social element out of the game. They had no disagreement about the need to cooperate in order to solve the professional, task-related problems, as it was in their individual best interest and the best interest of the team. This state of affairs enabled them to work together even though they actually continued to dislike each other personally.

As indicated earlier, the chairman and I essentially made a deal according to which I took responsibility for handling the players, and he had to handle the situation with the coach. The chairman, however, hesitated to fire the coach. Instead, he decided to do nothing, just wait another game or two to see what would happen. The result was devastating—despite the effective cooperation between players X and Y on the court, we lost another game because of the coach. At that point, he was fired at last and the team played much better in the last games under the new interim coach. Due to the lost game, however, we didn't have the home advantage in the last game of the semifinal playoff (best of five) which we lost two to three.

As for myself, I was told that I did a marvelous job but the club would not extend my contract. Wondering why, somebody from inside told me confidentially that the captain—X, a highly paid star—claimed that I had "undermined" him, despite the fact that my activities were professional and he had cooperated with them. Still, he gave the board an ultimatum: "Either he goes—or I do!" So I did.

Sociometry

Sociometry is an instrument intended to measure the structure of a small group, first proposed in 1934 by psychotherapist Jacob L. Moreno back in his classic *Who Shall Survive: A New Approach to the Problem of Human Interrelations*. Thinking about the zeitgeist in the 1930s, it is no wonder that a group of people was conceived similar to an atom: a group has positive and negative forces acting to pull or attract each other together (i.e., nuclear force), or to repel them from one another (i.e, electromagnetic force). Similarly, under certain circumstances, nucleons (i.e., protons or neutrons) may even be ejected from the nucleus, just as a member of a group or team can be removed.

In sociometry, participants are asked so-called sociometric questions that indicate with whom they would prefer to share or not to share a certain activity. The data concerning "who chooses whom" are then diagrammed as a "sociogram," in which the group members' choices are represented by circles and the connections (i.e., interrelations) between them.

As mentioned, I have used sociometry quite often with sport teams. In my first intervention ever (the one with the troublemaker in chapter 7), I decided to pose six questions, which I found to be very effective, and which I have used ever since. These questions can be tailored to fit any team, whether in sports or at work. For example, when consulting basketball teams, I ask the following:

1. Positive and negative *task*-related questions:
   a. Name a person with whom you would like to play on court with the most;

     b. Name a person with whom you would like to play on court with the least.

2. Positive and negative *social*-related questions:

     a. Name a person whom you like the most on the team (e.g., your best friend on the team);

     b. Name a person whom you like the least on the team (e.g., your least favorite person on the team).

3. The "captain question":

     a. Who is the most appropriate person to be the team's captain?

     b. Who is the least appropriate person to be the team's captain?

With just some small adjustments, these questions can then be applied to a business setting:

1. Positive and negative *task*-related questions:

     a. Name a person with whom you would like to work with the most;

     b. Name a person with whom you would like to work with the least.

2. Positive and negative *social*-related questions:

     a. Name a person whom you like the most on the team (e.g., your best friend on the team);

     b. Name a person whom you like the least on the team (e.g., your least favorite person on the team).

3. The "captain question":

     a. Who is the most appropriate person to be the team's leader?

     b. Who is the least appropriate person to be the team's leader?

Please note that when respondents state that they do not like or prefer one specific person on the team, this does not necessarily mean that they actively *dislike or reject* that person—for example, they simply may be indifferent. It is therefore necessary to make sure that it is clear to the participants that a. and b. refer to positive and negative *active* attitudes and that question 1 refers solely to the *professional* aspect, which does not necessarily correspond with the response in question 2, which refers solely to the *social* aspect.

Team members should be instructed to name one to three persons, as they like, for each question. They may answer the questions in a written form (ensuring confidentiality of the information), or in personal, discreet interviews. Then six sociograms can be created to tell the entire story of how the team members see themselves interacting professionally and personally with the others on the team (both positively and negatively), while also showing whom the majority feels should be considered a potential leader (and whom should not).

To better understand sociometry, it is helpful to see some examples of sociograms, as displayed in Figures 8.1 through 8.6 (which actually correspond with the case of the basketball team described on pages 154 through 156). The six figures correspond to the questions asked, and potential responses, for one team. The thick lines in the positive sociograms (Figures 8.1, 8.3, and 8.5) reflect mutual preferences. The thick lines in the negative sociograms (Figures 8.2, 8.4, and 8.6) reflect mutual rejections. The big numbers with circles reflect the players. The small numbers next to the lines reflect whether the choice was first, second, or third (they were allowed to choose a maximum of three names).

The six figures are an excellent springboard toward understanding the overall structure of a team, but sociograms do *not* explain the nature of the interactions discovered; they are used only to describe or depict the connections. To fully understand these interactions, the sociograms must be interpreted and handled smartly. After creating the socigrams, I usually sit with the coaches or managers to discuss the figures, explain the findings, and then interpret them. Because of the interpretations required to adequately utilize the sociometric information, I always recommend working with a professional, at least at first, to get a better understanding of the results. There are many small details that only someone with sociometry training will be able to find. In addition, misinterpreting sociograms may cause substantial damage.

The timing of the sociometric data collection is also of *immense* importance. For example, with a new team, or new team members, everyone needs to get to know each other before they can make any type of judgment call. If you perform the sociometric test too early, you may find later that many attitudes and feelings have changed—the leaders who were identified early on may have lost their standings, new friendships may have deteriorated, and people may find that they work better with others that they were initially skeptical of.

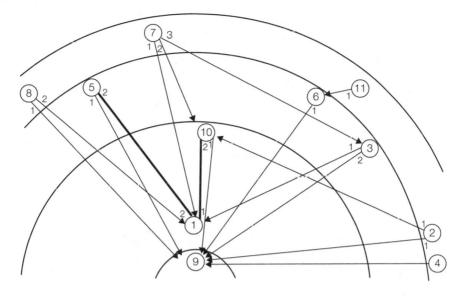

Figure 8.1 Positive Task Sociogram: person with whom you would like to work/play with the most.

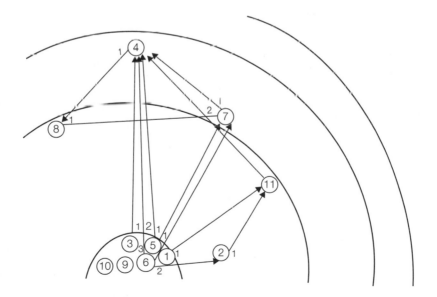

Figure 8.2 Negative Task Sociogram: person with whom you would like to work/play with the least.

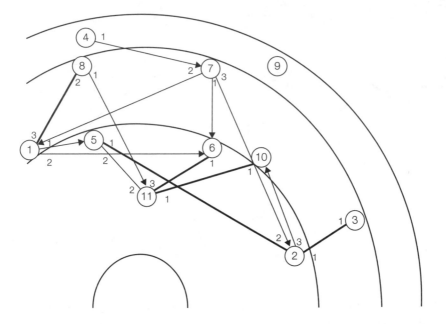

Figure 8.3 Positive Social Sociogram: person whom you like the most on the team (e.g., your best friend on the team).

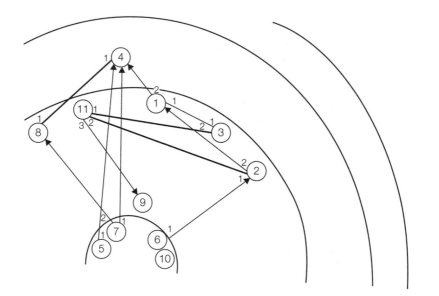

Figure 8.4 Negative Social Sociogram: person whom you like the least on the team (e.g., your least favorite person on the team).

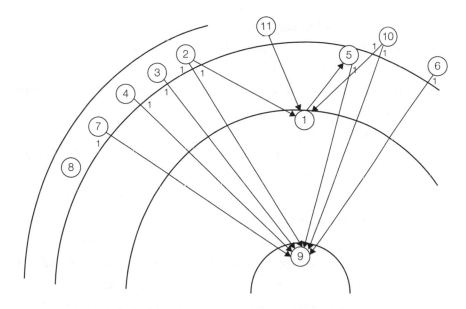

Figure 8.5 Positive Captain Sociogram: most appropriate person to be the team's leader/captain.

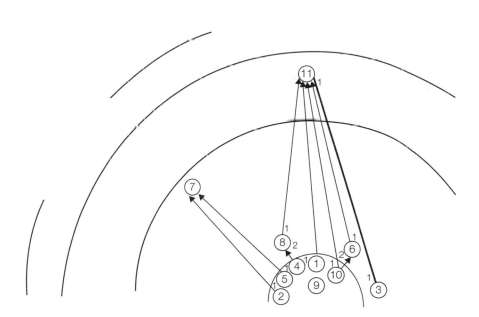

Figure 8.6 Negative Captain Sociogram: least appropriate person to be the team's leader/captain.

As mentioned, sociometry is especially effective with small groups. With larger groups, it may be quite difficult to map connections and create sociograms. In such a case, it's better to simply gather information about who likes or dislikes whom and then look for popularity without taking into account the connections.

Lastly, if not used properly, sociometry can be quite dangerous. For example, a particular person may be perceived and tagged as a "sociomat" (someone with a negative sociometric status) in one group, but in another context within another group, he would not be a sociomat at all. That is, one's sociometric status is dependent on the group that is involved in the evaluation. It may happen, however, that somebody is stereotyped as a sociomat in one team, creating a potentially negative reputation that will follow, even if that person switches to another team. For this reason, confidentiality is key—sociometric data are no different than any other medical or psychological data, and should therefore not be shared among the team members or used publicly.

Communication in Task-Oriented Teams

An interesting perspective in measuring team cohesion was suggested by my "academic twin" Gershon Tenenbaum, whom you met earlier in the book. Gershon presented a unique approach to measuring one important aspect of task cohesion, namely communication, using a discussion analysis tool (DAT) developed by his colleague Allan Jeong at Florida State. Allan developed and applied this instrument mainly for educational settings, but Gershon and his colleagues applied these procedures to analyze team communications in sports.[12] In doing so, they found substantial differences between the communication patterns of winning and losing teams.[13]

For example, in looking at doubles tennis teams, they discovered that winning teams exchanged messages more frequently; moreover, their communication was more significant (i.e., less trivial) than in losing teams. Winning teams tried to coordinate actions and solve problems instead of engaging in irrelevant or useless conversation (chitchat, or what I like to call "blah blah"). The winners were busy planning and discussing plays, more attuned to court conditions, and able to better share expectations and predict their partner's behavior. All of this communication contributed to better coordination and, ultimately, to more effective problem-solving.

Keep in mind that in cases like doubles tennis, factual interactions are necessary for task completion, similar to any office environment in which teams work interactively. When teams don't have to work interactively, however, these interactions are not always necessary. Hans Lenk, a Professor Emeritus of Philosophy at the University of Karlsruhe, Germany who was also an Olympic rowing champion, demonstrated this idea in a sports context in his classic 1969 article, "Top Performance Despite Internal Conflict." In this article, he described how German rowing crews became Olympic winners without extensively affiliating with others.[14] In the case of Hans Lenk's high-caliber, world-class rowing teams, they were highly successful *despite* being combative toward one another and consistently embroiled in internal conflicts. Why? Precisely because rowing is not an "interactive" but rather a "coactive" sport, as discussed in chapter 7 (this is similar to individual salespeople who sell directly to their own clients, though their revenues are pooled for the benefit of senior management). Of course the team's success partially came from the fact that they were excellent professional rowers to begin with, but the main point is that the team did not need to love each other to succeed. The coactive nature of the task meant they didn't even need to verbally communicate (which is good, since some of them were not on speaking terms with each other).

Gershon and I also conducted a study to evaluate the perceived effect of teammates' responses during competition among athletes participating in team sports.[15] In this study we looked at basketball, team handball, soccer, and water polo teams. Not surprisingly, we found that positive and negative peer responses were primary sources of influence on teammate's vulnerability to psychological performance crises in competition. These responses are considered social reinforcements (positive or negative) and are particularly influential in regards to a person's success or failure.

Of course, when team members perform a successful action, as a leader or a colleague you naturally tend to provide them with a positive response and praise. But what about when the opposite situation occurs? For example, how do you respond when teammates perform an *un*successful action (i.e., a mistake), particularly when you least expect it or it is atypical of your teammate, colleague, or employee? Though you may be angry and frustrated, this is exactly the moment to communicate *effectively*.

Your teammates know when they have messed up, and what they urgently need in such a situation is a good word, a positive response, or encouragement. Though people tend to say, "well, everybody knows that," many teammates too often discourage each other after they've made mistakes. This type of discouragement is demoralizing and detrimental to team performance overall. Keep in mind: athletes' perceptions of their teammates' responses on court are an active evaluative feedback, which is of crucial importance to the understanding of one's psychological state in competition. Through the teammates' responses, the athlete may experience substantial social reinforcements—whether positive or negative. These are particularly influential when players interact with success and failure in task accomplishment. Thus subjectively experienced success or failure perceptions are further amplified by teammates' responses. If the responses are negative, they act to amplify the devastating effect of failure. By contrast, if the teammates want to neutralize the devastating effect of failure on the player, they have to respond positively (which has the opposite effect to amplifying by negative response). Therefore, to build a successful team, keep in mind how important your comrades are and leave negative reinforcements out of everyday communication.

COMPETITIVE COOPERATION, COOPERATIVE COMPETITION

> Ask not what your teammates can do for you. Ask what you can do for your teammates.
>
> —Earvin "Magic" Johnson

It is usually assumed in elite sport that cooperative behavior is superior to individualistic behavior, not only for group performance but for the performance of individuals within the group as well. In essence, team-building rests on a similar assumption, namely that cooperative behavior is superior to competitive behavior for both individuals and group performance. But this is a somewhat simplistic approach.

Let's go back to the sports heroes mentioned in this chapter. I believe it's fair to assert that every Kokuc wants to be in the starting five; every Pippen wants to be a shining Jordan; and even every Katsche would like to be a glittering Kaiser Franz. It's only human: competition and rivalry are built-in elements of sport teams, especially when the rewards are high (in the case of famous athletes, don't forget the huge advertising contracts they can rake in). I mentioned Arsene Wenger as an example of a coach who clearly prefers the team over the individual players. At the beginning of the chapter, I also brought up Pat Riley: according to his famous 1993 book, *The Winner Within*, Riley based his big successes on the principle of "success through un-selfishment." This principle states that only team-oriented behaviors are encouraged, with all players being asked to put aside their interests and personal considerations to work primarily toward the good of the team as a whole. But in reality, is this what is happening when a team is performing at its highest levels? Not entirely.

For example, take a closer look at Pat Riley and star player Magic Johnson, who Riley coached while he was at the helm of the Los Angeles Lakers in the 1990s. Riley describes Johnson, and Larry Bird, as "most unselfish" players. He writes:

> They [Johnson and Bird] made it a habit to be unselfish. They taught
> a lot of other players what it is to sacrifice and to be unselfish by being
> passers and thinking "team first and team last" . . . what they brought
> was an incredible desire to win through making other players better
> and being unselfish. And they'll go down in history as that.

In my opinion, however, there is a little catch here: I believe a team's success is a matter of synchronizing the individual's interests with those of the team. Therefore, I think, it is perhaps no sacrifice on the part of the "unselfish" players at all—even though it looks better when presented as such. In the 1996 interview with Riley, for example, he said the following about the great 1960s–1970s UCLA and LA Lakers player Gail Goodrich:

> Gail was a perfect complement as a superstar. Now that, to me, is like a contradiction because what kind of superstar can be a complement? He's not a role player.

The implication is that Gail—a gifted all-time top scorer—was ready to sacrifice himself for the team, just like Johnson or Bird, but was that really what was happening? Riley mentions a contradiction, which leads me to my main point: as you've seen time and again in this book—and especially highlighted in chapters 5, 6, and 7—high team performance is actually a synthesis between thesis and antithesis, between black and white. Thus it is not a real contradiction—Gail's greatness came from his ability to encompass both ends of a seeming contradiction; Johnson also knew he had to work for his teammates before expecting them to work for him. Only in this way could these athletes reach their level of performance and stardom. So what we see here is a completely selfish reason to behave in an unselfish way.

Think about the paradoxical psychological situation faced by a player like Kokuc who made his living, and reputation, with the Bulls as being the "ultimate 'No. 6.'" Despite the likely desire of such a "sixth man" to promote himself to the starting five through better performance, the more successful he was in getting up off the bench, the more likely he was going to be stuck in the role of number six. He would therefore have never made it to the starting team, precisely *because* he was such a great sixth man! This state is of course an impossible one from a (psycho)logical point of view: the mythos says "let the best players play," but if you have somebody who is good at getting up off the bench, you don't reward him by putting him on the starting team—but rather by sticking him on the bench as number six for as long as the team needs this player. That all being said, however, this situation also allows players to synchronize their individual interests with those of the team: Kokuc was incredibly successful because his self interests were met as he accepted his role on the team.

In a February 11, 2015 lecture in Tel Aviv, FC Barcelona's sport psychologist Inma Puig claimed that team cohesion in soccer or basketball is often in danger after successes, because players tend to begin taking individual credit for winning games. This action, says Puig, creates a situation where competition is directed *inward* instead of *outward*, (in Jordan's words, the "I" prevails instead of the "team"). Even worse, however, is the state where cohesion starts to fall apart when teams *lose*—it becomes a truly tough challenge to remain united. Cohesion in this condition is probably a team's only hope to turn the situation around. In the epigraph of this chapter, we see how the Dutch team in 1974 began disintegrating into a group of individuals when they saw they were going to lose in the world championship final game. Indeed, despite their great efforts, these individuals who no longer functioned as a cohesive team, lost.

SUMMARY

There is almost unanimous consensus among experts that a successful team needs a clear hierarchy among its players, just as within any other organization. Of course, number one stars still need their teams—any organization needs their number twos and other helping hands. You can build a team around a player, but the player cannot build a team alone.

There are many types of organizational structures, but the there are two that are commonly implemented in an office or business setting: flat/horizontal, which has few levels of middle management between staff and executives, or tall/vertical, which is a more typical corporate hierarchal structure with many levels, in which every person, except one, is subordinate to someone above them.

When choosing talent, be it on the field or in the office, two approaches exist: one where you select good players and build a team from them (creating a system) or one where you choose a system in which you believe the select players will fit. This type of system-thinking supports the interplay and interaction between team members and contributes to their collective teamwork. More importantly, it will help you decide the best way to create a team: sometimes you're not only looking to bring on talent, but also someone who will fit within the culture and environment.

In essence, the main idea is to turn a group into a team, while focusing on the team structure, environment, and processes. Synchronizing the task-related interests of the individual and the team in an interactive setting is integral to building a highly functional, cohesive team. If individuals are committed to this team, then performance is enhanced. People will be willing and ready to do whatever is required to create a functional harmony within a group and succeed at a task, as a team, because they recognize their own self-interest.

I have also found in working with teams that it is possible to diagnose their problems and come to solutions through a number of implementable steps, such as profiling the team's performance, setting team goals, fostering mutual respect, developing role clarity (and acceptance), and promoting effective communication.

Understanding how to overcome the potential difficulties of team-building and how to craft the best team given the particular situation, and why, is of utmost importance and will lead to maximum levels of success.

DAILY PRACTICES

As an Individual

- Provide positive reinforcement and praise to colleagues and team members on a regular basis.
- Realize that your place in the office hierarchy is important even if you're not the star employee—understanding your role will help you work with your colleagues more productively and increase team performance.
- Make sure to communicate with your team when it counts the most—keep lines of communication open when you're working together under a tight deadline or on any major project.

As a Leader

- Decide what type of hierarchy is right for your team and business.
- When hiring new employees, take the return on investment into account, but also try to figure out how well this person will work in the given team environment and culture.
- Employ techniques such as sociometry and DAT to better understand how to improve team task cohesion and overall performance.

NOTES

1. YouTube, "World Cup, West Germany 1974: Netherlands–West Germany 1–2 (Final)–HD," www.youtube.com/watch?v=gQdK7v4Jpc.
2. "NBA Encyclopedia, Playoff Edition," interview with Pat Riley, April 16, 1996.
3. Ibid.
4. Andreas Burkert, "The Centre-Back of the Libero," *Sueddeutsche Zeitung*, May 17, 2010.
5. D. Schulze-Marmeling, *Die Bayern: Vom Klub zum Konzern—Die Geschichte eines Rekordmeisters* [Bayern: From Club to Concern—The History of a Record Champion] (Goettingen: Die Werkstatt, 1997), 144.
6. Richard K. Ronay, K. Greenaway, Eric M. Anicich, and Adam Galinsky, "The Path to Glory is Paved with Hierarchy: When Hierarchical Differentiation Increases Group Effectiveness," *Psychological Science* 23, no. 6 (June 2012): 669–677.
7. April Joyner, "Why Office Hierarchies Are Good for Business," *Inc.*, August 24, 2012, www.inc.com/magazine/201209/april-joyner/why-office-hierarchies-are-good-for-business.html.
8. Andre Lavoie, "4 Considerations When Determining the Best Leadership Structure for Your Business," *Entrepreneur*, June 2, 2015, www.entrepreneur.com/article/246770.
9. H. Kedar-Levy and M. Bar-Eli, "The Valuation of Athletes as Risky Investments: A Theoretical Model," *Journal of Sport Management* 22 (2008): 50–81.
10. Jim Belsoic, "5 Skills to Master Before You Even Think About Applying for a Social Media Job," *The Muse*, 2016, www.themuse.com/advice/5-skills-to-master-before-you-even-think-about-applying-for-a-social-media-job.
11. A. V. Carron, M. A. Eys, and S. Burke, "Team Cohesion: Nature, Correlates and Development," in *Social Psychology in Sport*, eds. S. Jowett and D. Lavalee (Champaign, IL: Human Kinetics, 2007), 91–101.

12. L. Domagoj, G. Tenenbaum, D. Eccles, A. Jeong, and T. Johnson, "Intrateam Communication and Performance in Doubles Tennis," *Research Quarterly for Exercise and Sport* 80 (June 2009): 281–290. Unfortunately, DAT for me are the initials of "Dopamine Transporters"; in the spring of 2013 I underwent a "DATscan"—a relatively new diagnostic imaging technology which helped my doctors to confirm that due to "reduced uptake in the putamen on both sides . . . dopamine transporter was clearly reduced and in accordance with Parkinson's disease" (as was written in one of the documents).

13. For a more in-depth look at the process behind DAT, I highly recommend reviewing Dr. Allen Jeong's *Discussion Analysis Tool* website, which provides further information: http://myweb.fsu.edu/ajeong/dat/.

14. H. Lenk, "Top Performance Despite Internal Conflict: An Antithesis to a Functional Proposition," in *Sport, Culture and Society: A Reader on the Sociology of Sport*, eds. J. W. Loy and G. S. Kenyon (New York: Macmillan, 1969), 224–235.

15. M. Bar-Eli, G. Tenenbaum, and N. Levy-Kolker, "A Three-Dimensional Crisis-Related Analysis of Perceived Teammates' Behavior in Competition," *Journal of Sport Behavior* 15 (1992): 179–200.

9

Leadership Values

Becoming a Head Honcho

Q: If you had a job description for an NBA coach, what would it be?
A: Insanity.

—Pat Riley[1]

Former professional baseball shortstop Derek Jeter will likely go down in history as one of Major League Baseball's top players of his generation. Between 1995 and 2014, Jeter helped lead the New York Yankees—the only professional team he played for throughout his career—to five World Series victories. As a powerhouse hitter, he became the Yankees' all-time career leader in hits, doubles, and at-bats, and he was also highly regarded for his base running and performance on the field. Jeter also played in fourteen All-Star games and received five Gold Glove Awards and five Silver Slugger Awards, among many others. Though he'll certainly be remembered for his success at bat and on the field, he will also always be remembered for his leadership skills.

Known lovingly as "El Capitan," Jeter embodied the role of a true leader in almost every way. He worked hard and was determined to succeed, inspiring and motivating those around him. As baseball analyst

Kevin Millar once commented, "This guy is amazing, and he makes the players around him so much better."[2] And "amazing" might be an understatement—Jeter notched more than 3,400 hits, attained a .310 batting average with a .377 on-base percentage, and stole nearly 360 bases during his professional career.[3]

Jeter always supported his team, even when facing losses. After winning the World Series in 1996, for example, the Yankees had a solid year in 1997 but lost the American League Division Series in five games to the Cleveland Indians. They learned a great deal from their losing season, and Jeter rallied his fellow team members to come back and win three consecutive World Series in 1998, 1999, and 2000 (they also won in 2009). Yankees owner Hank Steinbrenner pointed out that "Derek has always played with a relentless, team-first attitude. And that mind-set has helped sustain this organization's objective of fielding championship-caliber teams year after year."[4]

Through all of his success Jeter maintained a humble attitude, something he was known and respected for throughout the league. He had a lot to brag about, but he always refrained. He didn't badmouth other players or coaches and he was as loyal to his team as he was to his fans. After his last game in 2014, when he left the field to chants of "Thank You, Derek!" he stated in an interview, "Everybody, the fans, are saying, 'Thank you, Derek.' I'm saying to myself, 'For what?' I'm just trying to do my job. Thank you guys."[5]

In addition to being an effective, humble leader, Jeter has always been a positive one, too. As ESPN Senior Writer Howard Bryant wrote in a 2013 piece before Jeter retired, "He became the signature player for the game's signature team when it returned to power, and in an era of drugs and cynicism and ruined reputations, he never embarrassed the sport, his team, or, most important, his family name."[6] Jeter has carried on his legacy of leadership through Jeter's Leaders, a youth leadership social change program funded by Jeter's Turn 2 Foundation. This leadership development program empowers, assists, and recognizes the accomplishments of high school students who are making positive life choices, improving their community, and acting as role models to their peers and younger students.

The person who introduced me to organizational psychology was Zur Shapira, currently a notable professor of management at New York University. From Zur, I learned that effective leadership is a key determinant to any organizational success. In essence, leadership refers to one's ability to influence and guide a group of people toward the achievement of a shared goal. In everyday speech, the terms "leader" and "manager" are quite frequently used interchangeably; however, this is inaccurate. A *leader* has the primary function of providing and establishing the fundamental organizational mission (a vision that helps determine the direction that the organization or team pursues) and to formulate the strategy for its implementation, attaining the goals and objectives derived from that mission. By contrast, a *manager* is primarily responsible for implementing the organizational mission and strategy through others, increasing employees' commitment and effort, as well as implementing various organizational functions such as planning, scheduling, budgeting, staffing, and recruiting.

In 2015's *Leading*, mentioned in chapter 5, authors Sir Alex Ferguson and Sir Michael Moritz provide a wonderful definition of the difference between leaders and managers, based on Ferguson's experience in Manchester United ("Manu"):

> At United we had plenty of people who could manage aspects of our activities far better than I could . . . my job was different. It was to set very high standards. It was to help everybody else believe they could do things that they didn't think they were capable of. It was to chart a course that has not been pursued before. It was to make everyone understand that the impossible was possible. That's the difference between leadership and management.[7]

Indeed, management can be conceived as another variant of leadership as there are some overlapping functions that blur the distinction between leaders and managers in actual daily practice. Although the differences are not always evident, they are real and should be taken into account. As Felix Lebed and I pointed out in our 2013 book *Complexity and Control in*

Team Sports, at least three major leadership functions should be fulfilled in a sport organization:

- Managing—refers to the manager's role in developing the sport organization;
- Coaching—refers primarily to coaches' interactions with their athletes;
- Playing—refers to within-team relations, such as between the captain and peers.

These three essential functions are nearly identical to those required in a business setting: developing the team and its talents, interacting with individual team members, and producing positive relationships within the team. To properly perform these functions, leaders must be:

1. flexible and adaptable;
2. modest and humble ("ego-less");
3. able to act as teachers;
4. willing to learn from failure.

Otherwise, they will not succeed. I introduced this chapter with Derek Jeter as an example of the pinnacle of effective leadership because he performed these functions flawlessly. To understand why these attitudes and behaviors are so imperative to high performance, let's take a closer look at each one individually.

FLEXIBILITY AND ADAPTABILITY

> I don't have a clue where the courage to take this three-pointer came from, but I believe Pini's decision to play me, despite all my misses, gave me the confidence I needed.
>
> — Sarunas "Sharas" Jasikevicius[8]

Sport psychology and sport management literature repeatedly emphasize that effective leadership should consist of the appropriate response to various structural group dimensions (such as size, composition, and objectives), as well as to different group processes (such as cohesion, norms, decision-making, and conflict resolution) and the environmental or situational context in which that group is performing. Many times, leaders' appropriate responses rely on their flexibility.

For example, in a television interview following Germany's victory in the European national team handball championship, Coach Heiner Brand (whom you met in chapter 7) was asked to compare his leadership style during that particular tournament against his style in previous years.[9] Coach Brand, known for his strictness, answered that he had practiced a "loose" style of leadership during that tournament, delegating much responsibility to the players, who, in his opinion, were highly mature and deserved that type of freedom. However, he also said that the players knew very well that he could return to his strict ways, if necessary. In other words, he had practiced a leadership style that was appropriate to his players in that particular situation to achieve this unprecedented victory. In fact, Coach Brand used a so-called contingency model, making his own leadership behavior dependent upon the characteristics of his players and the situation in which the team was operating.

Much of the sport leadership research related to this idea has been connected to the name of Packianathan Chelladurai (aka "Chella"), a distinguished professor of sport management at Troy University, Alabama. Chella promoted the so-called multidimensional model of leadership, which maintains that situational characteristics, group member characteristics, and leader characteristics may produce three states of leader behavior: required, preferred, and actual. One part of actual leader behavior reflects the adaptation of the leader to the demands and constraints imposed by the situation; the other part is a function of the leader's response to group members' preferences.

The degree of congruence among the three states of leadership behavior determines the extent to which team members are not only satisfied, but more importantly, how they successfully perform as individuals and as a group. In fact, Chella considered a leader's behavior to be an "intervening variable"—one that creates links between "independent" and "dependent" variables. Independent variables in this instance are those that determine the leader's behaviors (the aforementioned situational, group members', and leader characteristics). The dependent variables (i.e., the output) are group performance and satisfaction.[10]

In principle, it is the *contingency* between leaders and the environment in which they operate that seems to be most crucial in determining leadership effectiveness. Thus, effective group leadership depends heavily on the congruence between leaders and their followers. There is no one best way to lead in all situations; effective leaders are advised to be tuned in to the needs of team members and provide the right balance between styles of leadership, maintaining flexibility in style (for example, strict versus loose) in order to facilitate maximal performance in the given situation.

Consider, for example, the style required by basketball coaches during time outs in stressful situations compared to the style required in relaxed, "peaceful" training sessions. At the end of a decisive game, where the score is close and stress is high, complex explanations are unnecessary, and even counterproductive, because the players' attention spans decrease and they cannot process too much information at once. In such a situation players need simple and clear directions, preferably based on well-trained moves and well-learned habits; thus a coach in this situation should be "autocratic," in the sense that the players get the feeling that "our leader knows exactly what she wants and we can rely on and trust her." In the peaceful environment of a regular training session, coaches are advised to use a more "democratic" style, where the emphasis is on improving athletes' performance by instructing them in the skills, techniques, and tactics of the game, letting them participate actively in the process.

Flexibility also includes an element of creativity to provide immediate and unexpected solutions to actual problems. For example, on March 3, 2005, the Maccabi Tel-Aviv basketball club was hosting the Montepaschi Siena Italian team in the EuroLeague. With 22 seconds left in the game, Siena was leading 84 to 82. Among other reasons, Maccabi was trailing because their superstar player Sarunas Jasikevicius (aka "Sharas") was having a terrible night—during the game, he had missed eight three-pointers in a row. Despite his repeated misses, Sharas was instructed by Maccabi's coach Pini Gershon to shoot a three-pointer—which he did. The end result: Maccabi won 85 to 84.

Sharas was beyond "cold" that evening—he was frozen. Coach Gershon therefore assumed that none of the opponents would expect Sharas to attempt such a decisive shot after eight misses. In fact, most coaches in that situation would prefer not to let a player on such an off night make another attempt. Gershon, however, rightly guessed that paradoxically, Sharas would be the freest, most unguarded player on court at that point of the game, precisely *because* he had already missed eight shots in a row. Gershon's creative—and paradoxical—thinking led the team to success.

This type of flexibility and creativity is essential to today's business leaders. Without a willingness to pursue exciting new projects, products, or services within changing business and social environments, you will be unable to lead your team. No leader may know this better than Larry Page, the cofounder of Google, who came up with the idea for the world's most powerful Internet search engine when he was still a twenty-two-year-old student at Stanford.

As his idea developed into a company with cofounder Sergey Brin, it was unlikely that Page knew how successful Google would one day become, along with the diversity of related products and services It offers, including YouTube, Chrome, and the Android. In a 2013 interview with *Wired*, Page told reporter Steven Levy that Google investors initially thought these types of products were "crazy," but that "if you're not doing some things that are crazy, then you're doing the wrong things."[11]

Page was flexible in the company's offerings, filling important tech niches and staying ahead of competition. He was the one who spearheaded the acquisition of the Android in 2010, which quickly became the world's most popular mobile operating system.[12] Maybe even more importantly, Page's flexibility has allowed him to assume numerous different roles at the company. Though he started as CEO in 1998, he was forced to step aside in 2001, at which time he became the president of products. By 2011, however, he was back in the CEO chair. In 2015, things were shaken up again when Google restructured and created a new holding company, Alphabet, with Page at the helm as CEO.

Though Page was more willing at certain times than others to move from position to position, he did so for the betterment of the company and the success of the overall organization. Throughout the process, he maintained a leadership role and helped steer Google to new heights. Though he could have been bitter or resentful for being demoted in 2001, his attitude when reassuming the CEO position was one of humility, another trait of today's top leaders.

EGO-LESSNESS: HUMILITY AND MODESTY

> Everything we said is cancelled . . . take the ball and bring the cup!
>
> —PINI GERSHON

The story of Apple cofounder Steve Jobs getting fired from the company he started—one that revolutionized home computing—is commonly discussed throughout business literature to showcase the importance of a truly superb leader. As the tale goes, when he was given the boot in 1985, he immediately went on to launch two new ventures: NeXT and Pixar Animation Studios. Over the next decade, Apple suffered, while Jobs thrived, and in 1996 he returned to the company when they purchased NeXT. By 1997 he had regained the position of interim CEO; by 2000 they dropped the "interim," and he led Apple toward the creation of its most ubiquitous and successful products.

What people talk about less is the humbleness Jobs showed when returning to lead Apple. He may have been known to work his employees hard and be difficult to get along with at times, but his ability to overcome his ego for the sake of the company he started is near astonishing. First, he simply could have refused to sell NeXT. He surely would have been able to continue to develop and create life-changing products on his own terms. Then when he was moved into an interim CEO position, he could have made a real fuss. Many people would find the "interim" label to be a slap in the face, something akin to saying "you're fine for now, but we're going to find someone better eventually," but Jobs persisted.

By the time Apple entered the new millennium, it was obvious that Jobs's leadership lay at the center of the company's success. In a 2005 Stanford commencement speech, Jobs stated, "I didn't see it then, but it turned out that getting fired from Apple was the best thing that could have ever happened to me."[13]

Humility and modesty, which I refer to as "ego-lessness," are necessary qualifications to great leadership. Business management author Patrick Lencioni, in his seminal *Five Dysfunctions of a Team*, described "inattention to results" owing to excessive focus on personal status and ego as a serious problem when it comes to teamwork. Many people in leadership positions typically feel threatened in situations where they believe members of the team they lead are smarter, more innovative, or all around "know better." Such an attitude, however, will only work against a leader's success and team performance. For example, think of Dick Fosbury's coach, Dean Benson, in chapter 6: if he had insisted that Fosbury stick with the traditional training he had implemented, Fosbury would not have been nearly as huge of a success, nor would the sport have moved forward by such leaps and bounds. Instead, according to Fosbury, Coach Benson "was pleased" for his success and encouraged him to proceed, even though "he was not sure exactly what" Fosbury was doing.[14]

Having mentioned Coach Gershon's ingenuity in discussing flexibility, I'd like to also show how the coach exhibited this concept of ego-lessness as well. In 1996 Hapoel Jerusalem, led by Gershon (the head coach at the time), won the cup after defeating Maccabi Tel-Aviv 67 to 65 in a last-moment basket by Adi Gordon. During what would become Israel's most famous basketball time out in history, Gordon, the star and symbol of Hapoel Jerusalem, insisted on acting contrary to Gershon's instructions.

In the video of that time out—broadcast many times over the years—you can clearly see Gershon planning the final play of the game and explaining it in detail to the players sitting in front of him. Jerusalem needed one basket, a simple two-pointer, to win the cup for the first time. Just before the players return to the court, however, assistant coach Erez Edelstein observes Gordon still sitting on the bench, in a silent protest. Edelstein then pokes Gershon with his elbow and points to Gordon. Gordon does not even say a word, but Gershon goes over to him and asks: "What do you want? You want the ball? O.K., everything we said is cancelled; Adi, take the ball and bring the cup!" Which he did.

Not only did Coach Gershon again show a great deal of creativity, while also adapting to the demands and constraints of his environment, but he also was willing to put his ego aside and "go with Gordon"—even though Gordon's behavior could have been interpreted as a threat to his authority as a leader. Instead, he preferred to "surrender" to Gordon, realizing that the main goal for *both* of them was to win the cup. For the sake of success, then, Coach Gershon threw away everything he had planned during that final time out, as opposed to many other coaches (or bosses, or leaders) who would have tried to save face in front of their team in similar situations, even though it would probably not have brought them the aspired success.

Ego-lessness is also regularly required when leaders are working with highly talented but somewhat unusual (or sometimes extraordinary) individuals. I warmly remember the late Professor Emma Geron, for whom I worked at the Wingate Institute as a research assistant back in 1979–1980 and for whom, I must admit, I caused a lot of trouble. Frankly, I was undisciplined, often arguing in an effort to prove that I was smarter than everybody else. Emma, one of the founders and pioneers of sport psychology, and a very wise woman, understood that it was mainly my somewhat low self-confidence which caused such a seemingly arrogant behavior. One day, she called me into her office at Wingate and told me she had been asked to write a recommendation for me. She said she would do it, leaving out any reference to my more "undisciplined" behavior, because she *knew* that I could succeed if I stayed focused and "behaved." This recommendation turned out to be a crucial key for my acceptance to the German Sport University Doctoral program.

From this experience, I learned an important lesson: today, if I see a "wild horse," such as I myself was about forty years ago, I try to contain her or his craziness and extract the talent. Such an approach requires much patience and ego-lessness on my behalf, because it is the very essence of such people to be often inconvenient for the system—and it is in many ways my duty as a professor to encourage their argumentative and questioning behavior. In fact, the ability to fulfill this role, acting as a teacher, is another main element of a productive and successful leader.

THE LEADER AS TEACHER: HELPING YOUR TEAM GO FROM ZEROS TO HEROES

A leader's most powerful ally is his or her own example.

—JOHN WOODEN

One of the most revered basketball coaches of all time is undoubtedly UCLA's John Wooden (1910–2010). During his time as head coach at UCLA, from 1948 to 1975, the team won ten NCAA national championships over a twelve-year period (1963–1975). Not only did he maintain an impeccable record and coach players who would go on to NBA fame, such as Kareem Abdul-Jabbar, but he was an inspiration to countless people due to his philosophy on success on the court and in everyday life.

In Chris Anderson's and David Sally's *The Numbers Game*, the authors point to Wooden as the model of what a good coach should be. Contending that good coaches—conceived as leaders—are highly important for organizational success, they detail how coach Wooden actually acted as a teacher, using the principles of deliberate practice to help his players reach their maximal levels of performance (a topic that should be quite familiar to you at this point). Interestingly enough, Wooden began his career as both an English teacher and a coach, which likely gave him insight into how to work with his players from a teacher's perspective. As reported by ESPN.com, Abdul-Jabbar once stated that "Coach [Wooden] taught us self discipline, and he was always his own best example."[15]

As teachers, leaders such as Wooden respond to the changing needs of the team members according to their stage of development. In fact,

Wooden's famous "pyramid of success" details how the main motives of success change as players, and people in general, develop their ability to handle and control increasingly complex tasks and situations.[16] The bottom of the pyramid starts with values including loyalty, friendship, and cooperation. Moving up the pyramid, you find self-control and initiative, followed by skill, team spirit, and confidence, leading to the highest point: competitive greatness. Wooden worked with all his team members to help them reach this pinnacle of success and performance.

In *The Numbers Game*, Anderson and Sally contend that in order to promote excellence, good coaches are strongly advised to continuously and repeatedly improve their players, motivating them and teaching them to perform old skills better, while also acquiring new skills:

> More than 10 percent of Coach Wooden's actions involved demonstrations of the correct or incorrect movement or both—showing the player the right way to do something. Training sessions were fundamentally about instruction for the UCLA coach: "I felt running a practice session was almost like teaching an English class. I knew a detailed plan was necessary in teaching English, but it took a while before I understood the same thing was necessary in sports. Otherwise, you waste an enormous amount of time, effort and talent."

Anderson and Sally go on to explain that good coaches such as Wooden script every practice and also monitor their own learning. Such notes help leaders learn from both their teams' and their own experiences. Through this process, coaches are themselves forced to improve, which in return helps the team further.

For example, in the early 1990s, I taught sport psychology to a group of team handball coaches working primarily with young players. The coaches reported having difficulties in explaining some actions to their junior players, in particular one specific movement: in team handball, it's necessary to know how to "fall" properly into the penalty area while throwing the ball to the goal. Though the coaches could automatically perform the movement in practice, they could not figure out a way to explain *how* they did it.

The typical response of average coaches in such a situation is to say to their players something like "don't do it that way," but they often can't go that next step to teach the team what *to* do; this is because in order to be able to teach something properly, coaches (and leaders in general) must fully control their own actions first. In the case of falling in team handball, the coaches may of course demonstrate the action, but they still need to think about how to demonstrate it correctly and effectively. This forces the coaches to self improve by considering their own optimal performance continuously, making sure the team does not acquire incorrect knowledge or bad habits.

In one study from the late 1990s, conducted in an educational, scholastic setting, my colleagues and I found that tutoring seems to benefit the tutors as well as the tutees, further supporting the point that if teachers have students who challenge them, they must improve to adequately fulfill their tasks to help students learn.[17] This idea can also be seen in offices or at companies in which team leaders, managers, and bosses are encouraged to incorporate a teacher-like aspect into their leadership methods. In a 2014 article in *Fast Company*, Ray Carvey, the executive vice president of corporate learning at Harvard Business Publishing, expressed this concept clearly. Carvey states that managers internalize the ideas or processes they're teaching, thereby reinforcing, and helping them take ownership of, their knowledge.[18]

By improving yourself as a leader first, you will therefore have a better chance of improving those you lead. The ability to do so relies on providing effective feedback to your team and helping them develop good habits.

Provide Effective Feedback

I have a special relationship with Mr. Basketball, the great basketball player and coach Nat Holman (1896–1995); after all, my chair in sports research at BGU is named after him. When Holman passed away he was described by Sam Goldaper, in the *New York Times*, as a professor whose students were actually his players.

According to the *Online Etymology Dictionary*, a "professor" is a person who professes to be an expert in a particular area, but is also a teacher of the highest rank. That is, he or she not only produces knowledge, but also shares it in the right way. This definition would fit Holman perfectly, being the author of the first valuable book on, and a great innovator in, coaching basketball.

Another person with similar attributes would probably be Arsenal's French Coach Arsene Wenger, nicknamed "Le Professeur" by fans and the British media, to reflect his studious demeanor. Wenger is responsible for innovating English soccer in the late 1990s by introducing changes in major elements such as diet and training methods. The well-known German goalkeeper Jens Lehmann, mentioned earlier in the book, vividly describes, in his 2010 book, how Wenger, his admired coach, constantly provided the players with ongoing feedback, insisting time and again on correcting "every wrong path" and "every senseless pass." As touched upon throughout the book, providing effective feedback is indeed essential to leading a team to perform at their highest capabilities.

I found this to be particularly true when investigating thirty-seven Israeli elite top athletes from basketball, team handball, soccer, and water polo (all "interactively dependent" sports). In this 1993 study—"A Three-Dimensional Crisis-Related Analysis of Perceived Coach's Behavior in Competition," published in the *Scandinavian Journal of Medicine and Science in Sports*—my colleagues and I assumed that from an athlete's point of view, a particular action on court can be either successful or not. However, we also took into account the question of whether a particular event was expected or unexpected by the athlete (remember chapter 4: people don't typically like surprises). The coaches' responses to the athletes' actions could be either positive or negative, or the coach could choose not to respond at all.

In this study, we found that nonoptimal psychological states (i.e., crisis) were strongly associated with a coach's negative response, an unsuccessful athlete's action, and unexpected events. In contrast, a positive response, a successful action, and expected events were associated with more optimal psychological states. The primary source of the coach's influence on the athlete consisted of positive and negative responses; that is, *active* modes as opposed to a lack of response. Such active responses provide highly significant feedback to the athlete. Great teachers, therefore, provide continuous feedback—and do it in the right way.

In the *Talent Code*, Dan Coyle describes quite a similar idea, based on Benjamin Bloom's classic study on talent development (1985's *Developing Talent in Young People*). Coyle states that good teachers are those that "gave much positive reinforcement and only rarely were critical of the child." He goes on to state that the teachers did, however, "set standards and expected the child to make progress, although this was largely done with approval and praise."

A closely related approach comes from the "inseparable intellectual twins" Ron Smith and Frank Smoll of the University of Washington. Since the late 1970s, these researchers have intensively investigated the role of individual differences, as well as of situational factors, in affecting leadership effectiveness, using the so-called cognitive-mediational model. This model was influenced by the authors' many years of investigating coaching behavior (in particular with young athletes) and emphasized the meaning athletes subjectively attribute to their leader's behavior.

At the very heart of this approach is the idea that coaches should try to create a positive psychosocial environment for the young athlete. Such an environment is based on the major learning principles associated with the application of positive reinforcement to enhance young athletes' mental well-being and performance outcomes. Smith and Smoll came up with the "positive approach to coaching," which presented an impressive list of do's and don'ts for the coach. For example, under the do's they include actions such as rewarding athletes immediately after a positive or successful performance, encouraging athletes immediately after they make mistakes, maintaining order by establishing clear expectations, and giving instruction. The don'ts include taking players' efforts for granted, punishing the athletes when things are going wrong, and reacting sarcastically or in a degrading manner in response to the athletes' performance.[19]

Today, Smith and Smoll are proponents of a practice they call the "mastery approach to coaching." This approach reflects both their accumulated research and practical experience. They actually aim at the development of a "master coach," or teacher, not only for children or youth, but much more generally, by trying to apply the idea to leadership practices outside of the realm of sports as well.

In my opinion, Smith and Smoll's mastery approach makes it even more evident why the role of the coach as teacher is so crucial. As a consequence, coaches are advised to regularly apply the mastery approach in order to improve the quality of coaching and become master coaches. In her seminal 2006 book *Mindset*,[20] world-renowned Stanford University Professor Carol Dweck recommends that such master coaches should praise the athletes' (or students') *effort*, not talent, emphasizing how abilities can be transformed through application. Needless to say, such motivational strategies can definitely be used complementarily with methods such as Ericsson's "deliberate practice" to improve coaching effectiveness and enhance athletes' performance.

Performers should be taught to see and interpret both challenges and failures as leverage rather than as threats and indictments. As Malcolm Gladwell puts it in *Outliers*, a setback often hides a golden opportunity that one should seek. According to Coyle, such performers then become self-regulated in the sense that they can exploit their talent to the maximum. To get to that point, however, they need to have leaders who are willing to help them see these failures and mistakes as learning opportunities.

LEARNING FROM FAILURE AND MISTAKES

> I have missed more than 9,000 shots in my career. I have lost almost 300 games. Twenty-six times I've been trusted to take the game winning shot and missed. I've failed over and over and over again in my life. And that's why I succeed.
>
> —Michael Jordan

On May 26, 1999, Manchester United played Bayern Munich in the Champions League cup final in Barcelona. Bayern scored a goal early in the game and began to clearly control the field. Toward the end of the second period it was seemingly obvious that Bayern felt the game was over and they had already won; important players were replaced so that they could receive their accolades and Bayern-ribbons were draped over the trophy in preparation for the presentation ceremony. Manu, however, did not give up, and managed to score two goals in injury time, unbelievably winning the cup. Manu's Coach Ferguson reports that he never lost confidence that his players would win.

Sir Alex attributes his ability not to lose hope until the very last moment to a positive attitude toward failure that he has cultivated over the years. In his book with Moritz, he has stated that his general approach to life "could be boiled down to the 101 seconds of injury time that it took United to turn what had looked like a 1–0 defeat by Bayern Munich in the 1999 Champions League final into a 2–1 victory." While his team was still trailing Bayern 1 to 0, Ferguson produced, in my opinion, one of the greatest half-time speeches ever:

> When that Cup is going to be presented, just remember that you can't even touch it if you're the losers—you'll be walking past it with your loser's medals, knowing someone walking behind you is going to lift the Cup.[21]

Bayern's coach at that exceptional game was Ottmar Hitzfeld, the tragic hero of the evening: for example, he was accused of playing a substantial role in that catastrophe by taking out two major players who could have controlled the ball in the remaining few minutes. Surprisingly, however, Hitzfeld took a positive lesson away from this stunning defeat.

In 2013, a special issue of the notable German soccer newspaper *Kicker Sportmagazin* was devoted to fifty years of the Bundesliga, the professional German soccer league. On this occasion, Hitzfeld was interviewed about his very successful career as a Bundesliga coach. In the interview, however, Hitzfeld didn't talk about his numerous national and international titles all that much. Instead, he focused on that 1999 Barcelona game and the effect it had on him as a leader. Though he saw the defeat as "immeasurable," he discussed how much he learned from it, specifically that "one must stand up again" after losing or failing. After learning this lesson, he made sure to impart this knowledge on all his teams throughout the rest of his career.

Of all his great achievements, including being selected twice as World Coach of the Year, Hitzfeld chose to talk about this formative experience, in which he had to mobilize all his knowledge and energy not only to overcome his own devastation, but also to help his team members cope with the difficult and trying experience of such a painful failure.

A more common approach to difficulties would have been simply doing nothing. Losses are too often taken for granted by many leaders and regarded as natural phenomena, like rainy days in the fall, snow in the winter, or earthquakes in California. Of course losses are indeed a part of the game, but successful leaders always try to perceive and interpret losses in relation to the personal development of players, processing them actively and constructively.

Without being aware of it, I assume, Hitzfeld applied a principle that in Jewish tradition is called *tikun*, which means "mending." Basically, *tikun* refers to the process of constantly refining one's mind and emotions in order to improve and make oneself increasingly better. This process never ends because nobody's perfect and we always make mistakes, but these mistakes should be leveraged for future successes. One top athlete who was extremely impressed and influenced by Ottmar Hitzfeld's coaching methods was Oliver Kahn, the well-known soccer goalie you met in part I. Kahn learned a great deal from Hitzfeld and attributed a significant portion of his success to Hitzfeld's positive influence.

On the evening of May 19, 2001, for example, Bayern Munich had to play a draw in an away game against Hamburg, in order to win the German championship. During the very last minute of the regular game, however, Bayern choked under the immense pressure and Hamburg scored a header shot, putting them up by 1 to 0. Bayern was stunned, but one person refused to give up: Oliver Kahn. Suddenly, Kahn ran out of his goal, grabbed the ball, and ran to the mid circle, screaming to his teammates: "Weiter! Weiter! Immer Weiter!" ["Go on! Go on! Always go on!"]. As he went, he literally pulled up some players who had collapsed in despair. Meanwhile, Bayern's assistant coach Michael Henke noticed how Hitzfeld's attitude changed from shock to something else. As reported by journalist Wolf Steiner, Hitzfeld clenched his fists and told Henke, "We will pull it off, we will pull it off."[22] Steiner goes on to describe how "suddenly all in the Bayern camp believe it. Skipper Stefan Effenberg shouts: 'We must try to get near their goal once or twice. Come on!'" Kahn's attitude in the first place was one that his leader, Hitzfeld, had originally instilled in him—now the feeling looped back around to his coach and the rest of the team. Bayern equalized the game in injury time and won the German championship. Four days later, they had to peak again—an awfully difficult task, which they successfully mastered: on May 23, 2001, Bayern went on to beat Valencia in the champion league final, making them European champs as well.

Just as Michael Jordan and Sir Alex Ferguson connected failure to success, Kahn draws a direct line between his team's 1999 defeat, the "trauma of Barcelona," to the team's 2001 achievements. He dedicates all of chapter 9 of his 2008 book *Ich* to the issue of failure, contending that failure includes the chance to learn something new, to further professionalize oneself. In writing about the 1999 Barcelona game, Kahn states:

> All an athlete dreams of was destroyed in a few minutes. Who knew if we would have another chance to play in the final? . . . However, retrospectively, I can tell you that we grew as a result of this defeat. We learned from this lesson, even if it had an ugly, bitter taste. Now, we had experienced, had earned the knowledge, that it is never over until the referee blows the final whistle. It is probably a trivial thing, but nobody learned and internalized it as we did.

Kahn calls this event "a club catastrophe" and contends that as a result Bayern developed an extreme ability to handle difficult situations—not as an expression of arrogance, but as a result of their own experience. With their 2001 success in Hamburg, they felt that anything was possible. Kahn attributed that achievement to their devastating loss in Barcelona, stating that "We learned our lesson and drew the right conclusions from the defeat of 1999."

Just as in sports, business leaders must be willing to confront their failures and learn to move forward with new knowledge. Sometimes these mistakes are small and potentially easy to fix; other times, they are so major they can affect how an entire company is run. For example, in 2014, General Motors began recalling cars due to faulty ignition switches that could mistakenly shut off a car's engine while people were driving. With the engine off, the airbags could not inflate or be deployed—eventually, 124 deaths were attributed to this malfunction.[23] If that wasn't bad enough, the recall itself was a debacle: starting with an initial 800,000 cars, a strategic nightmare in itself, GM ended up having to recall nearly 30 *million* vehicles worldwide.[24] Still worse yet, evidence surfaced that GM engineers had been receiving reports about problems related to the ignition switches as early as 2005.[25]

Though a longtime GM employee, CEO Mary T. Barra—the first woman to ever head a Big 3 automaker—had just taken the position two weeks before this crisis hit. In the face of shareholder pressures, the faulty ignition switch catastrophe, and the massive recall, she righted the ship and turned the company around. According to a 2016 *Wall Street Journal* article by Christopher Ross, in light of GM's failure, Barra found that there were flaws in the company's culture. She therefore brought on a former US attorney to perform an internal investigation to figure out just what went wrong and how potential negligence got so out of hand. In the process, she ended up firing fifteen employees and developing a way for engineers and others to respond quickly to potential safety violations.[26] In 2015 Barra also helped to rebrand the infamous Cadillac, increase growth in China, invest in technology, and create greater financial stability for GM overall.[27]

Without an ability to learn from missteps, mistakes, failures, and defeats, great leaders cannot fully develop their teams or themselves. These learning opportunities do more than just show you what to do correctly the next time around, they also lead to growth in character and in level of performance. LA Lakers coach Pat Riley described this idea simply, saying that his teams throughout the 1980s learned and grew from their losses.

He also believed "that the next champion always learns from the former champion how to get it done, what it takes to win."[28] Of course, it's also possible to learn lessons from other members of a *current* team—not just successful past players—those that act as peer leaders.

PEER LEADERS

> Y Respect!
>
> *—an enthusiastic, and telling, sociometric questionnaire response*

Oliver Kahn was a great athletic leader on the pitch, serving as captain of both Bayern Munich (2002–2008) and the national German team (2000–2006). Having been heavily influenced by Coach Hitzfeld, a substantial part of Kahn's leadership skills stemmed from his ability to cope well with difficult situations and failures (his "Immer Weiter" became legendary). Kahn is what is called a "peer leader"—someone who "emerges from" or "grows from within" the team. (Another good example of a peer leader is player Y from chapter 8, who had a high sociometric status; in fact, one of his teammates wrote only two words in his sociometric questionnaire: "*Y respect!*"). From my experience, a captain's ability to be accepted by the group members as a peer leader is integral to a team's task-related cohesion (which is decisive, as we saw, for the team's successful performance).

In their 2005 article "An Examination of Coach and Peer Leader Behaviors in Sport," published in *Psychology of Sport and Exercise*, Todd M. Loughead from McGill University in Montreal and James Hardy from the University of Western Ontario investigated the question of who acts as peer leaders in a wide range of team sports (e.g., ice hockey, soccer, rugby, basketball, and volleyball), wondering if it was the team captain or the teammates who exhibit leadership behaviors.[29] Loughead and Hardy found that 32.4 percent of the athletes studied indicated that team captains are the only source of peer leadership in their teams. Only 2.5 percent of the athletes indicated that teammates other than the captain served as peer leaders. Most of the athletes—65.1 percent—indicated that both team captains *and* teammates provided peer leadership to their teams. These findings indicate that although not all peer leaders are captains, all captains should have some kind of peer leadership (even if they are not the only peer leaders in their respective teams). What happens when this is not the case (that is, in the 2.5 percent of the cases)? From my experience, failure is, to a great extent, preprogrammed.

For example, back in the 1993–1994 season, I was appointed as a basketball team's sport psychologist in one of the leading first-division teams in the Israeli basketball league, before the start of the season. The team consisted of a patchwork of newly purchased players, and the question as to who should be appointed captain had arisen. I talked with some players and the coaching staff and got the impression that the big star—"K," who cost the team a lot of money—would be appropriate. However, as the team began playing, they were unable to achieve the expected level of performance. Even though he was highly respected by everyone, it turned out that K could do nothing to help solve the problems the team was facing; he simply did not have the right stuff to take the team where it needed to go to succeed.

However, I found out that another player, "N," a modest, introverted, and silent type (whose nickname was actually "the dumb one"), had the qualities and the authority needed to cope with the current problems. This situation shows that the so-called best player is not necessarily the best task-related leader. What I actually did in this particular case was to convince N to quietly undertake some of the captain's peer-leadership tasks without K noticing it. My consideration was that even if K would notice, he wouldn't mind (because he had a lot of respect for N as well), as long as his external status would be preserved. Indeed, in this respect, a noticeable improvement was observed, even though some of the team's problems were not completely solved yet (mainly because they were more of a professional nature which was beyond the scope of the captain's role).

Similarly, in any company, peer leaders are those that emerge from a group or department that help facilitate a team's performance. There are those leaders that are more formal, such as an official director, and there are those that are less so, such as a senior staff member who other employees turn to for advice or help on a regular basis. Peer leaders can be any age or at any stage in their career and you may be surprised to find that a person you least expected on your team is one of the most well-respected and sought-out peer leaders.

Mentors are somewhere in between formal and informal peer leaders, but they work with team members one-on-one to not only increase an individual's skills and knowledge—remember, great leaders act like teachers—but also to help the group function better. According to the Millennium Group International, a management consulting and professional services firm, mentoring programs have been proven highly effective in areas including retention rates, promotions, individual and group development, and in overall productivity.[30] For example, they found that 75 percent of executives indicated that mentoring played a key role in their careers; 71 percent of Fortune 500 companies use mentoring to make sure learning occurs in their organizations; 95 percent of mentees said the experience motivated them to do their very best; and 96 percent of executives consider mentoring to be an important development tool.[31] Such programs can also be official and set up by a company or organization, or some employees will simply seek out those peer leaders that they believe they can learn a great deal from.

No matter who they are, over time, peer leaders will emerge from the team. It's possible to discover this during group discussions and meetings, or just simply by quietly observing how team members interact with one another, seeing if there are one or two whom others consult consistently. Once you've identified them, make sure that you reach out to them so they know that you are willing to support them and work with them to help the team succeed. And, as mentioned earlier, keep your ego in check—there is no reason to be threatened by other leaders in the group: you're all working together toward the same goal.

SUMMARY

As stated in the epigraph of this chapter, Pat Riley once said that the appropriate job description of a coach boils down to one word: "insanity."

I believe this term can be applied to leaders in general. However, to make this job less "insane," attention should be paid to some important leadership values.

The three major leadership functions essential to any sports organization are nearly identical to those in a business setting: developing the team and its talents, interacting with individual team members, and producing positive relationships within the team.

The attributes of a great leader include flexibility and adaptability to the environment; humility and modesty; and the ability to act as a teacher. Coach John Wooden regularly comes to mind as a team leader who embodied this idea. Business leaders like Larry Page of Google, Steve Jobs of Apple, and Mary T. Barra of GM share similar attributes, shown by the exceptional success of their companies and organizations.

Leadership is not simply management, as it is imperative to support the group by providing and establishing the fundamental organizational mission and formulating strategies for its implementation. There are common values that contribute to a leader's success, and his or her team's performance, that must be developed and maintained continuously.

Learning from failure is certainly one, whether you're the head of a company like General Motors or Apple—both who were on the brink of destruction before coming back as major powerhouses in their field—or Bayern Munich's Coach Ottmar Hitzfeld.

A focus on deliberate practice and effective feedback is also needed, no matter if you're a head coach or a peer leader; a middle manager with fifteen people under you; or a mentor to a younger business associate.

DAILY PRACTICES

As an Individual

- Be flexible at work and in your own career path.
- Maintain a sense of humility—don't let your ego get in the way of making the right decisions for your company or team.

- No matter the circumstances, treat failure and mistakes as opportunities to learn and progress.

As a Leader

- Help team members learn new skills and develop new expertise.
- Provide effective feedback on your team's strengths, weaknesses, and general performance.
- Identify peer leaders within your team and give them the proper support and tools to increase overall team performance.

NOTES

1. NBA Encyclopedia Playoff Edition, "The NBA at 50: Pat Riley: A Conversation with the Heat Head Coach," *NBA.com*, April 16, 1996, www.nba.com/encyclopedia/playoff_edition.html.
2. Mike Kennedy and Mark Stewart, "Derek Jeter: What They Say," *JockBio.com*, 2011, www.jockbio.com/Bios/Jeter/Jeter_they-say.html.
3. Jason Fell, "Farewell Derek Jeter, A True Role Model and Leader," *Entrepreneur*, September 25, 2014, www.entrepreneur.com/article/237788.
4. Mike Kennedy and Mark Stewart, "Derek Jeter: What They Say," *JockBio.com*, 2011, www.jockbio.com/Bios/Jeter/Jeter_they-say.html.
5. Jim Merrifield, "Derek Jeter—5 Keys to Leadership Success," *AIIM Community*, October 15, 2014, http://community.aiim.org/blogs/jim-merrifield/2014/10/15/derek-jeter---5-keys-to-leadership-success.
6. Howard Bryant, "True Story," *ESPN.com*, May 17, 2013, www.espn.com/mlb/story/_/id/9227155/new-york-yankees-shortstop-derek-jeter-greatness-goes-numbers-espn-magazine.
7. A. Ferguson and M. Moritz, *Leading: Learning from Life and My Years at Manchester United* (New York: Hachette, 2015).
8. In reference to his winning three-pointer against Montepaschi Siena, in which Coach Pini Gershon gave him credit (and the ball) despite an embarrassing streak of previous misses.
9. "Eins: Eins-Talk," broadcast on the TV.NRW channel on February 5, 2004.
10. P. Chelladurai, "A Personal Journey in Theorizing in Sport Management," *Sport Management Review* 16 (2013): 22–28.
11. Steven Levy, "Google's Larry Page on Why Moon Shots Matter," *Wired*, January 17, 2013, www.wired.com/2013/01/ff-qa-larry-page/all/.

12. Nicholas Carlson, "The Untold Story of Larry Page's Incredible Comeback," *Business Insider*, April 24, 2014, www.businessinsider.com/larry-page-the-untold-story-2014-4?page=2.

13. Joel Siegel, "When Steve Jobs Got Fired By Apple," *ABC News*, October 6, 2011, http://abcnews.go.com/Technology/steve-jobs-fire-company/story?id=14683754.

14. M. Bar-Eli, O. Lowengart, M. Tsukahara, and R. D. Fosbury, "Tsukahara's Vault and Fosbury's Flop: A Comparative Analysis of Two Great Inventions," *International Journal of Innovation Management* 12 (March 2008): 21–39.

15. Mike Puma, "Wizard of Westwood," *ESPN.com*, accessed May 2017, www.espn.com/classic/biography/s/Wooden_John.html.

16. J. R. Wooden, *Practical Modern Basketball* (New York: Wiley, 1980). Wooden's teaching practices were also intensively investigated elsewhere; see R. Gallimore and R. Tharp, "What a Coach Can Teach a Teacher, 1975–2004: Reflections and Reanalysis of John Wooden's Teaching Practices," *The Sport Psychologist* 18 (June 2004): 119–137.

17. N. Bar-Eli, M. Bar-Eli, G. Tenenbaum, and C. Forlin, "The Tutoring Process and Its Manifestation in the Classroom Behavior of Tutors and Tutees," *British Educational Research Journal* 24 (January 1998): 283–300.

18. Laura Vanderkam, "Should Strong Leaders Also Be Great Teachers?" *Fast Company*, September 17, 2014, www.fastcompany.com/3035631/the-future-of-work/should-strong-leaders-also-be-great-teachers.

19. The principles of the positive approach to coaching are described in F. L. Smoll and R. E. Smith, "Leadership Research in Young Athletes," in *Psychological Foundations of Sport*, eds. J. M. Silva and R. S. Weinberg (Champaign, IL: Human Kinetics, 1984), 371–386. My Hebrew textbook in which the do's and don'ts are presented is M. Bar-Eli and G. Tenenbaum, *The Psychology of Sport and Exercise* (Netanya: Wingate Institute [Hebrew], 1996). It should be noted that Smoll and Smith updated and extended their leadership model over the years (e.g., to talk about "mastery approach to coaching"); see, for example, R. E. Smith and F. L. Smoll, "Social-Cognitive Approach to Coaching Behaviors," in *Social Psychology in Sport*, eds. S. Jowett and D. Lavalee (Champaign, IL: Human Kinetics, 2007), 75–90.

20. C. S. Dweck, *Mindset* (New York: Ballantine, 2006).

21. A. Ferguson and M. Moritz, *Leading* (London: Hodder, 2015).

22. Bundesliga Fanatic Staff, "Bundesliga Rewind—Schalke and the Four Minute Championship—2000/01," *Bundesliga Fanatic*, May 5, 2011, http://bundesligafanatic.com/bundesliga-rewind-%E2%80%93-schalke-and-the- four-minute-championship.

23. David Shepardson, "GM Compensation Fund Completes Review with 124 Deaths," *The Detroit News*, August 24, 2015, www.detroitnews.com/story/business/autos/general-motors/2015/08/24/gm-ignition-fund-completes-review/32287697/.

24. Jeff Bennett, "GM to Recall 8.45 Million More Vehicles in North America," *Wall Street Journal*, June 30, 2014, www.wsj.com/articles/gm-to-recall-7-6-million-more- vehicles-in-u-s-1404153705.

25. Sonari Glinton, "The Long Road to GM's Ignition Switch Recall," *NPR*, March 31, 2014, www.npr.org/2014/03/31/297312252/the-long-road-to-gms-ignition-switch-recall.

26. Christopher Ross, "A Day in the Life of GM CEO Mary Barra," *Wall Street Journal*, April 25, 2016, www.wsj.com/articles/a-day-in-the-life-of-gm-ceo-mary-barra-1461601044.

27. "The World's Most Powerful People: #65 Mary Barra," *Forbes*, 2016, www.forbes.com/profile/mary-barra/.

28. NBA Encyclopedia Playoff Edition, "The NBA at 50: Pat Riley: A Conversation with the Heat Head Coach."

29. M. T. Loughead and J. Hardy, "An Examination of Coach and Peer Leader Behaviors in Sport," *Psychology of Sport and Exercise* 6 (2005): 303–312.

30. The Millennium Group International, "Employee Mentoring Programs: Benefits/Risk Assessment and Business Case," *TMGI.net*, 2009, www.tmgi.net/white_paper/employee_mentoring_white_paper.

31. Ibid.

PART IV

Enhancing Your State of Mind

10

Mental Preparation I

*Incorporating Imagery and Visualization
into a Daily Routine*

I am accustomed to sleep and in my dreams to imagine the same things
that lunatics imagine when awake.

—RENÉ DESCARTES

In Western culture imagination is often dismissed as irrational; how often do we hear expressions like "stop dreaming, be realistic" or "dreaming is childish, you're an adult"? However, imagination is vital: for example, what happens to you when you visualize yourself conducting an important job interview or you imagine sleeping with an attractive partner? What happens when you let yourself dream about the future—your plans, hopes, and aspirations? History has recorded countless famous dreamers, some of whom made a major impact on the world around them. Think about Martin Luther King Jr. and his "I have a dream" speech delivered on August 28, 1963 at the Lincoln Memorial in Washington, DC. King's remarks that day were integral to pushing the US civil rights movement forward and his words still ring true today. Then there is John Lennon's "Imagine," which inspired people throughout the world with its call for peace and harmony. And there are the dream interpreters like Sigmund Freud or, much earlier, the Biblical figure Joseph of the "technicolor coat," who interpreted the Pharaoh's dreams.

In science, the most notable dreamer was probably Albert Einstein (1879–1955). When he won the Nobel Prize in 1921, he credited his own boyhood idea of riding on a beam of light with a spark as playing a pivotal role in the development of his theory of special relativity. Einstein thereby acknowledged the immense power of imagination in the scientific process. Furthermore, he regularly employed his imagination when utilizing what he called "thought experiments"—experiments carried out solely in the mind—to work out complex ideas. (If you want to try out a typical Einstein thought experiment, visualize yourself riding in an elevator that is in free-fall, which is a vivid and convincing example that gravity and acceleration are one and the same.)

Another famous example of the power of imagination in science comes from the prominent German chemist August Kekule (1829–1896). In 1865, Kekule was the first to suggest that the structure of benzene contains a six-membered ring of carbon atoms with alternating single and double bonds. Kekule reported later that he had discovered the ring shape of the benzene molecule after having a daydream about the cyclicality and circularity of the ancient Egyptian-Greek symbol Ouroboros, which depicts a serpent or dragon eating its own tail.

From a technical perspective, psychologists often use the terms "imagery," "visualization," or "mental rehearsal" as if they were the same to account for the systematic, controllable, deliberate, conscious, functional, and purposeful use of imagination for enhancing one's performance. However, this is inaccurate, because "visualization," which refers only to the sense of vision, is a *narrower* term, while "imagery" involves the kinesthetic, auditory, tactile, and olfactory senses as well. "Mental rehearsal" is *broader* because it encompasses a variety of other mental techniques employed beyond imagery to enhance performance (which I further discuss in chapter 11).

Imagery is, in fact, a form of simulation that is similar to a real sensory experience, but the entire process takes place solely in the mind. Imagery enables individuals to recreate previous positive experiences and picture new ones in order to prepare themselves mentally for performance. Think, for example, of a basketball player, imaging herself penetrating to the basket: she can not only "see" this scenario in her imagination, but also "feel" the bodily sensations of the associated movements, "hear" the sounds of the spectators, "smell" the stench of the opponents defending the basket, and even "taste" the saltiness of sweat in her mouth.

Strangely enough, even though imagery and visualization techniques seem to work, as evidenced from extensive research in this area, to be honest with you, psychologists don't know exactly why. Despite the fact that no less than *eight* theories have been suggested to explain why real stimuli and imagined ones have similar effects on our consciousness, almost no empirical support has been found for most of them.

IMAGERY THEORIES

The effective use of imagery is an art and a science.

—MARK H. ANSHEL[1]

One theory on why mental imagery is effective was suggested in 1874 by the English physician, invertebrate zoologist, and physiologist William Benjamin Carpenter (1813–1885). At that time, he published a book titled *Principles of Mental Physiology* in which he proposed the "ideomotor principle of imagery" as part of his "psychoneuromuscular theory." According to this principle, imagery facilitates the learning of motor skills because vividly imagined events innervate the muscles in somewhat the same way that physically practicing a movement does.

In the 1930s, R. S. Sackett provided another explanation as to why imagery may work in his so-called symbolic learning theory.[2] This approach states that mental practice and imagery cause individuals to literally plan their actions in advance. They cognitively consider motor sequences, task goals, and alternative solutions before a physical response is required. Imagery therefore helps in developing a mental blueprint by creating a motor program in the central nervous system. According to the theory, imagining what you believe must be done to achieve a goal can improve your performance.

In 1979 Professor Peter J. Lang, a member of the University of Wisconsin, Madison faculty at the time, promoted the "bioinformational theory," which assumes an image is a functionally organized set of propositions stored by the brain. The theory contends that a description of an image consists on both stimulus propositions (i.e., statements that describe specific stimulus features of the scenario to be imagined) and response propositions (i.e., statements that describe the imager's response to the particular scenario), which are designed to produce physiological activity.[3] In fact, imagery instructions that contain response propositions elicit far greater physiological responses than do imagery instructions that contain only stimulus propositions.

In a 2014 study, a group of German psychologists under the leadership of my good friend Professor Thomas Schack of Bielefeld University provided some evidence for Sackett's approach, using the term "mental representations."[4] That same year, however, in an up-to-date review of imagery, Jennifer Cumming and Sarah E. Williams from the University of Birmingham (UK) contended that "each theory has helped shape our understanding of imagery in different ways, but with the exception of the bioinformational theory, few of these have received empirical support."[5]

Cumming and Williams themselves propose an explanation, which is related to the way neural networks function. These authors claim that it is "the most contemporary explanation behind imagery's effectiveness."[6] They proposed that the effectiveness of imagery can be explained primarily by the partial overlap of some neural networks. These overlapping networks are responsible for the planning and execution of motor movements, for example, during both imagery and actual skill execution. This means that some areas of the brain that are active while visualizing a particular skill are also active when the skill is performed. This partial overlap has been referred to as a "functional equivalence" that exists between the visualized and the actual activities. Based on these similarities, it has also been suggested that imagery might be useful in priming skilled performance. In this case, neural networks are enabled to activate more readily or more accurately during actual task performance.

Though these are just a handful of the many differing theories, no matter how exactly the process works, it has been demonstrated that imagery can be used to improve concentration, control emotional responses, acquire and practice techniques and strategies, and build confidence—a variety of skills necessary to enhance our performance. To be effective, images should first of all be vivid, involving as many senses as possible and create, or recreate, the feelings associated with the skill to be learned or the task to be executed. In addition, the images should be controllable in the sense that they do what we want them to do. To increase performance, you must understand how you can effectively use imagery techniques to your advantage.

PICTURING POSITIVITY

> Once you replace negative thoughts with positive ones, you'll start having positive results.
>
> —WILLIE NELSON

When we use our imagination to execute a skill or action from our own vantage point, the perspective is referred to as "internal" or "first-person." However, when we view ourselves from the perspective of an outside observer, as if we are watching ourselves in a movie or video, the perspective is referred to as "external" or "third-person."

Initially, sport psychologists believed the internal perspective was more advantageous since it was supposedly a closer approximation to reality. Studies on that particular point, however, turned out to be inconclusive. Moreover, to date, athletes are more accustomed now than ever before to watching themselves externally, mainly owing to more extensive TV coverage and the advent of digital video on smartphones and other handheld devices. What I usually do with the athletes I consult is to advise them to start with the internal perspective, but if they don't feel comfortable with it, to then switch to the external perspective. Sometimes, they even use both depending on each athlete's individual preferences, which neither they nor I can tell in advance, but only discover through trial and error. All in all, however, whether performers use an internal or external image is much less important than its vividness—being as close to reality as possible, using all sensory modalities—and controllability—the ability to deliberately use the technique on command.

The events, actions, or successes you imagine should have a positive focus; that is, they should end up with a positive outcome (e.g., in sports, the performer successfully gets on base, kicks a field goal, or makes a basket; in business, the performer successfully completes a project, closes a deal, or aces a presentation). An important part of this positive focus is coping with mistakes. As the old saying goes, nobody is perfect and everybody makes mistakes, so realistic imagery should also be used to successfully cope with mistakes. For example, if basketball players visualize making foul shots, they should also see themselves missing some. From there they need to imagine recovering immediately by successfully shooting the next free throws. Similarly, if a new project goes awry at the office, it's necessary to imagine the development of a way to get it back on track.

Paradoxically, in order to attain the desired positive outcome, it is often necessary to focus not on the outcome itself, but on the process which leads to that outcome. Focusing only on the outcome may produce an unnecessary "*must*urbation effect" ("I must do it, I must do it, I must do it . . ."), which can be dangerous as it leads to self-imposed pressure. That is why I always recommend that athletes focus first on the *execution* of a movement or task. This does not exclude imagining the positive outcome of the movement, of course, but if you execute the movement perfectly, the positive outcome will usually follow.

For example, in the mid-1980s the late NBA basketball player and all-time leading NCAA Division I point scorer Pistol Pete Maravich came to Wingate to give a workshop to basketball coaches. Before starting, he shot a number of three-pointers. He'd simply shoot and turn away. The coaches, of course, followed the trajectory of the ball to the end. After about a dozen of these, Pistol Pete said, "Why are you looking at the ball?

If I threw it correctly, it's going to go in almost every time!" And it did. Maravich showed the coaches why it's important to focus mainly on visualizing an accurate process of execution, which will be followed by an increased probability of positive outcomes.

I had a similar personal experience when working with an excellent basketball player who I will refer to here as "M." I first learned to admire M because of the exceptional reasons he had for coming to and working with a sport psychologist. He was already twenty-eight years old, playing for a leading club and regularly for the national team. Although he didn't feel that he had any particular psychological problems, his wife convinced him to see *if* he could learn anything from, and be improved by, a sport psychologist—a unique motivation among elite athletes to begin with.

At that time, M was the ultimate sixth player on the team, much like Tony Kukoc from the Bulls discussed in chapter 8. However, like every sub, he was highly motivated to enter the starting five, and he hoped improving his game would increase the probability of becoming a starting five player (not being aware of the sixth man paradox we discussed in chapter 8).

While working with M, I soon discovered that he had a very high percentage of sinking free throws (80 percent to 90 percent on a regular basis in contest), so we did not touch those at all—it was one of those times in which doing nothing was optimal. More generally, through his rich experience and natural wisdom, M had developed self-made, intuitive ways of successfully regulating his arousal level on court, which functioned well and with which he was quite satisfied. After a while, however, we found one particular problem that he wanted to try and solve with my help. M complained that he had difficulties shooting the ball immediately after receiving a pass. More specifically, M contended that his problem was the extra 0.5 seconds needed in order to release the ball to the basket. Firing the ball too slowly means the defense has enough time to organize; the faster you shoot, the greater your advantage while they are still scrambling. Thus, 0.5 seconds was crucial.

After thinking it over, I realized the problem could be conceptualized as one of "attentional shift." Attention to external stimuli can be either broad, distributed among different environmental cues necessary for successful task performance, or narrow, focused on a specific target in the environment. Performance on court, however, often requires quick shifts between the two—which was precisely M's problem.

What M and I figured out together was that when running on offense, he would apply a broad or distributed attentional focus, causing him to concentrate mainly on reading the game and assessing the situation for relevant information, such as where to locate himself in order to be the best passing option for the playmaker. However, when he got the ball, he had to shift to a narrow attentional focus, locking onto a specific target in the environment—the basket. We therefore developed a procedure to cope with this problem, which was essentially based on two pillars:

1. Scenarios or scripts in which M imagined himself time and again getting the ball and shooting, including an emphasis on conducting the attentional shift as fast as possible
2. While on offense, he began to look at the basket from time to time even before getting the ball; I call it the "Abu-Samra procedure"—in honor of my decision to run to that particular bunker before the MiG attack that saved my life (discussed in chapter 1).

The combination of imagery techniques, picturing a positive outcome through execution of a movement, and the Abu-Samra procedure proved itself highly successful. After a short while, even basketball commentators in the Israeli media noticed his much quicker ball release and wondered how he did it. Soon enough, when another player was injured, M received his chance to get off the bench on a regular basis, and he became a solid, successful starter *despite* the sixth-man paradox.

Similar to the discussion in chapter 3 about short-term and long-term goals, visualization and imagery techniques can be employed in regards to immediate actions and for future aspirations. For example, you can visualize your next play while on the basketball court the same as you can visualize the next point you want to make in an office argument or debate. If you're preparing to meet a client for lunch or dinner, it's possible to picture in your mind how the conversation will proceed, what information you'd like to share or receive, and even how you'll comport yourself and your posture.

Imagining long-term success and performance is equally important. Take media mogul, philanthropist, and ultra-successful business icon Oprah Winfrey. *The Oprah Winfrey Show* ran from 1986 through 2011 and remains the highest-rated program of its kind in history. Winfrey is the chairwoman and CEO of both a production company and a network station, and she is worth a whopping $3.1 billion.[7] However, she was born into a low-income family in rural Mississippi, then raised in an inner-city neighborhood in Milwaukee, where she had to overcome a great deal of adversity.

In part, Winfrey attributes her nearly unparalleled success to positive thinking and visualization. When she was young, she would watch her grandmother nearly work her fingers to the bone, and Winfrey would repeatedly say to herself, "My life won't be like this, it will be better."[8] On her TV show, she regularly showcased success stories related to positive thinking and even discussed the creation of her own personal vision board—a board or piece of paper on which a person pastes or tacks up cut out images, pictures, phrases, and drawings that serve as an inspiration and representation of success.[9]

Such positive visualization techniques can only increase your performance, however, if you're willing to put in the time and effort. You can't *occasionally* imagine success—it needs to be repetitive, hardwired into your thoughts and actions. You must therefore try to develop an imagery routine and visualize success every single day.

EVERYDAY IMAGERY ROUTINES

> If you mentally see yourself in a scenario, you'll start to make decisions in your life that get you there.
>
> —Sarah Blakely

Imagery should be built into your daily routine and conducted in "real time," meaning that the time spent on imagining a particular skill or action should be equal to the time it takes to execute the skill or action in reality. It is especially effective when preceded by some kind of relaxation techniques (which I discuss and recommend in detail in chapter 11). Therefore, when you develop your own imagery-training program, try to "mentally warm up" first: choose a proper setting to begin with and try to combine imagery with a relaxation exercise. Maintain a positive approach by focusing on positive outcomes; however, don't forget to rehearse the process of optimal task execution. Furthermore, use imagery to prepare for the eventuality of making mistakes (be realistic: "nobody's perfect!"), but also to effectively cope with them.

As mentioned, imagery must be as vivid as possible and involve all the kinesthetic, auditory, tactile, and olfactory senses. So when developing a routine, first start by picturing the goal. What exactly do you want to accomplish and how do you see yourself succeeding? Remember, you want to imagine positive outcomes. Figure out where you are most comfortable when visualizing your success—is it at home? At the office? Maybe while you're going for a walk? In principle, there are no limitations as to when and where to utilize imagery: before or after you prepare for an event; before, during, and after the event itself; and during breaks in action (as discussed with "visualization holes" in the following section). In short, to produce quality training, use imagery whenever and wherever it suits you and helps you most.

Imagery is often invoked before an upcoming competition because athletes like to review exactly what they should do during a game or event. It is very important, however, that the process is not rushed or forced, but rather fit comfortably into the individual's pre-event routine. From my experience, integrating visualization and imagery into regular stretching exercises right before a contest, for example, is more than welcome by many athletes. The basketball teams I've worked with were proponents of this method and would perform this part of their routine directly on the court before playing an opponent. Such techniques help Olympians and other top athletes, such as soccer champ Carli Lloyd, swimmer Michael

Phelps, track and field athlete Jessica Ennis Hill, and tennis star Chris Evert, perform at their highest levels.

Jens Lehmann, an athlete you are undoubtedly familiar with at this point, also employed imagery and visualization regularly during his active career as goalkeeper. For example, in a June 30, 2006 game, the national soccer teams of Germany and Argentina met in Berlin in a tense quarter final game of the 2006 World Cup that ended 1 to 1 after extra time. In the penalty shootout Lehmann was the hero of the day, saving two out of four penalty kicks and thereby putting Germany on the cusp of victory. In his 2010 book, Lehmann describes how for about ten minutes before he took an afternoon nap, right after lunch, he regularly applied a routine comprised of elements from different mental preparation techniques, including imagery.[10] He describes how he visualized different game situations in which he successfully managed to stop the ball, catch it, and return it quickly into the game. On the occasion of that particular 2006 World Cup game against Argentina, Lehmann claims that he literally dreamed of how he would stop the decisive penalty kicks in the shootout; he maintains that this procedure, and particularly the amazing dream, helped him immensely in concentrating on—and successfully managing—the decisive penalties in that game.

Anecdotes such as this one are frequently reported in elite sports. They are encouraging, especially because they emphasize the importance that elite athletes attribute not only to imagery, but to mental preparation in general as an integral part of their success. Top athletes such as Formula One star Jenson Button and golfer Jack Nicklaus consistently use mental preparation routines, including imagery. In his 2008 book, goalkeeper Oliver Kahn explains in great detail how his coach Ottmar Hitzfeld (both whom you met earlier) insisted on the team maintaining a tight, strict routine of game preparation, which began one day before the game and lasted until the first whistle. Moreover, Hitzfeld also insisted that every player develop his own personal pregame mental preparation routine, which often included imagery. Kahn claims and reiterates that having a pregame mental preparation routine that includes imagery and visualization is one of the most important secrets of success.

Sara Blakely, the founder of the undergarment shapewear and linge-rie company Spanx, would likely agree. Take a moment to consider this fact: Blakely invested her $5,000 life savings to start the Atlanta-based company in 2000, and as of 2016, at age forty-five, Blakely had a net worth of over $1 billion.[11] Additionally, in 2015, she expanded outside of Spanx and became a co-owner of the Atlanta Hawks basketball team. Similar to Oprah Winfrey, Blakely attributes a considerable part of her success to imagination and the use of visualization—and she's not afraid to admit it. In an April 12, 2012 *Wall Street Journal* article, "Can You Get Rich By Visualizing Yourself Rich?," journalist Robert Frank tells readers that Blakely once stated, "I believe you can take mental snapshots of your future and what success looks like to you. If you mentally see yourself in a scenario, you'll start to make decisions in your life that get you there."

As an individual, visualizing your success can lead to positive concrete results. For example, say you need to prepare for a critical conversation with a coworker. Maybe you're in the position of having to let someone go or, on the opposite end of the spectrum, maybe you're asking for a promotion or other type of increased compensation. These types of con-versations can be highly stressful, so in an effort to hit your optimal level of stress and motivation (as discussed in chapters 1 and 2) you may want to employ visualization. Prepare by using as much detail as possible to imagine the expected situation: outline where the event will take place, the feelings and thoughts you may have, and what you have to do to achieve the desired result. Collect as much information about the situation as you can in advance.

For example, if you plan to ask for a promotion, make sure that you're able to identify why you deserve the additional responsibilities and com-pensation that come with the position. Figure out your boss's preferences; think about potential arguments that could be raised against your request, and then go into that meeting with an idea of how to reply to an array of responses. You should even keep the temperature in the room in mind; consider how to best dress for the conversation, and decide if you want to have a glass of water or a cup of coffee handy during the discussion. In short, consider yourself an agent for the FBI, CIA—or if you like, MI5,

MI6, or even the Mossad: you're collecting intelligence. Based on this information, try to imagine numerous scenarios of how such a discussion will play out and how you can use those scenarios to your advantage.

Now that you have all this information, compile a script that outlines the conversation you expect to have (the more intelligence you have collected the closer to reality the script will be). Once you have completed preparing this conversation in writing, you can record yourself to get a better idea of how you sound or might come across (the same technique can be employed before giving a presentation, for example). As most people do, you may want to listen to yourself and rehearse your imagery procedure as close to the event as possible. As you continue to use this imagery technique, you will likely improve on other psychological factors, such as your self-confidence and your ability to handle stressful tasks and mistakes.

In addition to visualizing your own success, if you visualize the success of your whole team everyday, it will help you all perform at higher levels. Compare your current situation with an ideal future situation and develop a process to attain the goals you visualize. Imagine the perfect team, then think carefully about how your *current* team interacts, who is the best at certain tasks or functions, and how everyone works together. Consider the disparities between perfection and the current state and find ways to close those gaps. Though you should consistently be working on your personal and team performance, a great time to step back and truly visualize success is during breaks in the action, which I refer to as "holes."

Visualization Holes

For athletes to stay on track during a competition, they must psychoregulate themselves. To do this, they are advised to use "dead time" or "holes" to visualize and prepare for what's ahead. From a psychological point of view, the game of basketball, for example, is a "game of holes" in which potentially devastating "nothings" may occur. One of the things I always do when working with players is explore these holes in the game and figure out how they can be filled appropriately with imagery-based

routines, helping the athletes self-regulate their psychological states during a contest.

One huge hole is created when an athlete sits on the bench during a
game. This situation occurs increasingly often in current elite sport where
the success of top teams is dependent, to a great extent, on the depth of the
team's bench (that is, on the number of good, available substitutes), and on
the ability of the coach to rotate players between or within games. A bench
can be a terrible place for the player, a real horror: nobody likes to sit on
the bench—even those players who are experts in coming off the bench.
If you ask players how they feel when sitting on the bench, they usually
report that they become frustrated and angry. When I have asked players
what they do about these feelings while sitting on the bench, the answer
is usually "nothing."

I therefore try to first help players reframe the subjective perception
associated with the experience of sitting on the bench. That is, I convey
to them the message that this hole actually provides an excellent opportunity to recover and better prepare themselves for entering the game.
Then, after having convinced them, I suggest a bench routine comprised
of different elements from various psycho-regulation techniques with an
emphasis on imagery and visualization. Such a bench routine includes
two essential parts:

1. Maintenance of a "readiness state"—that is, appropriate awareness and alertness to what is going on, while sitting on
   the bench;
2. Getting up—what the players do from the moment the coach
   calls them to enter the game until they actually start to play.

One great athlete who had a substantial influence on my development
of the "bench psychology" used by many of the athletes I have advised
was the Norwegian "Baby Face Assassin" striker Ole Gunnar Solskjaer
from Manchester United. Solskjaer made a living coming into matches as
a substitute late in a game and scoring decisive goals (such as the winning
goal scored in injury time—the 93rd minute—against Bayern in the 1999

final, which we discussed in chapter 9). This unique ability had to do with something very special in Solskjaer's mental preparation: former Manu Manager Sir Alex Ferguson remarked that Solskjaer would sit on the bench and study the game without taking his eyes off the action. Instead of wasting his time, Solskjaer used it to improve his upcoming performance on the pitch, thereby building his reputation as a "super sub."

In a report from 2012, Solskjaer—an active manager in the Norwegian soccer league by that time—is described as someone who tries to build the teams he coaches around players who are strong mentally (like he himself was as a player). The reporter continues:

> That was such an obvious part of his own make-up as a player and even his time on the bench as a regular substitute with Manchester United was put to good use as he famously spent it intently studying the opposition . . . That was not something he did lightly but with a very specific view to making the best of any situation he found himself in: "I probably didn't analyze the whole game. I had to think about myself, how can I do the most damage for the opposition if I come on? I sat there and I studied football games but I didn't exactly analyze their strikers . . . Instead, I would pay attention to what the defenders and full-backs were doing wrong."[12]

Instead of just sitting on the bench, getting frustrated and angry, Solskjaer saw this downtime as an opportunity to excel. He *imagined* what he would do the moment he entered the game. By doing so he kept himself aware and alert, having no problem whatsoever in getting up whenever called, going onto the field, and scoring crucial goals.

Even in today's hectic rat race, there are plenty of times when holes present themselves, providing an opportunity to visualize and imagine success. Sometimes these holes are quite brief—a morning commute, a coffee break, a quick walk around the office or floor—but they can still be utilized to picture the completion of projects and tasks, or even something as simple as a conference call you're dreading or an e-mail that you keep meaning to respond to. You'll also inevitably experience some type of down time at the end of a large project or a business cycle. That time is great for going over your past successes (or failures) with your colleagues or employees, but it's equally important to discuss what you see as steps forward for your team and the overall business. Let people know what you envision for the rest of the year, the following year, and five years out. Explain what you see when you talk about success, and help them visualize it as well. Regularly employing this type of "collective imagining" will keep you and the individual members of your team in tune and prepared for whatever comes next.

SUMMARY

Imagination, visualization, and dreaming (yes, even daydreaming!) are vital to enhancing performance. Imagery can be used to improve concentration, control emotional responses, acquire and practice techniques and strategies, and build confidence. Regardless of the differing theories on why the process works, it's been demonstrated time and again that integrating imagery and visualization techniques into a regular routine will help you reach your goals.[13]

Not only should mental imagery be built into your everyday life, but it is especially effective when preceded by some kind of relaxation. Taking a few minutes at the beginning of the day to take some deep breaths will get you started on the right foot.

Imagery should be vivid, involving as many senses as possible and creating, or recreating, the feelings associated with the skill to be learned or the task to be executed. Despite the fact that imagery is frequently referred to as visualization, it also involves the kinesthetic, auditory, tactile, and olfactory senses as well.

Visualizing the completion of a project, closing a deal, or acing a presentation will contribute to your success just like such techniques help Olympians and other top athletes, such as soccer champ Carli Lloyd, swimmer Michael Phelps, track and field athlete Jessica Ennis Hill, and tennis star Chris Evert.

Team athletes on the bench have the time to both maintain a ready state while also paying attention to all the details on the court. Similarly, taking a step back to visualize success in your career (say a move from assistant to senior manager over time) or a team of employees that works like a well-oiled machine, will help you relegate tasks and assign responsibilities. Down time on the court should be regularly used for such imagery, just as down time during a business cycle or after the completion of a large project can be a great time to take stock, recuperate, and visualize your future success.

DAILY PRACTICES

As an Individual

- Develop a routine that utilizes vivid, controlled visualization techniques every day.
- Despite Western culture's dismissal of the idea, don't be hesitant or afraid to use your imagination to improve your performance   remember that it's worked for everyone from Michael Phelps to Oprah Winfrey.
- Focus on properly and successfully performing an action or task, not necessarily on the outcome.

As a Leader

- Whether using an internal or external perspective, make sure the events, actions, and successes you visualize have a positive focus.
- Think about your team's (or company's) shortcomings, compare them to the ideal team you envision, and develop ways to close the gaps between the two.
- Use holes throughout the day or at the end of a project or initiative to hone in on what you envision for future success, both for yourself as an individual and your team as a whole.

NOTES

1. M. H. Anshel, *Sport Psychology: From Theory to Practice*, 5th ed. (San Francisco: Benjamin Cummings, 2011).
2. R. S. Sackett, "The Influence of Symbolic Rehearsal Upon the Retention of a Maze Habit," *Journal of General Psychology* 13 (1934): 113–128.
3. P. J. Lang, "A Bioinformational Theory of Emotional Imagery," *Psychophysiology* 17 (November 1979): 495–512.
4. C. Frank, W. M. Land, C. Popp, and T. Schack, "Mental Representations and Mental Practice: Experimental Investigation on the Functional Links Between Motor Memory and Motor Imagery," *PLOS ONE* 9(4) (April 2014): e95175.
5. J. Cumming and S. E. Williams, "Imagery," in *Encyclopedia of Sport and Exercise Psychology*, vol. 1, eds. R. C. Eklund and G. Tenenbaum (Thousand Oaks, CA: Sage, 2014), 369–373.
6. Ibid.
7. "The World's 100 Most Powerful Women: #21 Oprah Winfrey," *Forbes*.com, August 24, 2016, www.forbes.com/profile/oprah-winfrey/.
8. Anna Williams, "8 Successful People Who Use The Power Of Visualization," *MindBodyGreen*, July 8, 2015, www.mindbodygreen.com/0-20630/8-successful-people-who-use-the-power-of-visualization.html.
9. Ibid.
10. Jens Lehmann, *Der Wahnsinn Liegt Auf Dem* Platz [Madness Lies on the Pitch] (Cologne: Kiepenheuer & Witsch, 2010).
11. "The World's 100 Most Powerful Women: #90 Sara Blakely," *Forbes*.com, August 24, 2016, www.forbes.com/profile/sara-blakely/.
12. Amy Lawrence, "Old Celebration Gets New Outing as Ole Gunnar Solskjaer Sparkles Again," the *Guardian*, November 10, 2012, www.theguardian.com/football/blog/2012/nov/10/celebration-ole-gunnar-solskjaer-molde.
13. J. Cumming and S. E. Williams, "The Role of Imagery in Performance," in *Handbook of Sport and Performance Psychology*, ed. S. Murphy (New York: Oxford University Press, 2012), 213–232.

11

Mental Preparation II

Basic Principles of Effective Psycho-Regulation

Except for our own thoughts, there is nothing absolutely in our power.
—RENÉ DESCARTES

bout three and a half decades ago, I served for a short while as the sport psychologist for the German National Basketball team alongside the legendary coach mentioned often in this book, Ralph Klein. When discussing the issue of why players missed foul shots and what could be done to alleviate this problem, Ralph would say, "They should develop routines and practice them." However, this is only partly true: although it is crucial to have a routine, its content is of utmost importance.

I have already emphasized that I am in favor of Ericsson's (and Syed's) deliberate practice, or Coyle's deep practice, but an appropriate application of these approaches would mean that in addition to the amount being crucial (i.e., the so-called "10,000 hours rule" popularized by Malcom Gladwell on the basis of Anders Ericsson's work), so is *what* is practiced, *how* it is practiced, and *when*. The same goes for foul shots, for example: players should practice their routines, but only after they understand why and how they help them specifically. As I have reiterated time and again, the key is to master the disturbance occurring *before* the throw.

Too often, I have seen players imitating a motion or action in which they don't truly understand what it is, how it can be used, and why it helps, if at all. This is evident, for example, with "dry shooting," in which players practice the shooting movement—mostly just with the arms, but sometimes with both arms and legs, known as the "extended version"—without a ball right before they take an actual shot. Players sporadically perform this motion to cope with potentially missing foul shots. Even though some great foul shooters have applied dry shooting (including NBA basketball player Steve Nash, who used the extended version, in my opinion), dry shooting is, as it is called, above all, dry—this is because it rehearses the motor movement, not the problem that occurs before the throw. This reminds me of the early 1990s when Pat Riley was extremely popular in Israel; at that time, many young coaches used to put a great deal of styling gel in their hair, a la Riley, as if the goo would penetrate their skulls and make them genius coaches just like him.

When seeking to improve performance in any endeavor, it's necessary to understand the process behind your methods, pulling back the curtain to get to the heart of a problem. This typically begins by developing your psychological skills and understanding first. Psychological skills are like physical skills—they can be taught, learned, and practiced. Still, many top athletes, who alot many hours weekly to physical practice, neglect the mental component, as do many of us on any given day. Lack of time is a common excuse, but in fact, it is an issue of priorities: if you believe that mental skills are important you will find the time to practice them. In sports, quite often, it is much more a matter of ignorance: if a coach tells his athletes to relax or concentrate, the implicit assumption is that the athletes already know how to do so, but the assumption is often wrong—they cannot implement what they don't have the skills to do.

More successful athletes seem to differ from less successful ones in their effective use of psychological skills. Even though athletes may acquire intuitive psycho-regulative measures over time, and these may even be successful, they are not innate and typically need to be taught

systematically and professionally. This is often done from an educational perspective to avoid the impression that psychology is only
good for "problem athletes," or "problem employees" for that matter,
who actually need clinical treatment. Anyone's psychological needs can
be addressed through a process that does not include the application
of clinical knowledge. This process is referred to as "mental preparation," and it can be applied to help you fulfill your maximum potential,
especially when you enter a state that I call "psychological performance
crisis."

CRISIS STATES AND OPTIMAL
PSYCHO-REGULATION

> To the extent that people can regulate what they think, they can influence
> how they feel and behave.
>
> —ALBERT BANDURA[1]

In general, any crisis state is usually perceived as an extremely acute,
intense event—or chain of events—that is unpredictable and often surprising in nature, typically occurring for a short point in time. In one way
or another, "crisis" refers to a turning point, where a person—or a system,
in a more general sense—must decide where to go and what to do.

In my 1984 doctoral dissertation, I tried to extend the Yerkes-Dodson
law (discussed in chapter 1) to account for the continuous organization,
or disorganization, of an athlete's behavior *during* competition. To do
so, it was necessary to add the dimension of time to the inverted U, in
order to include and conceptualize the dynamic changes in the athlete's
psychological state on court over time. I argued that athletes in contest
are essentially moving between two extremes: at the one extreme, their
performance may be maximal because their arousal is optimal, while at
the other, performance can deteriorate into a performance crisis—either
because of too much, or too little, arousal. Thus it is actually a theory of
crisis development, which requires the inclusion of time within a dynamic

view of the inverted U, instead of the rather static or timeless nature of the original Yerkes-Dodson law.

The crisis model assumes that during competition, athletes frequently experience psychological stress that can elevate their arousal levels and negatively affect their performance. Under extreme arousal levels athletes may enter a psychological performance crisis, a state in which their ability to cope adequately with competitive requirements substantially deteriorates (as discussed in chapter 1).

Disturbances, which can cause substantial drifts from the optimal level, may of course be real sometimes. From a psychologist's point of view, however, what is much more important is that these drifts may often exist only in a person's mind, such as with the player from chapter 2 who said he became mad every time he saw that referee on court, leading him to get two fouls even before the game started. While working with Gershon Tenenbaum in the research department of Wingate in 1987–1993, we studied what we called "crisis-related factors"—those mental factors that may affect the athlete's state in contest in a way that may increase the probability of performance crisis at the expense of the probability of maximal performance.[2]

In order to identify these crisis-related factors, the athlete's state in competition was systematically decomposed into its various facets or building blocks. Essentially, these building blocks may be divided into two groups, each of them related to a particular basic question:

1. Basic question No. 1: What happens to the athlete *before* the contest begins? This issue had been dealt with extensively in many previous applied contexts, especially in the former Eastern Bloc, and has been known as "prestart-state."[3] Thus, the first factor to be investigated was the athlete's prestart susceptibility to crisis, that is, what the athlete brings to the contest (I discussed part of this idea in chapter 2 in regards to an athlete's motivation).

2. Basic question No. 2: What may affect the athlete *during* contest, to increase (or decrease) crisis probability? Here,

I discussed the time phase in which the athlete experienced
the disturbance, the game standing at that time (with a strong
emphasis on the concept of momentum, which you got to
know in chapter 4), the frequency and intensity in which the
athlete violates rules or norms of the game (something to be
discussed in more detail in chapter 12 on aggressive behavior
and morality), and the athlete's subjectively perceived social
environment (i.e., teammates, coach, spectators and referees,
which I also discussed to some extent throughout part III of
the book, "Working Together").

It is of course impossible to predict exactly which specific combination of
events will occur in each moment of a particular contest. When certain
events occur, however, we can categorize them in terms of these "crisis-
related factors" and then combine or synthesize them together to diagnose
the athlete's psychological state (i.e., crisis probability) in each moment of
the game. This can be done with the help of a computer, using what we
call Bayesian statistics, but in principle, also without it. Based on such a
diagnosis, we can than match the required psycho-regulative measure to
be used at that moment.

As we have seen throughout the book, optimal arousal is a necessary, albeit not necessarily sufficient, precondition for maximal performance. When performing a task, a person's psycho-regulation must also
be optimal. Look at it this way: performers of any kind are conceived of
as systems. As such, they function in line with the classical principles of
"general systems theory," developed in the 1940s by the Austrian-born
theoretical biologist Ludwig von Bertalanffy (1901–1972). Systems are
"self-regulating," meaning they self-correct through feedback. The concept of feedback, in turn, has been intensively studied in cybernetics, the
science of communication and control in self-regulating systems, which is
closely associated with the famous American mathematician and philosopher Norbert Wiener (1894–1964). (Many of the ideas presented by von
Bertalanffy's general systems theory and Wiener's cybernetics are very
similar, even complementary.)

There are five psycho-regulative dimensions that are, in essence, the key to understanding mental preparation in this context:

1. Stabilization versus modification;
2. Relaxation versus mobilization;
3. Prevention versus compensation;
4. Self versus others;
5. Intuitive versus professional.

The most fundamental question in terms of psycho-regulation relates to stabilization versus modification and follows as such: Is the psychological state of the performer favorable or not in terms of accomplishing a particular task in a specific situation? If the answer is yes, then this psychological state should be maintained or stabilized, perhaps by—you guessed it—doing nothing. If the performer's psychological state is *not* favorable any more, then it should be modified in order to re-establish the desirable psychological state. Whether to stabilize or modify, and to what degree, depends on the extent of deviation from the optimum.

However, to account for a person's possible energizing problems, there is also the question of the direction of the deviation: as we saw earlier, one's psychological state can deviate from optimum in two different directions—either the performer is overaroused or underaroused. To overcome overarousal, relaxation is required, whereas in the case of underarousal, mobilization is required (relaxation versus mobilization).

The prevention versus compensation differentiation relates to the dimension of time: events that actually happen during the course of a performance—whether a basketball game or business strategy meeting— may require "compensation," or a response after the fact. However, the events might also have been anticipated at an earlier stage; in that case it's important to consider how they could have been prevented.

Notice that this differentiation also relates to the beginning and end of one's action: at the first moment of performance, compensation can be made with respect to the performer's "prestart state." For example, when a basketball player is nonoptimally aroused, and is not feeling confident before the game starts, she or he may try to open the game by deliberately conducting two to three successful actions in order to gain confidence and enter a state of perceived or actual positive momentum (see chapter 4).

Evidently, prevention can take place prior to actual performance with regard to events that are anticipated to occur during the performance itself. However, in order to prevent future negative events, compensation can also be used at the end of the previous performance. For example, in the Olympic Games, Judokas—professional Judo competitors—have to compete in a series of contests in one single day, which psychologically can be quite demanding. At the Rio 2016 Summer Olympics, Israeli heavyweight Judoka Or Sasson lost in the semifinals to the dominant French Judoka Teddy Riner, who went on to win the gold. Right after the contest a TV camera caught National Coach Oren Smadja, a 1992 Olympic bronze medalist himself (and a student of mine, by the way), attempting to compensate by reframing the defeat into success. Intending to give Sasson confidence, instead of mourning the loss of the contest and the gold, Smadja said to him, "Or, you managed to give Teddy a real great fight!" Sasson came back to win the next contest and thereby, the bronze medal.

When in an office environment, it's easy to find yourself deviating from optimal arousal and maximal performance levels. Whether you're the CEO or the lowliest assistant, you're bound to find yourself under immense stress at one time or another. Some days you'll get to the office late, sit down at your desk, boot up your computer, and before you've even had the chance to take a sip of your morning coffee, someone is asking you about an upcoming meeting, if your team is going to make an impending deadline (which just got moved up the day before), or when you plan on reviewing a document that just landed on your desk. By the end of the day it feels as if a million things are due, you haven't answered even ten of the one hundred e-mails you've received that day, and the caffeine from your morning coffee, which you finally got to drink, has worn off. The pressure and stress builds up and you're ready to scream.

In this case, when it all just seems a little bit *too* much, relaxation is required to get you back to an optimal arousal level. Better yet, if you start your day with some simple relaxation techniques, you're likely to maintain a better, more relaxed attitude throughout the day. When you sit down at your desk first thing, take a moment to deeply inhale and exhale. This type of deep breathing will increase the oxygen flowing to your brain and help you enter a more calm state. In fact, the American Institute of Stress (AIS) widely recommends deep breathing as one of the best ways to relax, stating that "abdominal breathing for 20 to 30 minutes each day will reduce anxiety and reduce stress."[4] Breathing techniques work as they help you connect more with your body and refocus your mind away from your worries. Of course, if you don't have time to do this in the morning, take the opportunity at lunch or even before you get to work.

The Harvard Medical School suggests a number of techniques to keep your stress in check, including taking a break at your desk to check your body for tension.[5] They suggest relaxing your facial muscles, dropping your arms to your sides, and letting your jaw open slightly. Then let your hands loosen, opening space between your fingers. Get comfortable in your chair and then take some deep breaths. Let your mind focus on your cramped fingers or sore back as you loosen up and begin to relax. After only three minutes, you should feel refreshed and ready to tackle whatever problem is waiting around the bend.

Of course, when it comes to office life there's the flip side, too: the contemporary work world can occasionally be, well, boring. Everyone hopes that they have the opportunity to do interesting, exciting, and valuable work and that they are on a career path toward some ultimate goal, but it's unlikely that you look forward to *every single* daily task. And on those slow summer days where you find yourself dozing off, daydreaming about lying on the beach with a cocktail in hand, the last thing you want to do is sit in front of your computer, pretending to look busy.

In that situation, it's time to *mobilize*. Get up and go for a walk around the office—get your blood flowing. Going out for a cup of coffee or taking a break to socialize for a few minutes can also be effective. Though it may sound cliché, laughter can help. As reported in *Forbes*, "A hearty chuckle stimulates circulation and soothes tension" and "laughter also increases endorphins released by the brain."[6] Journalist Amy Morin, who reports on the psychological aspects of business, suggests surrounding yourself with some items that make you laugh—such as a folder filled with funny photos or some of your favorite jokes.[7] Stop by a friend's desk and share a humorous story and see if they have one in return.

These are simple techniques, but they're also effective in helping you re-enter a state of equilibrium. Some can be performed on the fly, before a big meeting or presentation, while others will require more time. No matter what, it's important to figure out the best way for you to personally re-enter that optimal state when you've gone adrift. At times you may be able to do this all on your own, and at others, you may need some help.

Self-Regulation versus Regulation by Others

In mental preparation and psycho-regulation, it's also important to consider *who* is regulating the performance: the individual performer (e.g., soccer player or sales associate), also known as "self-regulation," or someone on the "outside" (e.g., a coach or a boss), also known as "regulation by others." Ideally most coaches or bosses would prefer to work with people who can completely regulate themselves throughout the process of task performance. However, it turns out that in reality, we can hardly live without any outside regulation.

In the late 1970s, the psychology institute of the German Sport University in Cologne conducted an extensive investigation to find out how athletes intuitively conduct self-regulation and how others intuitively regulate them.[8] It is extremely important to gain information about these intuitive techniques, because good sport psychologists will never go against the athlete's or coach's intuitions; instead they will build on them, as in Judo, when you use your opponent's power to help you. But it also turned out that the differentiations of psycho-regulative states can be applied not only to intuitive psycho-regulation, but also to professional measures undertaken upon a psychologist's advice (intuitive versus professional).

The five psycho-regulative dimensions discussed can be visually depicted as in Figure 11.1.

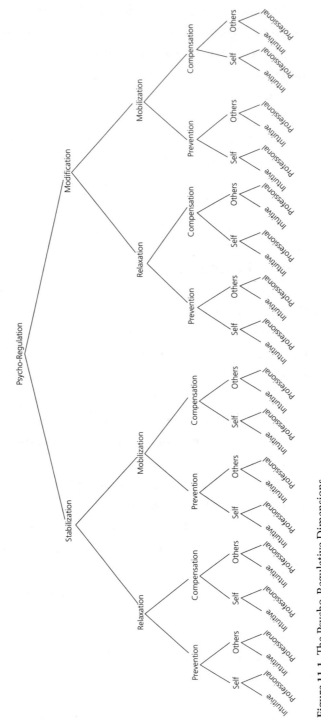

Figure 11.1 The Psycho-Regulative Dimensions.

Let's assume, for example, that I am performing my daily anti-Parkinson's exercises as prescribed by my devoted doctors, Professor Nir Giladi and Dr. Yair Zlotnik: I begin by walking as quickly as I can through my neighborhood. While doing so, I primarily aim to remain safe, clear of cars and other hazards. I do this by visually monitoring the road for traffic and by maintaining ample room to walk safely between regular traffic and the curb or edge of the pavement. What happens if a large moving truck approaches me or if I find that the shoulder on the road has disappeared? I deal with such a disturbance by continuing my walk through the neighbor's front lawn until the moving truck has passed or the shoulder reappears. During any given walk, numerous disturbances that require my response may occur; if I control them appropriately, I can be considered a self-regulated walker.

Self-regulation is an integral part of participation in any sport or exercise. For example, it includes my urge to stop during some of the intense exercises I do twice a week with my personal anti-Parkinson's trainer, or a similar urge a professional elite athlete feels during difficult strength and conditioning training. In fact, self-regulation is part of any performance. For example, it's imperative that you maintain focus while giving a presentation; that John McEnroe tries to reduce his angry outbursts on the tennis court; that you explain concepts or processes clearly during a meeting; or that Tiger Woods attempts to ignore feelings of excitement and focus on a putt to win a tournament. Simply put, self-regulation is the process by which we consciously attempt to cope with and constrain unwanted thoughts, feelings, and behaviors and bring these in line with goals and expectations.

Failure to self-regulate may have severe consequences; for example, if you are on a diet and exercise plan and you don't stick to it properly, you may spiral out of control into obesity and ill health, instead of reaching your ideal target weight. In elite sport or in a business setting, such a failure may be reflected in emotional outbursts, poor decisions, and a reduction in performance. By effectively regulating your thoughts, feelings, and behaviors—those that can distract you from achieving an important goal—there will be a greater probability for success over failure. Self-regulated performers essentially function without external controls; almost as if they are on automatic pilot, they will utilize mainly self-perceived feedback from their environment.

The ability to self-regulate, however, may be depleted as your coping resources are exhausted by constant use. In such cases, outside help might be necessary. Regulation by others is also important from an entirely different, much deeper perspective: as I mentioned earlier, performers cannot really live without at least *some* outside regulation—a situation closely linked to the concept of hierarchy.

In this context, hierarchy refers to our "standards of comparison," or reference points, that are actually determined by a system of goals, which vary, like layers, from lower order to higher order. According to the "lower-higher" order hierarchy notion, achievement of lower-order goals is essential for the achievement of higher-order goals. A simple example will illustrate the point: when kids or teens are taught to dribble a basketball, regulation from the outside is necessary to learn the action correctly. When they learn to self-regulate their dribbling they can then become a playmaker, provided all the other necessary skills are present. They can then pay more attention, as they have more free resources and energy, to on court problem-solving and decision-making.

The latter tasks must also first be regulated by the coach through instructions and feedback. Only afterward, as the players gain experience and learn to self-regulate in increasingly difficult tasks on court, do the tasks regulated from the outside become higher in terms of complexity and goals to be achieved. For example, the coach can then regulate complex tactical maneuvers that couldn't be done while the coach was busy regulating the players' dribbling. This is probably what famous coach John Wooden (whom you met in chapter 9) meant when he said "It's the little details that are vital. Little things make big things happen." In other words, if you can't control the little things, don't expect to be able to do the big ones.

When working with top athletes as a psychological consultant, I first have to teach them basic mental preparation skills; then, I show them how to apply them. Even after they learn how and when to use them appropriately, athletes continue to come to me for consultation because, though they were already successful automatic pilots on the lower level psycho-regulative tasks, they need help with the more complex ones.

But at the end—or the beginning, as observed by Descartes centuries ago—it is only our thoughts that we are able to control. Thoughts stand in the center of psycho-regulation; they are, as Descartes said, under our absolute power. If used appropriately, you can do wonders with them to shape and enhance your performance through effective psycho-regulation.

ENHANCING FREE THROW PERFORMANCE, AND MUCH MORE

> I just have to go to the line and hit them and make them pay, and I will, I'm not worried.
>
> —Shaquille O'Neal[9]

When I was working with IAF pilots, I used to tell them that they are essentially no different from soccer players. Why? Because both combat pilots and elite soccer players have to deal with extreme pressures frequently. Other professional populations are exposed to similar extreme pressures as well: think, for example, of traders in the stock market, students taking timed exams, surgeons conducting risky all-or-nothing operations, or fire fighters trying to save lives under dangerous conditions. How can such people deal with these everyday extreme pressures?

There are many psychological skills training programs that utilize a "toolbox" of measures available to the performance psychologist trying to consult the performer, be it a pilot or an athlete, a business manager or an employee, a teacher or a student, a surgeon or a fire fighter. Such toolboxes can be reduced to more or less three basic pillars from which an effective mental preparation program aimed at *individual* performance enhancers can be composed.

1. Thought control: the way performers think, in terms of their own definition of the situation (see chapter 6); motivation

and commitment (see motivation in chapter 2 and goal-
setting in chapter 3); expectations (see self-confidence in
chapter 4); and attention and concentration (e.g., attentional
shifts, chapter 10).

2. Arousal regulation: mainly relaxation to combat overarousal,
but also psyching yourself up (see chapters 1 and 2).

3. Imagery: imagining actions and success (as discussed in detail
in chapter 10).

The way in which performers define the situation they are facing is critical to any potential improvement of their psychological state. Therefore
the process of reframing, discussed in chapter 6, is crucial. Recall the
example I gave you of the young playmaker who developed a fear of
shooting as well as of penetration? Only after I reframed the situation for
him could we begin the process of mental training. For obvious reasons
I cannot reveal his name, as he is still quite famous in Israel, so I'll use his
initial: "C."

C reported that in practice he would score about 90 percent of his free
throws, whereas in contest, the percentage decreased to under 50 percent.
C's coach advised that he simply needed more practice, suggesting that
he stay after workouts and throw a few hundred more foul shots. This,
however, only aggravated the problem, since the coach's advice in no way
addressed the actual issue. Just like player M in chapter 10, it was obvious
that C had no motor problems since he was sinking 90 percent of his free
throws in training. This means that the issue lay not in the movement but
in some disturbance affecting him *before* the throw itself.

To further explore the problem, I asked him: "How much time do
you have to get ready to throw?" "Five seconds," he said, referring to the
European basketball rules that allow free-throw shooters five seconds
to ready themselves and initiate the throw during a foul shot. However,
from a psychological point of view this answer was inaccurate, because
the *actual* time period before shooting a foul is much longer. The player
did not count the time lapse between the moment the foul was called and
when he received the ball from the referee (about ten seconds). In other

words, adding those ten seconds to the five allotted, means he had about fifteen seconds to prepare, not five.

My next question was: "And what do you do during these fifteen seconds?" By now, I'm sure you know what he said: "Nothing." As discussed, doing nothing in such a situation is devastating because it creates a vacuum that is immediately filled by anxiety and worry. As I always say, this state of affairs is like putting sand into your car engine and expecting it to drive smoothly. If this rationale seems strange or exceptional, consider for a moment the former professional basketball player Shaquille O'Neal.

Over his nearly twenty-year professional NBA career, "Shaq" won the NBA Rookie of the year award (1992–1993), the 1999–2000 MVP, three Finals MVP awards, and more. In one year alone, 2000, he won the NBA MVP, the All-Star game MVP, and the Finals MVP awards—one of only three players to have done so throughout the history of the NBA.[10] Shaq ranks seventh of all-time in points scored, fifth in field goals, and thirteenth in rebounds. That all being said, even though he was known for his impressive dunking ability, he will also be remembered for his *weakness* in free throws, which he himself considered a mental issue. After a particularly horrendous free shot performance in a June 2006 game, Shaq stated, "It's probably just a matter of concentration. I actually shot the night before pretty well, so I'm probably just, you know, thinking about it a little too much."[11]

His free throw issue became so bad, however, with a career average of 52.7 percent, that his opponents would regularly foul him on purpose to force him to shoot free throws—a technique that became known as "Hack a Shaq." In December of 2008 Shaq missed his 5,000th shot from the foul line, the only player aside from Wilt Chamberlain to have done so professionally.[12] Shaq attempted 11,252 free throws during his 1,207 game career, which means a waste of 5,322 throws (compared to 100 percent accuracy), or of 3,072 throws if you take 80 percent as a standard for comparison.[13]

Another great NBA player was a little bit more efficient in that respect: Karl Malone—often called "The Mailman" because of his consistent delivery—led the NBA in free throws, making a league record seven times. During his early years in the NBA, Malone raised his free throw shooting percentage from below 50 percent to 75 percent, a huge leap.[14] I always wondered how Malone was able to perform with such accuracy, though I had my theories: I remember very well watching NBA games in the 1990s and seeing Malone mutter something to himself while preparing for foul shots. I assumed this was some mantra-like repetition given to him by a sport psychologist, and it piqued my curiosity.

In 2002 I was invited to Guangzhou, China, to give a keynote address. While there, I met Keith Henschen, a sport psychology professor at the University of Utah. I knew that Keith had served for many years as a psychological consultant to the Utah Jazz, and I asked him if he knew what Malone was saying when he stood on the foul line before shooting a free throw. This is what Keith told me: "This is for [my wife] Kay and the baby." According to Keith, it was a trigger to get Karl ready to shoot.

Coming back to C, I instructed him to apply an agreed upon mental routine to incorporate in the fifteen seconds he had to prepare for a foul shot and to be used without exception in every game. The procedure was comprised of different elements taken from well-known mental preparation techniques in sport, including contracting and relaxing his hands, taking one or two deep breaths, and calling up images of succeeding (e.g., first, looking at the basket, then seeing himself successfully shooting a free throw twice). These were the steps he performed in the first ten seconds before receiving the ball. Once he had the ball in his hands, he had five seconds to bounce the ball three times, call up one more successful image, and then shoot while exhaling and engaging in an appropriate mental follow-through.

After learning these techniques and rehearsing them at home, they were first applied on court in isolated, quiet training sessions, attended only by myself and C: I used to foul him while dribbling, then count the seconds he had to prepare to shoot. He soon started to use the procedure, which had developed into a routine, in team training sessions and, only later, in real competitions. Thus, learning the psychological skills enabled him to successfully shoot fouls, and progress from practices and simulations to actual competitions. In this way the routine was gradually taught, rehearsed, tested, and stabilized; it continued—as mental training should—until it became an integral part of his repertoire during his whole career.

Player C's free throw percentages improved dramatically, exceeding 80 percent in contest. As a result, he started to penetrate often to the basket, gaining confidence in his ability to score when fouled.[15] Paradoxically, as seen in chapter 6, C also found himself free more often to shoot from the outside (precisely because he was doing the opposite, that is, penetrating). His general performance improved and this problem, along with some others, was solved.

Performers as Tailors: Matching Mental Preparation to Individual Needs

Note that C's training, just like any mental training program, was tailored to meet a person's individual needs. The consultant may provide general advice but must also customize the individual program to suit the performer's needs.

Traditionally, performance psychologists have advocated two major categories of relaxation strategies: physical and mental. "Progressive relaxation" is a good example of the first category in which the performer focuses on progressively tensing and then relaxing different muscle groups, one after the other. Through this progressive relaxation technique, the individual learns the difference between high and low levels of tension and how they affect his or her body. Consequently, the performer becomes aware of where and when tension occurs and tries to reduce it by relaxing the relevant muscles. In principle, this form of physical relaxation is expected to also decrease mental tension.

From my experience, the progressive relaxation method is quite effective with athletes, because their bodies are actually their "working devices" and they are therefore often highly aware of minor disturbances (e.g., tensions) in even a tiny, hidden muscle, one that a nonathlete like me would not even know existed. Since they are working with their muscles all the time, athletes usually prefer a combination of some elements from progressive relaxation, breath control, and imagery. Progressive relaxation also speaks to athletes since such a muscle-based procedure often seems natural to them: it is very similar in its nature and spirit to exercises such as stretching, which are often conducted by the athletes anyway. Thus it is reasonable and useful to apply the technique with athletes.

With other populations (such as musicians, surgeons, or trial lawyers), however, I have found that *mental* relaxation techniques such as relaxation response are more effective. Even though the physical element is not always entirely absent in such groups (e.g., musicians play instruments and surgeons use their hands to operate), the dominant component is not the physical one, but rather, the cognitive-emotional one. Such is the relaxation response: it applies the basic elements of meditation, but eliminates the spiritual or religious aspect. This technique teaches users to quiet the mind, concentrate, relax, and reduce muscle tension. It requires that users passively focus on, or imagine, a single relaxing word, thought, picture, or color. If you sit in your office all day, this exercise is quite useful.

Needless to say, I cannot guarantee that if you are a typical office-sitter relaxation response techniques will *always* help you. Moreover, you might even prefer to use progressive relaxation instead or in addition to relaxation response techniques (just as it's possible that an athlete will prefer relaxation response). Our scientifically based principles are probabilistic rather than deterministic in nature: they apply only to majorities (i.e., most of the people most of the time), but not to *everyone*. That being said, I can still advise most modern day business professionals to act according to the following guidelines:

1. Become exposed to, and aware of, the toolbox that works best for you, resting on the three pillars.
2. Through a process of trial and error, try to find out what is most effective for you, taking into account your personal preferences, the task to be performed, and your environment.

Your can discover your preferences by asking questions such as:

- What speaks to you the best?
- When do you feel mostly well?
- In which part of your body is your most effective response?

- Where in your body or mind do you experience the most substantial positive change?

Consider your tasks by asking:

- Is it a motor task?
- Does it involve many muscles (such as with athletes), just a few (such as with a musician or surgeon) or none at all (such as with lawyers, professors, and other people with desk jobs)?
- Is it simple or complex?

Think about your environment or situation in which the technique should be applied:

- Does it take place at home?
- Is it practiced in training?
- Is it during competition?
- Is it a job interview setting?
- Are you preparing for an exam or a romantic meeting?

Try first to train at home, in a quiet atmosphere. This could be enough for you to help you achieve your best performance level. If you'd like to apply it outside of your home, you may want to simulate it first. Let your friends, family, or close colleagues play the jury and critically assess your performance, whether you're conducting an important speech or giving a presentation. Then let somebody watch your performance directly prior to the event in the very place where you'll be giving the speech or presentation. Similarly, if you're a musician, have someone attend your practice prior to an important concert in the very hall in which it is going to take place. Then use those critiques—and your response to them in the rehearsal—to help you psycho-regulate when you actually give the presentation or perform the piece.

There are three important principles to keep in mind here:

1. There is no absolute or ultimate means to success! The keyword here is "matching": whether you're an athlete or a CEO, the

mental preparation procedure should match your particular performance of a particular task in a particular environment.

2. Use the procedure "from the light to the heavy": first try it out at home, then outside of your home, then where it should be applied at last, and finally, in the event itself.

3. If a procedure doesn't fully work for you, don't hesitate to optimize by updating, changing, and revising it; remember, life is dynamic.

Similar principles have guided me when fighting my Parkinson's. After being diagnosed, I soon discovered that there are vastly different ways in which the disease expresses itself—doctors even talk about a "family of Parkinson's" (what a "nice" family), which they have to carefully treat on an individual basis. This also requires Parkinson's patients to intimately understand their disease and actively cooperate with their doctors. Otherwise, even excellent doctors such as Nir Giladi and Yair Zlotnik may have a hard time helping.

Then there is the specific profile of *my* Parkinson's, which can be quite different than someone else's, even if it is in the same family. For example, I may respond completely differently to the same cocktail of medications than another patient. The disease is also dynamic: unfortunately, it deteriorates all the time, so that what works today should probably be revised tomorrow, or in a month, a year, and so forth. Often, I also have to train some coping modes at home before applying them "on court." For example, I practiced injecting myself with a certain medication time and again at home before I dared to do it outside, first in the privacy of my room at the university, then also in public (e.g., while traveling on the train).

Therefore, just as personal preferences, the task to be performed, and the environment are crucial to business or sports performance, they are also essential in many everyday life occurrences. This type of mental preparation helps individuals prepare, or compensate, on many levels and can be incorporated into a regular, daily routine to help reach maximal performance.

LIMITATIONS TO MENTAL PREPARATION

But Miki, it was *so* beautiful!

—O, *Israeli water polo national team's penalty shooter*

Unfortunately, even the best mental preparation has its limitations. For example, while I was the team psychologist for the Israel national water polo team in 1992, the team played Egypt—a very sensitive event, for obvious reasons—in the small Belgian city of Mouscron during the Four Nations Tournament (which consisted of Belgium, France, Israel, and Egypt). In the very last minute, we had a penalty kick in our favor. In penalty kicks in water polo, a player throws the ball from a distance of about 16 feet (5 meters) from the net, though at the time it was only 13 feet (4 meters).

The shooter was an extremely talented player and highly intelligent guy—let's call him "O"—who was a real problem athlete when I first started working with the team (in fact, to this day I think I was hired mainly to handle him). O was our regular penalty shooter. Before the game started, we warned him not to shoot penalties to the center of the goal, right below the bar, as it is considered a humiliation to the goalie (plus, it can hit his head). But alas, O, who had played an almost perfect game until that moment, shot the last ball exactly where he shouldn't have, to the center, right under the bar and . . . he scored. After the game (which we clearly won, by the way), curious about his decision, I asked him why he couldn't restrain himself for just a few more minutes. His answer was so original that I couldn't be angry with him: he said, "But Miki, it was *so* beautiful!" So you see, even the best mental preparation in the world may have its limitations: it held during most of it, but not throughout the entire game.

In chapter 2, I discussed the issue of overmotivation, including the resulting effects of choking under pressure. Though mental preparation should help you overcome this dreaded response and its potentially devastating consequences, it's still possible to fall victim to overmotivation during the action you're performing.

For example, in 2000 I worked for a soccer team in the Israeli first division. When I started working with them, they were placing last in the league and in danger of relegation to the second division. The coach was a young ex-player, who had just been appointed and was rather lacking in confidence. After I administered sociometric tests (in the form of interviews; see chapter 8) and implemented some social changes based on the results, the coach, recognizing the limitations of his offensive players, decided to change his tactics. From then on they would play a "bunker" defense, in which they essentially tried to "steal" a goal and win. Amazingly, this tactic worked, and slowly but surely we began to collect points and rise slightly above relegation level.

Then came a decisive game against another relegation candidate. We played at home and were ahead of the team in the league; all we had to do was not lose. The worst thing for us would be if the other team scored an early goal, which meant we had to attack—just what our players were unable to do. The opponent's playmaker happened to be a tall guy. We assigned a player to stick to him and cover him throughout the game. However, our "player leech," I'll call him "A," had one major disadvantage: he was short. That's why we instructed him to leave his player during corners and stick to the goal post—if he stayed with his player in corners, his taller opponent would easily be able to head in a ball.

Essentially, A's instructions for that game were painfully simple: "Stick to that player throughout game, don't leave him alone for a minute! But in corners, *then* leave him alone and stick to the goalpost!" How much simpler could it be? We gave him these instructions at least three times: first in the locker room, then before the players went out to warm up, and finally, because I was still uneasy as I watched the players before the first whistle, I advised the coach to explain the task to A a third time. The coach didn't really believe it was necessary, as the task seemed so simple, but he followed my advice. I also decided to give A a good cue, also known as a "trigger." Trigger words or images are short, vivid, and positive reminders intended to help someone focus on a specific target or the performance of a given action. I asked A to think of his wife every time a corner was called against the team and embrace the goalpost as if he were embracing her. A good trigger, right? I thought it must at least be worthy of a sport psychology textbook. But fifteen minutes into the game the first corner was kicked against us. The ball flew high to the penalty area, A's main opponent heads it directly into the corner where A should have been. But where was A? You guessed it: far away from the goal, *next to* "his" player, with the goal side wide open.

How do you explain such actions? Well, it is possible that the player was *so* stupid that he could not understand simple instructions after hearing them three times. But this was not the case. Perhaps his wife was a bad trigger—maybe they were on bad terms at that time and A actually wanted to forget her? This, too, however, was not the case. A much more probable explanation was that he simply *choked*, despite all our efforts. Needless to say, we had to open the game and go on attack; soon enough, we gave away a second goal and lost 0 to 2. Not surprisingly, right after the game, the coach was fired, along with the psychologist.

No matter how mentally prepared you feel, the possibility of failure still exists. As discussed, however, failure provides the opportunity to learn and come back stronger. If your day doesn't go as planned, if a project falls by the wayside, if your boss yells at you for a missed deadline, don't fear. Go back to step one, reconsider how to move forward, and develop a plan for action. Remember, it's all in your head, and the more you can regulate your thinking and your psychological state in general, the better your performance will be.

SUMMARY

More successful athletes usually differ from less successful ones in their effective use of their psychological skills, and the same can be said for business leaders and other professionals. Psychological skills are like physical skills—they can be taught, learned, and practiced. Yes, the movements of dribbling, passing, shooting, and scoring can be mastered in practice, but when the game arrives, mental preparation takes precedence.

The same goes for the business world: being psychologically prepared for any obstacle, challenge, or task, will lead to better performance. Methods of relaxation and concentration are often overlooked in favor of more concrete preparation, such as rote memorization, overpracticed speeches, or incessant e-mails, but mental preparation is key: the secret to top performance lies in the optimal psychological regulation of the performer's arousal.

DAILY PRACTICES

As an Individual

- When you're experiencing stress and anxiety, take a minute to relax by employing deep breathing techniques.
- If you're feeling disengaged, get up from behind your desk and take a break with coworkers or friends.
- Incorporate relaxation responses in your everyday routine.

As a Leader

- Develop a personal mantra and before addressing your team, or your superiors, take a moment to repeat it quietly to yourself.
- Talk to your team to understand why individual members' performance may be deviating from maximal levels—once you've figured that out, be willing to help them get back on track.
- Even if a project fails or a presentation falls apart, learn from the experience and mentally prepare yourself for the next challenge ahead.

NOTES

1. A. Bandura, *Self-Efficacy: The Exercise of Control* (New York: Freeman, 1997), 131, 145.

2. I extensively reviewed these mental factors in M. Bar-Eli, "Psychological Performance Crisis in Competition, 1984–1996: A Review," *European Yearbook of Sport Psychology* 1 (1997): 73–112.

3. In German, "Vorstartzustand"; I read this material in German, which was translated from Russian mainly by DDR writers.

4. Kelly Marksberry, "Take a Deep Breath," *AIS: Daily Life Blog*, August 10, 2012, www.stress.org/take-a-deep-breath/.

5. "Mini-Relaxation Exercises: A Quick Fix in Stressful Moments," *Harvard Health Publications: Healthbeat*, November 2012, www.health.harvard.edu/healthbeat/mini-relaxation-exercises-a-quick-fix-in-stressful-moments.

6. Amy Morin, "5 Powerful Stress Relievers You Can Do At Your Desk," *Forbes*, July 29, 2015, www.forbes.com/sites/amymorin/2015/07/29/5-powerful-stress-relievers-you-can-do-at-your-desk/#72f913583bc3.

7. Ibid.

8. The findings of the self-regulation project were published in J. R. Nitsch and H. Allmer, "Naïve Psycho-Regulative Techniken der Selbstbeeinflussung im Sport" [Naïve Psycho-Regulative Techniques of Self-Influence in Sport], *Sportwissenschaft* 9 (1979): 143–163. The findings concerning regulation by others were published in D. Hackfort, "Techniken der Angstkontrolle von Trainern" [Coaches' Techniques of Anxiety Control], *Leistunssport* 10 (1980): 104–110. The possibility of applying the intuitive psycho-regulative categories to professional psychological consultation was mentioned when I first published the theory of crisis: M. Bar-Eli and G. Tenenbaum, "A Theory of Individual Psychological Crisis in Competitive Sport," *Applied Psychology* 38 (April 1989): 107–120.

9. Shaquille O'Neal, interview on KTAR radio, Phoenix, AZ, October 16, 2008.

10. "Shaquille O'Neal NBA Stats," *Basketball-Reference.com*, 2016, www.basketball-reference.com/players/o/onealsh01.html.

11. Jeff Dengate, "Free Throw Woes," *NBA.com*, June 9, 2006, www.nba.com/finals2006/freebies_060609.html.

12. Bob Baum, "Mason's 3-Pointer Gives Spurs 91–90 Win Vver Suns," *NBA.com*, December 25, 2008, www.nba.com/games/20081225/SASPHX/recap.html.

13. "NBA & ABA Career Leaders and Records for Free Throw Attempts," *Sports Reference*, 2016, www.basketball-reference.com/leaders/fta_career.html.

14. "Karl Malone," *Sports Reference*, 2016, www.basketball-reference.com/players/m/malonka01.html.

15. Remember what I told you about self-confidence in chapter 4: for example, about Bandura's notion (based on his theory of self-efficacy) on how performers increasingly gain confidence through successive enactive mastery experiences or performance accomplishments, where success breeds success? That's what happened here.

12

Moral Performance

Is Winning Really Everything?

My ruthless desire to win at all costs served me well on the bike but the
level it went to, for whatever reason, was flawed.

—LANCE ARMSTRONG[1]

I t was the erstwhile Aristotle who opined that striving for excellence
lies at the heart of virtue and drew on sports, as well as the crafts, to
illustrate this idea.[2] Aristotle argued that humans achieve happiness
when they exercise their physical and intellectual capacities to the full-
est. He also contended that sports provide a rich opportunity to excel and
experience this happiness, which is intrinsic to striving, excelling, and
succeeding. However, the desire to develop one's capacities in pursuit of
worthy ends may be endangered by an exaggerated emphasis on winning.

The founder of the Modern Olympic Games, Baron Pierre de Coubertin,
asserted that "the most important thing . . . is not winning but taking part
[in the Games]." However, I bet that many coaches over the years would
disagree. Take American football coach Vince Lombardi for example, who
once stated that "winning isn't everything; it's the *only* thing." Then there
was legendary Liverpool FC soccer coach Bill Shankly, who said, "If you

are first you are first. If you are second you are nothing." Geoffrey Chaucer, the great English poet of the Middle Ages, coined a phrase we use to this day to describe these type of people who are ready to obtain something by any and all means, saying that they are willing to "beg, borrow, or steal." Of course, Chaucer's beg-borrow-steal principle doesn't only relate to sports; Lombardi's and Shankly's quotes could have come just as easily from any politician, corporate titan, businessperson, or even child on the playground. In today's culture, like it or not, winning—anything from a promotion at work to an argument with a spouse—has become the end-all and be-all.

Whether in sports or in business, everyone wants to be successful, but what many people don't realize is that a single-minded pursuit of victory can often undermine long-term performance. Though cheating, lying, stealing, or taking part in any other form of deception may temporarily lead to seemingly better results, over time they will decrease performance and can potentially lead to disastrous effects.

COGNITIVE ANXIETY, AGGRESSION, AND PERFORMANCE

> Stay calm and aggressive.
>
> —GABRIELLE REECE

As reiterated throughout this book, intense levels of arousal are frequently accompanied by high anxiety, which can be detrimental to performance. One major reason for this decrease in performance is so-called cognitive anxiety, characterized by worrisome thoughts like "What if I fail?" Cognitive anxiety misdirects your attention from task-relevant cues— those necessary for task accomplishment—to task irrelevant cues—those that are more concerned with self- or social-evaluation, such as "How do I look?"

As I'm sure you recall, this can be seen with penalty kickers who shoot nonoptimally because they don't want to look like Roberto Baggio (after shooting the ball sky-high; see chapter 5) or with free-throwers like Shaq being afraid of missing (see chapter 11). Outside sports, it may happen with a student, who starts to worry about what her parents and friends would think of her if she doesn't succeed in an important exam—instead of focusing on just completing it—or with an employee, who begins to imagine the boss's potential furious response if he doesn't complete the task on time, instead of concentrating purely on task fulfillment.

As you saw in the last chapter, in my crisis theory I proposed the idea that in contests, as compared to in training, athletes may experience more difficulties in their self-regulation system.[3] This means that because of increased pressure, they will have more problems making the adjustments required between their actual actions and previous expectations due to overarousal. When individuals are overly aroused not only is their performance impaired, but they will increasingly behave in a *task-irrelevant* manner, many times resulting in aggressive behavior.

As I indicated in my 1997 review of crisis theory, studies have repeatedly found that high levels of arousal do indeed tend to instigate and magnify aggressive behavior. As a result, in a contest, athletes may become more "socially deviant" (as sociologists would say), tending to violate rules and norms of conduct more often and more severely. In such cases, increased arousal will be associated with the use of illegitimate, forbidden aggressive modes of behavior. A little aggression can lead to small gains in performance, because it is related to increases in arousal, but at a certain point you become so overly aroused that your performance suffers. Therefore, the near-sighted pursuit of victory that often leads to aggression can undermine performance.

That being said, aggression exhibited in a contest is sometimes employed deliberately, even cold-bloodedly, because it is *functional* for goal attainment. This behavior is called "instrumental aggression" and is used as an effective means of completing a desired task performance. Instrumental aggression is *not* indicative of nonoptimal states or even crisis. On the contrary, it is precisely what the instrumental aggressor is expected to do. Such is the mild case of a tactical foul committed in basketball toward the end of the game, which is typically considered fair, but it can certainly be worse (e.g., when an athlete is instructed to deliberately harm or even injure somebody else). This type of aggression is based less on emotion and more on strategy—it calls to mind the character of Michael Corleone in 1990's *The Godfather III* when he states, "Never hate your enemies. It affects your judgment."

A famous example from sport is Werner Liebrich's brutal tackle against Ferenc Puskas during the 3 to 8 defeat of West Germany against the Hungarian "golden team" in one of the first-round matches of the 1954 world championship, causing Puskas a hairline fracture of the ankle. (Rumors have it that Liebrich was assigned to do so by Coach Sepp Herberger.) Later on, being in a very questionable condition, Puskas played only in the final game, which ended in the sensational "Miracle of Bern," with West Germany winning the World Championship after defeating Hungary 3 to 2.

Instrumental aggression, however, is different from so-called hostile aggression. This kind of aggression is an end rather than a means, and is therefore task-irrelevant. In other words, it contributes nothing to task accomplishment and is "aggression for the sake of aggression." Therefore, it is detrimental to task performance because aggressors are busy with something they should not be doing, instead of focusing on task completion.

Crisis theory argues that the more substantial an athlete's deviation from optimal arousal in competition, the higher the probability of impaired task performance and of deviations from official rules and normative athletic behavior. When arousal is extremely high, violations become increasingly unexpected in the sense that they occur too frequently or too intensively, in comparison to an athlete's regular, normal behavior in a contest, which is expected to be assertive but not inappropriately aggressive. In this case, such violations indicate a high probability of performance crisis—that is, far-from-optimal functioning.

Back in the 1970s, the Germans invested a great deal of effort in fighting an increasing violence in sports, especially in soccer. In 1976 Hartmut Gabler from the University of Tuebingen published a book titled *Aggressive Actions in Sport*, in which he demonstrated that athletes from different interactive sports were able to clearly differentiate among modes of behavior which were against the rules, but were judged either as "fair" or "unfair" by the athletes in regards to the "norms" of the game. I took this notion further and considered whether the violation was "called," or sanctioned, by the referees or not. The idea was that sanctioning a behavior is a form of negative environmental feedback to the athlete, which may provoke or increase frustration and thereby increase the probability of nonoptimal states and crisis.

Rule and norm related violations were then defined by two dimensions:

1. Fairness, or the "degree of violation": either the violation was normatively minor or major;
2. Sanctions, or "referees' response": either the violation was called or ignored.

Gershon Tenenbaum and I studied this idea by investigating twenty-eight German basketball experts and forty-five Israeli team handball experts. We found that high crisis vulnerability was associated with unexpectedly poor performance, and with unexpected violations such as unfair and called behaviors. Later on, we conducted a similar study in tennis with thirty-one tennis experts in Israel. We found that vulnerability to crisis was associated with unexpectedly poor performance, with unexpected and major violations, and with unexpected behaviors to which the officials respond. The results were in line with crisis theory. However, all these studies were based only on questionnaires; therefore we also conducted two interesting studies on this topic, which relied on observations of real athletes' behavior on court.

In the first one, Israeli basketball experts observed sixteen basketball games in a tournament of fifty-three teenage boys who belonged to selected regional teams.[4] A list of violations was presented to the experts prior to the observational procedure. These violations were classified as "minor" (such as small personal contact or obstruction) or "major" (such as tripping or assaulting the opponent without trying to get the ball) and were agreed upon among the experts. Pairs of observers then had to choose one player each and observe him throughout that game. When one of the violations occurred, the observers had to note the exact time of its occurrence.

We found that these behavioral violations, which were directly derived from the crisis concept, could be used as crisis indicators in competition, meaning that it was possible to infer players' psychological state just by observing their behavioral violations. Players who commit too many violations, especially severe ones, are apparently in nonoptimal states of arousal and their performance deteriorates accordingly. In such a situation, coaches should probably take action at that time, for example, by taking the players out of the game, letting them relax and regain their concentration before sending them back in.

Though aggression can take the form of flat-out violence—players deliberately knocking others down in the race for the ball or puck—nonviolent forms of aggression in the pursuit of a win can be just as damaging. Think of one business partner stabbing the other in the back to obtain the lion's share of profits or a high school student spreading a hurtful rumor as a ploy to steal a peer's boyfriend or girlfriend. As our research shows, acting this way doesn't just hurt the object of the aggression; it sometimes hurts the aggressor. A case in point is our second study on this topic, which used data on real athletes' behavior on court. In our 2006 *Journal of Sports Sciences* article on the red card, signifying an ejection from the game in soccer, we analyzed archived data of the First German Bundesliga, from its establishment in 1963 to 2004 (41 seasons), and found that the frequency of red cards, which was directly related to levels of aggression, was also highly correlated with poorer performance.[5]

This poorer performance tends to result in a vicious-cycle phenomenon: performers in an inappropriate arousal state lose their concentration; as a result, their performance declines because they are too distracted to attend to the right cues and too frustrated to concentrate on the task. This in turn causes more frustration and aggression, heightened arousal, and further deterioration in performance. Of course, in a business setting, aggressive thoughts or behavior may not lead to actual physical blows— let's hope not at least—but still affect performance in the same way. Once you become overly aroused, whether you're angry with a business competitor or fellow team member, it can be hard to get back to what's important: namely, the completion of a task. Understanding your own behavioral violations, when they occur and why, or those of the members of your team, will help you avoid the problem before it starts. Similarly, understanding the thought processes behind cheating and deception, and the unfortunate outcomes, will keep you from becoming distracted and increase your overall performance.

DECEPTION: TO CHEAT OR NOT TO CHEAT?

I have no problem with cheating. Whatever you can get away with.

—Joe Torre

Very often, our culture *encourages* deception. There is an ancient human dilemma that people have faced since the beginning of mankind, at the center of which is this question: "Does it pay to commit a crime?"

Some argue that it *never* does, while others might respond with, "Well, would I get caught?" Still, others weigh the potential upsides and downsides, considering a type of reward–punishment matrix. For example, say you are the chief financial officer of a major Fortune 500 company and you have considered embezzling funds from the organization. You would likely think about what you would do with that money, what satisfaction it may bring or what good you could use it for in your own life, versus what could happen if you get caught, how long you'd end up in jail, or what other punishment you'd receive. You may think that you could get away with it, but something inside you says to stop, as you know you'd be filled with guilt.

I would argue that overall, it has been shown that dishonesty or deception doesn't truly pay—just as too much aggression will lead to underperformance over time, so will cheating. My colleagues' and my 2014 paper "Deception and Decision Making in Professional Basketball: Is It Beneficial to Flop," published in the *Journal of Economic Behavior and Organization*, investigated this idea based on "flopping" on the basketball court (i.e., faking offensive fouls).[6] Flopping occurs when an offensive player initiates sufficient contact with a defender who has established a stationary position. The defensive player may exaggerate the effect of this contact by purposely falling. In this situation, the referee must decide whether a legal stationary position was achieved and the contact initiated was sufficient to call a foul against the attacking player. The behavior of players on defense, exaggerating their reactions or intentionally falling to elicit offensive fouls, can be considered cheating. Recently, flops received much attention from the NBA, with the enforcement of a policy involving a warning, then fines, and threats of suspension.[7]

Five hundred incidents with the potential of meeting the criteria of an offensive foul were recorded from the 2009–2010 season of the Israeli Basketball Super League and were analyzed by top basketball referees. One important finding was that falling intentionally in order to improve the chances of being awarded an offensive foul is common behavior among defenders—these consisted of almost two thirds of the recorded falls. This action resembles deception in other fields, where people habitually "deceive without remorse," such as used car sales, poker games, and tax returns.[8] Moreover, falling seems to be rational and helpful at first, increasing the chances of getting an offensive foul—when a defender does not fall, his chances of receiving an offensive foul are very small at only 2.8 percent. However, a more careful analysis showed that the *entire* impact of an intentional fall on the team is rather negative.

More specifically, the picture changes if the narrow thinking that focuses only on the potential offensive foul is extended to consider other aspects of the game more comprehensively. For example, a fallen defender is less helpful to the overall team than the one standing. More generally, falling intentionally was not, on average, a good decision. This surprising statement is based on detailed calculations of game outcomes following collisions. In particular, we defined "events with *positive* impact on the defense team" (P) and "events with *negative* impact on the defense team" (N); a higher PN ratio is therefore better for the team on defense. Interestingly, despite the higher chances it gives to get an offensive foul, falling intentionally when it is relatively clear that the fall was intentional (known as an "active intentional fall") hurts the team on defense significantly: the overall average PN ratio in stays and falls is 0.89, whereas in the case of an active intentional fall it is only 0.45—a decrease of about half, which represents the *worst* strategy for the defending team. Thus, in the long run, intentional falling is dysfunctional.

It is not quite clear whether rational reasons or rather biased decision processes (or possibly both) may surprisingly lead highly motivated, professional, and experienced players to frequently act against their team's interests by intentionally falling. But one thing is *definitely* unclear: why coaches do not instruct their players to stop cheating by falling. One reasonable explanation is that these professionals still don't know our findings about the detrimental effect of falling. Indeed, we did not find any evidence of awareness of such findings either in the academic literature, or in basketball discussions, forums, or websites. At any rate, the conclusion is that the practice of cheating by falling should definitely be thought through more carefully—if not for moral reasons, than for sheer self-interests for successful performance.

As mentioned, we also found that referees almost never call an offensive foul if the player remained on his feet (only 2.8 percent of the cases). Generally speaking, they call fewer fouls than those judged by our experts as deserving of a call. This "conservative" behavior can be explained again both by rational reasons and biased decision processes. However, essentially, basketball referees also seem to manage the game, rather than administer the rules, to avoid impeding the flow of the game. Such an approach is more than evident in a 2012 *New York Times* interview with former NBA referee, Joey Crawford. Upon Crawford's retirement after thirty-five years of officiating, speaking about the three game sevens in the NBA finals he had refereed, he stated that he knew how well he did: "When you go through those three games and nobody is saying a word about the three of you afterwards, that's the pinnacle. For a referee, that's the absolute best."[9]

This makes referees' officiating mistakes—such as not calling something which should have been called—not only understandable, but also, though paradoxically, rational. In his unique, genius way, Ofer Azar summarized the results of this study in one sentence: "We show that the players try to cheat, have some success, hurt their team on the way, and the referees are conservative."[10] This negative environment, and the negative feedback that performers experience, only further exacerbates the situation. Sanctioning negative or unethical behavior in the workplace can also create nonoptimal states, while leading to systematic unethical behavior. This situation typically occurs slowly over time.

For example, in any vendor relationship, in which one business buys products to sell to other businesses, the practice of giving and accepting small gifts may seem harmless, but can give way to more substantial kickbacks, awarding a company or employee with money in exchange for a favor, say picking one company's product or service over another competitors'. Then there is theft—an employee may think nothing of bringing home an extra pad of paper or a few pens from the office supply closet, but this can be a slippery slope. Not to say that just because you threw a pack of paper clips into your bag means you'll be embezzling money in no time, but most unethical behavior starts small, then gets larger.

According to a 2014 *Harvard Business Review* article, "How Unethical Behavior Becomes Habit," many of the largest business scandals over the years follow a pattern of ethical behavior eroding over time.[11] In fact, the authors found that when growing opportunities for unethical behavior are present, participants are more likely to rationalize their conduct than those that experience an abrupt change (i.e., an immediate large opportunity). The authors of the article point out that when employees rationalize minor incidents, they may end up committing more major offenses down the line that they would have not considered originally. They also found that people are more likely to overlook unethical behavior if it is gradual. Such an environment is not only due to a few unethical employees, either. As the authors state, "Unfortunately, the assumption that unethical workplace behavior is the product of a few bad apples has blinded many organizations to the fact that we all can be negatively influenced by situational forces."

One of the most extreme recent examples of unethical business behavior is the 2015 Volkswagen emissions scandal, in which it was discovered that 11 million VW vehicles were equipped with software that cheated on emissions tests. Researchers from West Virginia University first realized the problem when they road-tested two VW models; some of these cars emitted almost forty times the permitted levels of nitrogen oxides into the air.[12] The more naïve may first give the benefit of the doubt and assume this was some oversight or mistake, but 11 million cars later and the verdict was in: VW knowingly included the software and employees decided to cheat on the emissions tests more than a decade before the scandal—this was when it first came to light that they could not meet US clean-air standards.[13]

Civil and criminal investigations were opened in the United States and Europe, while VW's chief executive Martin Winterkorn stepped down as he, too, came under investigation for market manipulation. Not only did the company's stock plunge 50 percent after the scandal, but it was reported that their liabilities associated with the scandal could be as high as $45 billion.[14] The answer to "to cheat or not to cheat" seems obvious in retrospect for VW, as their brand, reputation, business, and profits have taken a pummeling. Still, people are convinced they can get away with all types of deception in an effort to succeed, only to find that their performance has faltered and they have, in the end, failed. Look no further than athletes and the ever-increasing doping epidemic.

Games and Doping

In the sporting world, one of the most common and highly publicized forms of cheating is "doping," the use of performance-enhancing drugs. From American track and field athlete and WNBA player Marion Jones to MLB professional shortstop Alex Rodriguez and from US sprinter Justin Gatlin to Lance Armstrong, every day seems to bring a new story about some top athletic performer implicated in doping. And this isn't just a recent phenomenon: as the late eminent Israeli sport historian Dr. Uriel Simri once claimed, the "real story" of elite sport is that "almost everyone is drugged."[15] According to Thomas Kistner's 2015 book *Shot*, soccer, the most popular sport in the world, even has an intensive "secret doping history," dating back to at least the early 1950s.[16]

One of the most interesting people I have met during my career is Gunnar Breivik, a professor at the Norwegian School of Sports Sciences in Oslo. Gunnar is a true scholar in the traditional sense of contributing to different subject areas—albeit mainly related to sports—such as psychology, sociology, and philosophy. I had lots of discussions with Gunnar about "Gott und die Welt," as the Germans say ("God and the World," meaning almost everything), but most interesting to me were his ideas about the problem of doping.

My interest in Gunnar's ideas grew out of my own preoccupation with the (ir)rationality problem. As I discussed earlier (for example, in chapter 6), one of the central modern concepts of rationality is based on the effectiveness of a person's actions. Within this framework, the game theory of decision-making can be discussed as an "ideal type," providing a reasonable model for real-life situations, such as doping.

Originally, game theory—invented in the mid-1940s—focused on the (often mathematical) study of conflict and cooperation between decision-makers, who are assumed to be intelligent and rational. Today, this approach applies to a wide range of behavioral relations and is regarded by many as the science of logical decision-making, not only in humans but also in animals and computers. What is particularly interesting, however, is that participants in such games—who supposedly act according to rational principles—may end up being locked in a completely irrational game. And vice versa: you sometimes see people playing a seemingly irrational game, but if you look carefully you understand the covert forces underlying this conduct, which turns out to be quite rational (e.g., the soccer goalies in chapter 5). These phenomena made game theory applicable for understanding doping in sport.

While doping seems to be effective in increasing athletic success, modern doping increases the economic costs for athletes and sport organizations, damages athletes' health, and raises many moral problems. Gunnar assumed that all athletes experience a Hamlet-like situation—similar to others discussed earlier in the book—and have a choice between two basic alternative strategies: to dope or not to dope. He also assumed that athletes will act rationally, maximizing their subjective expected utilities when choosing between the alternative strategies to reach their goals. In 1987, he analyzed the doping dilemma and found that the so-called prisoner's dilemma exists in sport. He also discovered that there are strong and widespread preference structures among athletes that inevitably lead to doping. In 1991 he presented some possibilities for cooperation against doping, based on these analyses.[17] A simple illustration of these ideas, derived from the very basic version of the prisoner's dilemma, follows as such.

"U" and "S" are the two best 100-meter (328-foot) sprinters in the world and should come up against each other in the next most important championship. For years, both have focused all their efforts on becoming the best. Now they must decide whether they dope or not: their decision is made taking into account 4 possible outcomes: 4 = the best one, 3= the second-best, 2 = the third-best, and 1 = the worst one.

In this state of affairs, several outcomes are possible. For example, one of the athletes could dope and the other not, in which case the doper would get the highest possible payoff (4), whereas the other would lose and get the worst (1). However, if both use a no-dope strategy, competition would be hard and winning would be uncertain for both; the moral, health, and career costs would be less, which would, for both, be the second-best result (3). If both dope, competition would be hard and fair, winning would be uncertain, and costs greater, which would lead to the third-best outcome (2).

This payoff matrix is presented in Figure 12.1.

The preferences of these two sprinters are regulated by two principles:

1. Winning is more important than fairness. Therefore, a certain but unfair victory is preferable to an uncertain and fair competition.
2. Fairness without cost is preferable to fairness with cost, even if absolute performance decreases.

		No Dope	Dope
S	No Dope	(3,3)	(1,4)
	Dope	(4,1)	(2,2)

Figure 12.1 The Lombardian Game.

Will these athletes dope in the championship or not? To reach a no-dope outcome (3, 3) in the championship, cooperation is needed. However, the danger that one's opponent will defect and dope, making the other a sucker, is always present. U may think that S will cooperate and not dope, but U may get his best outcome, a probable victory, by defecting and choosing to dope himself (4). If U thinks that S will defect, and U therefore chooses to dope, he will only end up with a payoff of (2). But U is even worse off if he chooses to cooperate *and* not to dope, ending up with the sucker's payoff (1). This means that whatever S does, U is better off choosing to dope and defecting from a cooperative no-dope strategy. S, however, will reason in exactly the same way. Both athletes will end up choosing defection and dope, which gives them their third-best payoff (2, 2). The paradox here is, of course, that by mutual cooperation they could have reached their second-best outcome (3, 3).

This type of game also plays out in the economy as businesses compete with one another for larger market share and profits. It can most easily be seen in how companies price their products. Take two major fast food restaurants: Burger King and McDonald's. Of course people may have their particular preferences, but the chains both sell similar food at fairly low costs to a wide-ranging demographic. Each burger joint has a version of a value menu that not only provides cheap eats, but also lures in customers who may end up spending more money on additional items.

What happens if Burger King decides to drop the price of its value menu in an effort to pull customers away from McDonald's? In doing so, it's possible that Burger King will win customers, earn more incremental profits by selling more value menu items, and the highest possible payoff (1).

McDonald's, however, will get the worst (4). If the companies maintain an implicit agreement and do not drop prices, then both will continue to earn a similar level of money and maintain a similar number of customers (3). If, however, Burger King lowers prices and in response McDonald's does too, this could lead to less profit for both companies since they are selling their products for cheaper (2).

Of course, pricing products is much different than cheating, but the same type of game theory applies. For example, what if one of VW's competitors, say Toyota, had been facing a similar problem with its cars' high levels of emissions, but then found out about VW's software that could cheat the test? If the company decided to implement the same software, they would be able to keep that competitive edge with VW. Of course we all know what happened to VW, and Toyota would have likely sealed its own fate as well.

In essence, what I am describing here is what Gunnar called "the Lombardian Game," which reflects the basic idea that victory is the most important thing—excuse me, the *only* thing—named, of course, after Vince Lombardi.

According to Gunnar, although such a game would encourage doping, it will not *ensure* it. "Deep dopers," however, would adopt the following principle: "Winning is the only thing and all means are 'kosher' to achieve it." Now you have become truly Machiavellian! This is the "Niccolo-based" game: an optimal state in which both athletes don't dope is practically impossible, because both players will always prefer to win at all costs (Figure 12.2).

In this kind of game, from the perspective of player U, the best happens when he dopes and his rival does not (1, 4). It is evident that each of the two would like his opponent to adopt a no-dope strategy, but since each one of them assumes that the other is "a little Niccolo" like himself—that is, Machiavellian—the entire system will end up being stuck in the state where both play the dope–dope game (3, 3) and neither ever reaches the potential top payoff (4). According to this reasoning, the no dope–no dope option exists as third best, but only theoretically; with both athletes holding such an attitude, it is highly unlikely in practice. This state becomes

		U	
		No Dope	Dope
S	No Dope	(2,2)	(1,4)
	Dope	(4,1)	(3,3)

Figure 12.2 The Machiavellian (or "Niccolo-based") Game.

somewhat surrealistic: at the beginning it appears tempting and inviting, but in the end, it turns out to be quite nightmarish. This idea is beautifully depicted in the final phrase of the Eagles' immortal song "Hotel California": "You can check out any time you like, but you can never leave" (just ask Lance Armstrong).

In an excellent article published in 2008 Michael Shermer, an American science writer, science historian, and ex-professional competitive bicyclist, extended some of Breivik's ideas.[18] Shermer analyzed the pervasive doping in competitive cycling using a game-theory view of the dynamics driving the problem. He studied how players in the doping game choose strategies they hope will maximize their return in anticipation of the strategies chosen by the other players in that game.

Shermer explains and illustrates why—from a game-theory perspective—doping is often a *rational* choice for elite athletes (specifically cyclists, in his case). First, there is opportunity, as the drugs are extremely effective in performance enhancement and are difficult to detect. In addition, the payoffs for success are huge, so as more athletes dope, there is greater incentive for "clean" athletes to stay competitive by doping as well, or risk being cut from a team. Basically, Shermer explains that cycling is typically in a state of "Nash equilibrium" where nobody will come forward as long as everyone has something to lose by coming forward; that is, where cheating is common throughout the entire system.

Toward the end of December 2016, sports websites around the world were flooded with headlines concerning a new scandal mentioned in sixty-five-year-old former NBA head coach George Karl's memoir *Furious George*. The 2013 NBA Coach of the Year created waves around the league by accusing the NBA of not being clean of performance-enhancing drugs, such as steroids and human growth hormone. While noting that the NBA has tougher drug testing standards than some other professional leagues, such as the NFL or MLB, Karl contends that the league is often slow to stop, or discover, the widespread cheating. Without mentioning explicit names, it could eventually be understood that he was referring to top stars such as Kobe Bryant, Dwayne Wade, Dwight Howard, and Deron Williams. In his words, it is "obvious" that many players are doping with the newest hard-to-detect blood boosters and performance-enhancing drugs (PEDs).[19]

Needless to say, Karl's provocative book has been heavily criticized. Critics argue, for example, that no major doping affair has been revealed thus far in the NBA (even though several players have been busted for PEDs), to which George Karl responds that Lance Armstrong never failed a drug test. Indeed, for me, the real question to be answered has always been how *did* a cheater like Armstrong manage to pass more than five hundred drug tests successfully? For years, I have been arguing that the influential sport bodies around the world have no interest in actually fighting doping, but rather in *looking like* they are doing their best to handle the issue. This is because on the one hand, the wonderful Olympic motto "Citius—Altius—Fortius" ("Faster—Higher—Stronger") becomes existential for the sport bodies in terms of the huge TV revenues, strongly dependent on ratings that come from sensational sporting achievements. This implies a continuous pressure to produce "unbelievable records" at all costs.

On the other hand, however, nobody likes "dirty" sports—and not only for moral or ethical reasons. Simply put, once doping is involved, sport becomes a competition between teams of medical doctors, sport physiologists, pharmacologists, and biochemists, not athletes. Why do people admire Jamaican sprinter Usain Bolt's unbelievable achievements? Precisely because they are something special, extraordinary, and "super-human." What would happen if Bolt were found—God forbid—guilty of doping? Fans would not only be angry with him because he cheated, but more deeply, they would be disappointed that he wasn't so special.

One eminent example for this argument is sprinter Ben Johnson's steroid scandal in the 1988 Olympics, which was a huge ordeal. After setting a new world record and winning the gold, he tested positive for steroids and he was stripped of his gold medal, making news around the world. Similarly, everyone loved Lance Armstrong because he was so remarkably unbelievable, and now many people feel betrayed. But an even deeper emotion is simple disappointment: his fans lost a hero. It turned out that Armstrong was simply an excellent "doping organizer," able to hide his drug usage. No one wants to sit in front of their TV for hours and waste their time admiring a pharmaceutical miracle.

Related to this is the fact that high-performing athletes risk not only their reputation, but their health as well. This idea is close to the very definition of irrational behavior—aside from being immoral, the risks are huge and do not necessarily justify the gains. As Lance Armstrong said in his good old days: "The riskiest thing you can do is get greedy."[20]

The fact that the NBA, for example, never had a real serious doping scandal can of course be attributed to incredibly rigorous testing; ironically, it can also be attributed to having relatively weak testing, thereby avoiding scandal. Skeptical people will tell you that they are unsure whether everything is being done to fight doping in sport: I, however, suspect that everything is being done *not* to fight sport doping effectively. More recently, economist Berno Buechel and colleagues—a team of German economists—came to similar conclusions, using three-player games.[21] Analyzing the games being played between sport organizations, athletes, and customers, Buechel and co. argued that such games result in what they call "the doping equilibrium," which is precisely what I've been talking about for years.

So what can be done to fight doping? First and foremost, it is necessary for athletes to change their basic attitudes; for example, adopt, and act according to, the rationale that fairness is most important. In addition, they must prefer to suffer from injustice than to do injustice to others. Sound familiar? Idealistic? Naïve? Maybe, but it comes directly from the Barron Pierre de Coubertin. This idea represents the classical values of fair play or gentlemanlike behavior in sport. Fairness is of utmost importance, together with the value of conducting a high-quality, exciting, and enjoyable game. In Breivik's terms, a "Coubertinian" game is then played (Figure 12.3).

If fairness is indeed above all, then the two preferred outcomes should in principle be no dope–no dope or dope–dope. However, because of high risks and the price involved in the second option, no dope–no dope will be preferred (4, 4) over the dope–dope (3, 3) option.

Interestingly, athletes applying the fairness principle will prefer the no dope–no dope option even to a situation in their favor, which would include doping (where the opponent does not dope). In such a situation, the fair athletes would have gained an unfair advantage over the opponents, a state of affairs that is not permitted by the athletes' fair value system. Moreover, they would even prefer to suffer from injustice (i.e., losing without doping, while the opponent dopes), than to cause one (i.e., dope, while the opponent does not).

The fairness above all principle can also be applied to teams with independently acting members, as discussed in chapters 7 and 8. For example, say a year-end bonus is based on sales team members' performance. In the Lombardian game (see Figure 12.1), if one team member moves in on another's client and makes the sale, his likelihood of receiving that bonus will increase (4), while the other's decreases (1). If they both stick to their own clients and work hard toward the year-end bonus, they both have a good chance of hitting their numbers and they also maintain a positive work relationship with one another and the rest of the team (3). If they both decide to snake clients from each other, they may get the bonus, though it's an uncertainty. In the meantime, there is likely a great

		U	
		No Dope	Dope
S	No Dope	(4,4)	(2,1)
	Dope	(1,2)	(3,3)

Figure 12.3 The Coubertinian Game.

deal of animosity forming between the two while their reputation as back-stabbers grows, leading to adverse effects on the team as a whole (2). In the Coubertinian game, however, if both team members consider fairness above all, they will not go around stealing each other's clients. In fact, they may even create a stronger bond among the team through cooperation.

DEVELOPING CHARACTER AND A MASTERY CLIMATE: DON'T CUT CORNERS WHEN YOU ARE RUNNING ALONE

> You can never do your best, which should always be your trademark, if you are cutting corners and shirking responsibilities.
>
> —OG MANDINO

In the early 1990s, I was teaching sport psychology in the coaches' school in Wingate; by Israeli law, all coaches must attend for certification. (Participants in these soccer courses include many ex-stars whose egos are sometimes much bigger than their career achievements.) That's where I met Gili Landau.

Gili was a big star in one of Israel's leading clubs, Hapoel Tel-Aviv, for seventeen years. He had quite a successful career as a striker, winning three Israeli championships and one national cup. In this final cup game in 1983, Gili was accused of using his hand to score the decisive goal and win the cup for Hapoel. Gili is also known for having scored a decisive last-minute goal in 1986 from a position that was "suspiciously" offside, effectively "stealing" the championship for his team.

Gili is also known for using spicy language and turning the witty phrase. I had to test the students at the end of the course, and there was strong evidence of them copying from each other. Unfortunately for me, I was proctoring the test (which I *hate* doing), but didn't really want to punish these basically nice guys. At the end of the exam, when Gili submitted his booklet, he uttered a sentence that has become immortal for me: "Miki, you taught us that soccer is a *team* sport . . . Well, this was a very original application of what you taught in class, don't you think?"

This anecdotal example goes to show that even highly successful sport veterans, educated for sportsmanship, fair play, and all these nice slogans, may not only cheat but also do many other immoral things to get what they want, whenever they can. Sometimes, the moral code of top athletes is quite bizarre. Remember Toni Schumacher's remarkable code of honor discussed earlier in the book? According to Schumacher, a penalty shot to the middle, whether successful or not, discredits the shooter because of dishonorable or unsportsmanlike behavior just as does the goalie's behavior of not diving. At first sight, it may seem that this guy has a particularly developed sense of morals, but before jumping that far, consider his conduct during the 1982 FIFA World Cup semifinal.

The game took place in Seville, with France facing off against West Germany. Having been on the pitch for exactly five minutes, the French defender, substitute Patrick Battiston, was following a long pass by Michel Platini. Battiston was clear through the German defense racing toward the German goal, when Schumacher, making no attempt to play the ball and defend the shot, raced toward Battison and jumped directly at him as he took the shot, making him shoot wide and miss the goal. Schumacher leapt into the air, twisting his body, and collided with Battiston, smashing Battiston's face with his hip and forearm. Battiston collapsed on the ground unconscious, with damaged vertebrae and a few teeth knocked out. He later slipped into a coma. Emergency medics had to administer oxygen on the pitch. Platini later said that he thought that Battiston was dead, because he looked extremely pale and seemed to have no pulse.

The Dutch referee Charles Corver did not call a foul for the incident, or even send Schumacher off the field. Instead, he decided on a goal kick. Schumacher then proceeded to take the goal kick and play resumed. Germany would eventually go on to win the game on penalty kicks after the match was tied at 3 to 3. After winning the game, Schumacher caused even more controversy: upon being told that Battiston had lost three teeth, he said, "If that's all that's wrong with him, I'll pay for the crowns." Even though Schumacher later apologized in person to Battiston (the apology was accepted), a French newspaper poll later asked who was the least popular man in France. Schumacher was ranked number one, even beating Adolf Hitler, who came in at number two. The incident was elected as the worst tackle ever by the *Observer*.[22] Indeed, a man with high moral standards!

Until the 1960s, belief in the character-building nature of sport was not subjected to serious doubt. However, accumulated evidence, at least on the intuitive level, have indicated that sport participation may have the opposite effect. Incidents such as Schumacher's tackle; Tonya Harding's involvement in the assault on Nancy Kerrigan before the US Figure Skating Championship in 1994; the "misbehavior" of "bad boys" in sports, such as John McEnroe in tennis, Jack Tatum in football, basketball's Charles Barkley spitting on fans he did not like; or serious crimes committed by a number of NFL players—such as Michael Vick running a dogfighting ring or Aaron Hernandez committing a first-degree murder—appeared increasingly more often in the media. This process, on the one hand, led to the public questioning of athletes' moral character. On the other hand, however, attempts have been made to see how character can be improved.

Much of human character in competition comes down to how individuals perceive success. Going back to Aristotle, mentioned at the beginning of this chapter, people developing their talents and performance in pursuit of a worthy goal can be ruined by an overemphasis on winning. Such ideas are reflected in the current concept of "achievement motivation theory," advocated mainly by educational psychologist and Purdue University professor John G. Nicholls, and applied to sport by Joan L. Duda, currently professor of Sport and Exercise Psychology at the University of Birmingham (previously at Purdue).[23]

These authors proposed that individuals can approach "achievement context," referring to how success is understood, by either a task or an ego orientation. All people are motivated to develop and display competence, but perceptions of competence vary: task-oriented persons feel successful when they meet or exceed self-referenced goals as well as when learning and mastering a task. By contrast, ego-oriented individuals evaluate success through social comparison, feeling competent only to the extent that their performance is better than others. These two orientations are "orthogonal"—that is, one can be high or low in both or high in one and low in the other.

Accumulated evidence reviewed by sport and exercise psychologist Maria Kavussanu from the University of Birmingham indicates that ego orientation has been negatively linked to a variety of moral variables, whereas task orientation has been found to be associated with increased sportsmanship and greater emphasis on morality.[24] This is in line with Nicholls's basic notion that the focus on demonstrating superiority over others—which characterizes ego-oriented people—may result in a lack of concern about justice, fairness, and the welfare of opponents in a competitive setting.

Put more simply, if you concentrate on fulfilling your own tasks, you have neither the time nor energy to look around, compare yourself to others, and then try to win through immoral means. If you focus on fulfilling *your* goals, always attempting to exceed them, and thereby improving *yourself*, you don't need to cheat or act aggressively toward others—it's simply irrelevant. In other words, the only person against whom you are constantly fighting to excel is yourself.

Needless to say, coaches (and bosses alike) play an important role in encouraging, or discouraging, a task-oriented mindset. Such a motivational climate—a concept similar to the positive or negative environmental feedback discussed earlier in the chapter—plays a major role in understanding performers' conduct. Paradoxically, coaches who help athletes focus on fulfilling their potential, as well as on trying to improve themselves and doing their best to meet their goals and tasks, will probably end up with better results—both in terms of the athlete's performance and ability to win—than in cases where coaches just push their athletes to high performance by a "must win at all costs" attitude. Such an attitude may often cause just the opposite (recall the *must*urbation effect from chapter 10).

Joan Duda and social sport psychologist professor Isabel Balaguer, from the University of Valencia in Spain, outline in detail how the performers' environment can be structured and strategies can be developed to enhance a task-oriented climate.[25] Among these, they suggest that coaches provide athletes with tasks that emphasize individual challenges and achievements, encourage the athletes' participation in the decision-making process, involve athletes in self-evaluation, and spend equal time with each team member. These actions also facilitate moral interpretations and responses to the performers' experiences. As Duda and Balaguer state in discussing a coach's influence on an athlete: "Whether this influence is more positive or negative appears to depend on the degree to which the motivational atmosphere the coach establishes is more or less task-involving and ego-involving."

This atmosphere should of course include more sportsmanship and morality, thereby decreasing irrelevant ego-related considerations. David Light Shields and Brenda Light Bredemeier, leading researchers in the area of sport character, would probably advise purposefully creating a positive, moral atmosphere in which everybody, for example, is committed to cultivating a moral culture by conforming to moral values and avoiding morally unacceptable actions and behaviors.[26] In other words, we cannot "just do it," but rather, "do it justly!" This means conceiving teams as "communities of character," in which character is actually taught, developed, and practiced.

What is important to emphasize here is that task-orientation has been associated with sportsmanship and higher morality for the most part because of the emphasis on the concept of mastery. As Shields and Bredemeier correctly note, a mastery climate encourages or augments task motivation, whereas a performance climate encourages or augments ego motivation. A mastery climate is associated with participants' use of effective learning strategies, a preference for challenging tasks, positive attitudes, and the belief that effort leads to success. Such a mastery-oriented achievement climate will be more effective in producing not only better performances, but also more sportsmanlike athletes or fair employees. Moreover, it seems that coaches who operate this way will have a greater chance of becoming what I have referred to as ego-less master coaches.

Two of the psychologists to first doubt the belief that sports builds character were Bruce Ogilvie and Thomas Tutko, professors at California's San Jose State University. In one of their most popular publications, back in 1971, they contended that sport does *not* build character, at least not in the traditional meaning of the idea originally developed in the United Kingdom and United States in the nineteenth century. Instead, I tend to agree with John Wooden (one of the great master coaches discussed in chapter 9), who said: "Sports do not build character, they reveal it."[27]

Task and mastery orientations may definitely help in creating athletes who are *both* focused on the task and fair—Wooden himself, as shown earlier, knew that very well. In my opinion, really good athletes are those who apply all these principles after having appropriately internalized them. For example, at the beginning of the 2000s I was consulting with a talented young soccer player for quite a long time. As our relationship developed, we once discussed the general state of Israeli soccer—which in my opinion, and that of many others, is far from satisfactory, to say the least. I stated that there was and is no real soccer in Israel, and never would be. When he asked me why, I replied by asking: "When the team runs around the pitch before practice without the coach being present, do you 'cut the corners' or not?" He smiled and said: "Not only do I cut, but even when I plan not to cut corners, the veterans tell me: 'Come with us, don't be a fool.'" "That's why there will be no soccer in Israel," I said. "I rest my case."

Even without the presence of the coach, a true good athlete, one who internalized all the principles discussed earlier, will not cut corners. Today, in my opinion, too many Israeli soccer players are not really focused on the task, nor are they fair; they cheat by cutting the corners. But whom do they cheat? Only themselves, with the obvious outcome of decreased performance. Similarly, if I did not perform my daily physical exercise drills required by the doctors to fight my Parkinson's, whom would I actually be cheating? Not *them*! I'd just be cheating *myself*.

Acting morally, in the sense of knowing that cutting corners will only hurt yourself in the end, makes you a better performer. Whether in sports or business or in life in general, don't cut corners, don't cheat yourself, and you'll find that your performance, as a professional and simply as a human being, will increase.

SUMMARY

In today's culture winning has become the end-all and be-all, but this unhealthy obsession can take a toll on long-term performance. Whether in sports or in business, everyone wants to be successful, but a single-minded pursuit of victory can often lead to negative decision-making, aggression, and cheating or deception of all kinds. According to crisis theory, such aggression or negative actions leads to a more substantial deviation from optimal arousal in competition, impairing task performance or normative behavior.

As a leader, whether you are a CEO, a middle manager, or a head coach, sanctioning unethical behavior is a form of negative environmental feedback, which may provoke or increase frustration and thereby increase the probability of nonoptimal states, as shown with referees and players. In the office, unethical behavior can become systematic, leading to disastrous results. To succeed, and avoid a decline in long-term performance, it's necessary to change both the individual and group attitude, while purposefully creating a positive, moral atmosphere, in which everybody is committed to cultivating a moral culture.

Such a mastery climate encourages or augments task motivation (as compared to a climate that encourages or augments ego motivation). Task and mastery orientations will help create athletes and employees who are both focused on the task *and* fair, leading to higher performance and levels of success throughout their careers and in their personal lives.

DAILY PRACTICES

As an Individual

- Avoid the vicious cycle of poor performance by recognizing when and why you experience aggressive, or otherwise negative, feelings and compensate for them by using mental preparation techniques discussed in chapters 10 and 11.

- Set your own task-related goals and then concentrate on fulfilling them and improving yourself, instead of constantly comparing yourself to, and trying to get ahead of, your colleagues and competitors.
- Remember that what may first seem rational in your pursuit of success, may end up being irrational, and vice versa—using morality as a guide, however, will keep you on the right track.

As a Leader

- Help your team, company, or other enterprise adopt and act according to the rationale that fairness is not only important, but necessary to success.
- Develop a task-oriented, mastery climate and moral environment to keep your team focused and decrease irrelevant ego-related considerations.
- Support effective learning strategies, a preference for challenging tasks, and positive attitudes at all levels of your organization.

NOTES

1. "Lance Armstrong Quotes: 25 Memorable Statements from Oprah Interview," *Huffington Post*, January 19, 2013.
2. Aristotle, *Nicomachean Ethics*, trans. Irwin, (Indianapolis: Hacket 1985).
3. M. Bar-Eli, "Psychological Performance Crisis in Competition, 1984–1996: A Review," *European Yearbook of Sport Psychology* 1 (1997): 73–112.
4. M. Bar-Eli and G. Tenenbaum, "Observations of Behavioral Violations as Crisis Indicators in Basketball," *The Sport Psychologist* 3 (September 1989): 237–244.
5. M. Bar-Eli, G. Tenenbaum, and S. Geister, "Consequences of Players' Dismissal in Professional Soccer: A Crisis-Related Analysis of Group-Size Effects," *Journal of Sports Sciences* 24 (October 2006): 1083–1094.
6. E. Morgulev, O. H. Azar, R. Lidor, E. Sabag, and M. Bar-Eli, "Deception and Decision Making in Professional Basketball: Is it Beneficial to Flop?," *Journal of Economic Behavior and Organization* 102 (April 2014): 108–118.
7. B. Golliver, "The Mavericks' Rick Carlisle: NBA to 'Stay the Course' on Flopping Policy," *Sports Illustrated*, 2013, http://nba.si.com/2013/06/16/nba-flopping-policy-david-stern-rick-carlisle-dallas-mavericks/.

8. P. Batigalli, G. Charness, and M. Dufwenberg, "Deception: The Role of Guilt," *Journal of Economic Behavior and Organization* 93 (September 2013): 227–232.

9. S. Borden, "Whistling His Own Tune: Joey Crawford Sounds Off on 35 Years as NBA Referee," *New York Times*, May 6, 2012, www.nytimes.com/2012/05/06sports/basketball/joey-crawford-sounds-off-on-35-years-as-an-nba-referee.htmi_r=2.

10. Personal communication to me, August 24, 2014.

11. Francesca Gino, Lisa D. Ordóñez, and David Welsh, "How Unethical Behavior Becomes Habit," *Harvard Business Review*, September 4, 2014, https://hbr.org/2014/09/how-unethical-behavior-becomes-habit.

12. Guilbert Gates, Jack Ewing, Karl Russell, and Derek Watkins, "Explaining Volkswagen's Emissions Scandal," *New York Times*, July 29, 2016, www.nytimes.com/interactive/2015/business/international/vw-diesel-emissions-scandal-explained.html?_r=0.

13. Ibid.

14. Paul R. La Monica, "Volkswagen Has Plunged 50%. Will It Ever Recover?" *CNN Money*, September 2015, http://money.cnn.com/2015/09/24/investing/volkswagen-vw-emissions-scandal-stock/.

15. U. Simri, *(Almost) Everyone is Drugged* (Tel-Aviv: Shalgi, 1993).

16. T. Kistner, *Schuss: Die Geheime Dopinggeschichte des Fussballs* [Shot: The Secret Doping] (Munich: Droemer, 2015).

17. All these publications are reviewed in our "psycho-philosophical" book chapter (M. Bar-Eli, Y. Lurie, and G. Breivik, "Rationality in Sport").

18. M. Shermer, "The Doping Dilemma," *Scientific American* 298 (2008): 82–89.

19. G. Karl with Sampson, *Furious George: My Forty Years Surviving NBA Divas, Clueless GMs, and Poor Shot Selection* (New York: Harper, 2017).

20. Good Reads, "Lance Armstrong Quotes," https://www.goodreads.com/author/quotes/1544.Lance_Armstrong.

21. B. Buechel, E. Emrich, and S. Pohlkamp, "Nobody's Innocent: The Role of Customers in the Doping Dilemma," unpublished working paper (University of Hamburg, Germany, 2013).

22. "The 5 Worst Tackles," *Observer Sport Monthly*, Sunday, May 19, 2002.

23. J. G. Nicholls, *The Competitive Ethos and Democratic Education* (Cambridge, MA: Harvard University Press, 1989); J. L. Duda, "Motivation in Sport Settings: A Goal Perspective Approach," in *Motivation in Sport and Exercise*, ed. G. Roberts (Champaign, IL: Human Kinetics, 1992), 57–91.

24. M. Kavussanu, "Morality in Sport," in *Social Psychology in Sport*, eds. S. Jowett and D. Lavallee (Champaign, IL: Human Kinetics, 2007), 265–277.

25. J. L. Duda and I. Balaguer, "Coach-Created Motivational Climate," in *Social Psychology in Sport*, eds. S. Jowett and D. Lavallee (Champaign, IL: Human Kinetics, 2007), 117–130.

26. D. L. Shields and B. L. Bredemeier, "Can Sport Build Character?" in *Character Psychology and Character Education*, eds. D. K. Lapsley and F. C. Power (Notre Dame, IN: University of Notre Dame Press, 2005), 121–139.

27. Torin Koos, "The 23 Most Inspirational Quotes from Exceptional Athletes," *Desert News*, September 25, 2014, www.deseretnews.com/top/2748/12/12-Sports-do-not-build-character-They-reveal-it.html.

Conclusion

People who say it cannot be done should not interrupt those who are doing it.

—*attributed to* GEORGE BERNARD SHAW[1]

ndeed, in sports, in business, and in life, achieving our best performance is like a long-distance run—or a marathon—in which you survive, even if you are in a state of crisis. It's a long, hard, but rewarding journey. You'll never make it to the finish line without training, which often requires guidance. That guidance is what I hope this book has offered you, dear readers. I hope that it has been not only an engaging, enlightening look at the fascinating psychology of performance, but also a tool for overcoming those psychological barriers standing between you and exploiting your full potential. As Vince Lombardi said, "Perfection is not attainable, but if we chase perfection, we can catch excellence." And excellence is truly what we are all striving for at the end of the day, whether in our professional careers or personal lives.

So what does it take to succeed? There is no better definition, I think, than that of Colin Powell, former US Secretary of State, chairperson of the

Joint Chiefs of Staff, and National Security Advisor—in short, a man, who surely knows something about success: "Success is the result of perfection, hard work, learning from failure, loyalty and persistence."

As I discussed throughout the book, even the greatest inspiration is, to a large extent, an outcome of hard work. An outstanding artist like Pablo Picasso, for example, attributed much of his own ingenuity to hard work— in other words, to deliberate or deep practice. In order to succeed not only do you need to practice, but you've got to learn how to swallow failure, being prepared to cope with the frustrating, sometimes maddening process of endlessly rolling the stone uphill in an effort to reach its top. (For this, Sir Alex Ferguson would say you need "three P's": Preparation, Perseverance, and Patience, which sum up to one big "C"—Consistency.) However, you should also be ready to cope with aftermath feelings of meaninglessness, emptiness, and sometimes even melancholy.

Paradoxically, this is exactly what keeps you going. Real achievers, dedicated top performers, will, as Sir Winston Churchill said, "Never give in, never give in, never, never, never."[2] Why? Because they manage to overcome our greatest weakness, which according to Thomas A. Edison, lies in giving up: "The most certain way to succeed is always to try just one more time."[3] When should one stop? French writer and aviator Antoine de Saint Exupéry, "father" of *The Little Prince*, gave us this beautiful advice: "Perfection is achieved, not when there is nothing more to add, but when there is nothing left to take away."

I do not expect you to believe everything I have written in this book. On the contrary! As I preach with regard to the ideas of others, I also preach about my own ideas: be *critical*, think of what I said, use your grey brain cells, and ask questions. Figure out how you can apply these lessons in new ways, which ones work the best for you, and decide which ones may not work for you at all. Even if you follow my advice and you do everything correctly, you must always remember that, by definition, any scientific know-how can only be probabilistic in nature. That is, based on my knowledge as a scientist and practitioner, I can responsibly provide you with general principles to guide your conduct, but they are subject to individual variations that, at the end, only you can be aware of.